# I Sight:
## The Power of Perception

*by*
*James Eliol Mercer*

**DORRANCE** PUBLISHING CO
EST. 1920
PITTSBURGH, PENNSYLVANIA 15238

Dorrance Publishing Co
585 Alpha Drive
Pittsburgh, PA 15238
Visit our website at www.dorrancebookstore.com

ISBN: 979-8-8860-4410-2
eISBN: 979-8-8868-3831-2

# Dedication

This book is dedicated to the loving memory of my mother, the late Mildred Mercer, who believed in the importance of family support and family values.

# Acknowledgements

If not for the support and assistance from those listed below, the writing of this book would not have been possible. Thank you all.

1. To my adorable wife, Valerie, who constantly provides ongoing support in all I do and all I need, especially her assistance in writing this book. For you sweetheart, I extend an extra special thank you with all my undying love.

2. To my daughter, Valerie Deanne Mercer Lawrence, a special thank you as well for your critique ability, your constructive criticism, your editing skills. And endless support. Thank you, Deanne, where would I be without your help.

3. To my son, James Scott Mercer, a special thank you as well for all your assistance and support with your technical skills when needed. If not for your support and technical skill I would be lost in cyber space. Thank you, Scott.

4. To my brothers and sisters who provided much needed support throughout my life, Thanks guys.

5. To the eye clinic and clinical trials staff at the Health Sciences Complex St. Johns, NL., which include secretaries, technicians, nurses and doctors all of which were involved in the identification of the RLBP1 affected gene and the insuring Novartis clinical trial on the RLBP1 gene, I wish to extend my appreciation for your professional support and assistance going forward. Thank you very much.

6. Finally to the Publisher for having the insight in helping bring this story to life. Thank you very much.

# *Biography – About the Author*

I currently live in Conception Bay South Newfoundland. My previous home was in Bishops Cove Newfoundland and Labrador. I was born at home on September 21st, 1951 in Upper Island Cove and moved to Bishops Cove in 1954. I come from a family of seven, including my parents. I have an older sister and brother as well as a younger sister and brother. I am married to Valerie Louise Lambert of Little Heart's Ease, Trinity Bay. We have two children and four grandchildren.

In 1970 I attended Memorial University of Newfoundland and Labrador, (MUN), but on the advice of an optometrist, I had to leave my studies early due to the continuing onslaught of legal blindness. I was also advised by that same person to seek work and live my life utilizing what sight I had.

I found work in construction but mostly in retail sales; however, in the mid 1980s I suffered a work-related back injury which led to surgery forcing me to join the ranks of the unemployed.

In the mid 1990s, unable to work in retail or construction anymore, I decided to return to school. This time however I had great adaption skills and felt confident in being successful. Because most of my early work was in retail, I felt a Business Management program was my best option and so I enrolled at Keyin Technical Collage where I successfully completed a Business Management Program with honours. I then secured work with the Federal Government as a public servant until I was forced to medically retire in 2006 due to continued failing sight.

I am a member of the Royal Canadian Legion and enjoy working as a volunteer for worthy causes; since my retirement, as a hobby, I chose to start writing. This will be my second novel to be published. Some of my other writings include published and unpublished poetry as well as two other incomplete novels.

# *Foreword*

The following is a true story based on the life of a legally blind person, James E. Mercer. The story begins with his first knowledge of having a sight problem in 1957. It follows him from the early age of 6 years old up to age 66 years where he felt he had sufficiently brought forward his story.

It also brings to life all of the emotions attached to dealing with a permeant sighted disability and the power of perception associated with it. The reader identifies with all the positivities and negativities attached to self adaptations and accommodations which he developed in an effort to adapt to society and life in general.

V. Deanne Lawrence, BA, C.EcD, C.AL
Economic Development and Tourism Officer
Town of Torbay, NL

# *Prologue*

The pixels of daylight gradually disappeared as dust encroached upon the landscape. The reflection of the hardened bleached snow still maintained enough light for me to remain somewhat mobile. Finally, the three of us left Rachel's Marsh and headed west towards Leslie Peddle's house. It was a short walk from the small make shift hockey rink to Leslie's house. Of course, I could have left Rachel's Marsh on the east end down over the hill and within three minutes I would have been home. But being six years old, the stories of fairies and the impending darkness played significant factors in my decision making to follow my buddies. Besides, they were afraid of fairies as well and security in numbers boosted our confidence.

After Leslie went in for the night, both Raymond and myself continued west down a small drung lane. It was a short cut from Peddles Hill to the main road. At the left of the drung lane which intersected the main road was Raymond's home. I was still no more than three to four minutes from home, but with the disappearance of my companion, my confidence left me also. It was just a short walk along the main road in a northeast direction, a walk I now dreaded. By then the daylight pixels had completely deteriorated, leaving me shrouded in total darkness. The light pixels which reflected from the snow had disappeared as well. Dust had fallen to the power of darkness. Shadows loomed large and the imagination of a scared little boy ran rapid. It was only a thousand feet or so from Raymond's house to my home, so I mustered up what courage I had left and turned towards home.

Still, I stood motionless enshrouded in total blackness. The only sign of light were the narrow beams of yellow light escaping from behind dark blinds or curtains of the nearby houses. I felt a little better as there was some small comfort in seeing those rays of light. Still, it wasn't enough light for me to see properly. The white marbled finished snow still had the capability of reflecting light. However, even though the narrow beams of yellow light were absorbed and reflected back into the darkness, it still wasn't enough for me to see. The light came from inside the houses and I was outside; my focus was on the beams of light for it was the only thing I could see. I was on my own, alone, blinded by fear and darkness. I knew I couldn't stay where I was and yet I dreaded to move on, so move I did. In the daylight, I knew the way home but confidence in my adaptation to darkness was not yet developed. It would be many years before that skill would be so. As each step drew me closer to home, my feet became heavy; it soon became even more difficult to move. The road was clear in the daytime when I could see, but it was dark and I couldn't see. Where exactly I was standing on the road I didn't know. I searched my brain and tried to imagine where I was but to no avail. In my thoughts if I could make it to my grandmother's house I would be halfway there.

# *Author's note*

Out of respect for the privacy of certain people, I have intentionally omitted or changed some of the names; thus, ensuring their privacy is protected.

The information for this story was gathered through my own memories along with the memories of other extended family members, neighbours and friends. Beyond those memories I researched both private and public documents. To further my research, I also utilized the internet and other external sources regarding a disabling eye disease and ongoing research for a treatment or cure.

# Table of Contents

*I Sight*
*The power of perception*

# Chapter 1

# A Terrifying Demon

The urge to know the future is always overpowering. We are only mere mortals; thus, our visual perception is limited only to the perimeters of our imagination. Before I try to decipher the pending future, I must have a beginning. Everything has a beginning; a parsec segment in time to mark something, whatever it may be.

For me, the memories of my early childhood are as vivid and fresh as the newly minted buttercups of spring. Before I digress back into the past, I should explain the reasons why.

I am a legally blind person who has faced many challenges in the ongoing journey through life, a life that has spanned more than six decades thus far.

All children face adversity in growing up. In my case the adversity I faced was not of any normal childhood upbringing. This adversity came to me early in life as a terrifying demon; it was then I realized I couldn't see at night. Initially my brain couldn't assimilate that fact. Being a young child, I thought all people both young and old couldn't see after dark.

It was a cold evening, late December in 1957, and the snow magnified the failing light of the retiring day. A major marsh hockey game had come to a successful end. It didn't matter who won the game as long as everyone enjoyed the fun. Soon, the games participants slowly disappeared anxiously awaiting another day and the next game.

The Christmas holidays provided an opportunity for all children to enjoy unbridled play in winter's wonderland. The sled riders were gone from the nearby hills. Several of us, myself included, were bystanders. Fans you might say, just watching the bigger boys play. With the game complete, I found myself, for some reason, waiting for a couple of my friends to head home. Along with myself, my closest friends Leslie Peddle and Raymond Lynch were the last to leave the ice-covered section of Rachel's Marsh. Rachel's Marsh is nestled in a hollow behind aunt Julie's hill.

I had told my mother I would be playing with my friends on Rachel's Marsh. My mom insisted I must be home before dark. I agreed, but the fun time spent playing with my friends seemed more important than heading home before total darkness. Besides, Rachel's Marsh was just up over Aunt Julie's hill just behind our house. It would have taken only few minutes to be home. Procrastination has always been my nemesis and so I stayed much longer than I should have.

The pixels of daylight gradually disappeared as dust encroached upon the landscape. The reflection of the hardened bleached snow still maintained enough light for me to remain somewhat mobile. Finally, the three of us left Rachel's Marsh and headed west towards Leslie Peddle's house. It was a short walk from the small make shift hockey rink to Leslie's house. Of course, I could have left Rachel's Marsh on the east end down over the hill and within three minutes I would have been home. But being six years old, the stories of fairies and the impending darkness played significant factors in my decision making to follow my buddies. Besides, they were afraid of fairies as well and security in numbers boosted our confidence.

After Leslie went in for the night, both Raymond and myself continued west down a small drung lane. It was a short cut from Peddles Hill to the main road. At the left of the drung lane which intersected the main road was Raymond's home. I was still no more than three to four minutes from home, but with the disappearance of my companion, my confidence left me also. It was just a short walk along the main road in a northeast direction, a walk I now dreaded. By then the daylight pixels had completely deteriorated, leaving me shrouded in total darkness. The light pixels which reflected from the snow had disappeared as well. Dust had fallen to the power of darkness. Shadows loomed large and the imagination of a scared little boy ran rapid. It was only a thousand feet or so from Raymond's house to my home, so I mustered up what courage I had left and turned towards home.

Still, I stood motionless enshrouded in total blackness. The only sign of light were the narrow beams of yellow light escaping from behind dark blinds or curtains of the nearby houses. I felt a little better as there was some small comfort in seeing those rays of light. Still, it wasn't enough light for me to see properly. The white marbled finished snow still had the capability of reflecting light. However, even though the narrow beams of yellow light were absorbed and reflected back into the darkness, it still wasn't enough for me to see. The light came from inside the houses and I was outside; my focus was on the beams of light for it was the only thing I could see. I was on my own, alone, blinded by fear and darkness. I knew I couldn't stay where I was and yet I dreaded to move on, so move I did. In the daylight, I knew the way home but confidence in my adaptation to darkness was not yet developed. It would be many years before that skill would be so. As each step drew me closer to home, my feet became heavy; it soon became even more difficult to move. The road was clear in the daytime when I could see, but it was dark and I couldn't see. Where exactly I was standing on the road I didn't know. I searched my brain and tried to imagine where I was but to no avail. In my thoughts if I could make it to my grandmother's house I would be halfway there.

The cold stillness of a frosty evening added too the mounting fear inside me. The sound of snow crunching underneath my feet became the focus of my attention. I tried blocking out all other sounds but they became louder and louder. Animals in nearby barns and stables moved about grumbling to each other in their own language. Unable to see in the darkness, the imagination of a scared little boy, the recollection of my grandfathers stories about fairies soon became overpowering as the release of hot tears threatened to freeze my eyes shut.

Through extreme effort I laboured forward. Somewhere in my heart I knew home had to be close. I hadn't gone very far when my body refused to go any further. I was frozen in my tracks—not from the cold but from fear. As luck would have it, I found myself in front of my grandparents' house. Through my fear-fogged brain I knew this to be true, because I could hear the familiar voices coming from inside.

It was then I lost it! The sound of familiar voices inside! The fear of being alone outside! The fear that fairies might take me. The cloak of total darkness with its scary shadows, startling noises and not knowing if I was on the road or about to fall over its steep embankments finally paralyzed me. I wanted to be home, nestled in the comfort and security of my mother's arms and I wanted it to happen immediately. My tears continued accompanied by vocal outbursts of crying and sobbing which became louder and louder. How long I stood there I don't know; any movement at all was completely impossible.

A door opened and a familiar voice spoke to me. I don't know what was said;

I only knew I was beyond answering. The consumption of one's own fears had taken me over the edge. I was shaking frantically when the gentle hand of my aunt Margarette encircled my hand and held it tightly.

I knew it was her because of the softness and compassion in her voice. "I will take you home," she said. It had taken forever to travel some 500 feet from Raymond's to Grandmother's house but the next 500 feet from Grandmother's to home went quickly. It's amazing what compassion and love can do to relieve fear and loneliness. All my fears disappeared when Aunt Margarette took my hand. It would be a while before the crying and sobbing stopped but I would be safe from the darkness as the yellow warm glow of an incandescent light bulb brought sight back into my eyes. I saw the relief in my mother's eyes as both my mom and aunt chatted briefly on my condition. My aunt explained how she found me and decided to bring me home. It didn't take long for my older brother and sister to make fun of me for being a scaredy cat, while my younger sister watched in amazement.

My father, James, for whom I was named after, worked in the iron ore mines on Bell Island and wasn't home. I wished he was, for he would have put my older siblings in their place but some choice scolding words from our mother seemed to settle them down. My four-year older sister Dorothy and my two-year older brother Leslie never again taunted me about darkness and the perceived fear of all the unknowns which were under the cloak of darkness. My sister Greta, who was two years my younger, hadn't yet felt the heartache of being the target of a fun maker. However, I am sure she took stock of what had transpired that night and filed it away for future reference.

It wasn't the first time I found myself in darkness but it was the first time I was outside alone and scared. I have never forgotten that night; it would become the foundation of how I would perceive and adapt to my life in general. I tell you, Mom didn't have to enforce the rule of being home before darkness ever again. I had learned my lesson that was for sure; the one thing about it, looking back opened my eyes beyond the power of perceived sight. The perception I had of everyone not able to see in the dark no longer held water. I had to accept the fact I was wrong in my postulation of everyone being the same.

From that point on, my earliest memories of not being able to see in darkness were always the same; as a child I was never alone in the darkness but always around my family. My parents kept me close to them. It seemed myself and my younger sister Greta were given more attention than my older siblings. I know

now the reason why but being a child, I hadn't acquired enough knowledge to know the difference. I really don't know when my parents knew of my affliction but they loved and cared for me, never making any fuss over it. To them I was a normal child who had a night vision restriction. I remember that winter very well; it was a winter we had lots of snow and I enjoyed playing in it but the realization I was somehow different in some way began to unravel in my head. My older siblings could always stay out later after dark and I along with my younger sister were kept inside. It ever so slowly became apparent that my sister and myself were not only different but unique in our family unit.

While my older siblings braved the darkness outside whenever they wanted to, I became accustomed to the dim yellow glow of incandescent light bulbs. In time, I became more observant of where everything was and paid close attention to all my surroundings. Although when the electrical power went out and I felt my body freeze from fear of lost mobility, I drew some comfort in the existence of the narrow beams of light emitting from beneath the dampers of the wood and coal-fired kitchen stove. My eyes would remain fixed on that light until the kerosene lamp was lit. Once the lamp was lit and its light flooded the room, my frozen posture relaxed. In no time the stiffness in my body left allowing freedom of movement once again. Still the perimeters of free movement were restricted to the diameter of a lamp's projected circle of light. To go beyond that point would be terrifying. There were unknown shadows, lurking demons and nocturnal monsters awaiting my entry into their realm of darkness.

When it was my bedtime, my mother encouraged me to follow her up the stairs. She removed the oil lamp from the kitchen and held it in her hand. The stairs lit up opening a path upstairs to my bedroom. The lamp was then left to rest on a table between the bedrooms in the hallway. Its yellow golden beams of light shone through my open bedroom doorway providing a fixed point of illumination for my eyes to focus on. How often I thanked God for that comfort. Still, the darkness within the bedroom was terrifying. How I dreaded bedtime yet my mother was only a call away she would tell me. It was during this time the monsters of my imagination came to life and each night I stood my ground holding them at bay until sleep erased them for another night. Sometimes I would call my mother for support, which she willingly offered, while other times I overcame those fears myself.

The introduction of darkness and the slow fading of light at the end of a day

5

became a transition place for me to adapt to the world of darkness. Unlike my older siblings who lived in a world where darkness and light were the one place, I lived in a place where darkness and light were two different worlds. In the morning my eyes opened to the glorious light of a new day. The true facts soon became clear to me. I could see really well during the daylight hours and was able to maintain the life of a normal child. However, the deterioration of my sight slowly consumed the healthy cells in my eyes leading me towards eventual blindness. Not to be outdone, refraction of my visual acuity also became a factor on my vision; it too would have to be addressed sometime in the future.

Oh, the fun I had growing up in the world of daylight. I was always a part of everything with all of my friends doing everything I possibly could given my limitations. Still, each day came to an end just before the world of darkness came alive. My friends never questioned why I always went before dark. I like to think they assumed my parents wanted me in before dark. Many times, I had to leave a game of whatever was being played at that instant and headed home before it ended. This sometimes frustrated my friends as they counted on me to be there until the end. It would be many years before my friends knew anything about my affliction and then only my closest trusted friends were privileged to that secret.

I did almost everything my siblings and friends did. However, my parents knew my limits and strictly enforced their parental guidance. If I wanted to exceed my limited capabilities, I would have to prove to my parents it was possible. Thus, I soon fell into a pattern and never objected or rebelled against my parental direction.

Schooling in the early years was never a problem. I was able to absorb, consume and digest my school work easily. This was because I paid strict attention to what was taught. This of course would lay a solid base for my future educational development. The one problem I had was doing homework. It seemed the yellow glow of the incandescent light bulb played havoc with my ability to see properly while doing homework. It was during this time I suffered greatly with the three R's of schooling not because I didn't want to learn but because of a barrier—a barrier beyond my control at that time. Because of this barrier I fell into the same rebellious traits of my peers. After all, most of my friends detested homework and often neglected doing it. How was I to be any different? I thought everyone was like me—boy was I wrong. They had the ability to do their homework but often felt it was an unnecessary chore. Whereas my ability was restricted and often my homework was unfinished but not because of neglect. Looking back, I can see my father or mother sitting near me at night time strongly encouraging me to do my homework. Other times, when my father wasn't home, I could easily fool my mother into thinking I had my homework completed. It didn't seem to matter when it came to homework for if I had it done, it was often wrong and I would have to redo it during early school hours while my remaining classmates moved forward with regular class instruction. Thank goodness for natural morning light. My eyes adapted well to this light and my vision improved greatly affording me the luxury of completing my homework in no time flat allowing me time to join regular class instruction. Of course, this meant I was always in catch up mode with the rest of the class. Schooling for me would always be a challenge and as my sight slowly deteriorated, I met the challenge head on and adapted whenever was necessary. It was through this self-adaptation I was able to carry on my educational training. All wasn't fun growing up; attending school was a necessity and like all children I detested it very much. It interfered with all my fun time, but I wasn't alone in that dilemma. All my peers suffered the same fate. Still, there were some bright spots in attending school; we socialized, grew as individuals and developed our own unique personalities. There was always the preschool play time, recess time, lunchtime and of course after school. We played all sorts of games. Some of my favourites included frozen ghost, three corner puss, Tilley, marbles, pitching coppers and an exhausting game of chasers. Of course, time constraints restricted us in how long we could play. Still my eyesight in daylight wasn't restricted or limited on my ability to function normally. Yes, my daylight sight was great. I could see things other children could see or at least I thought I could.

In school, I stumbled over reading and writing even though my focus on my school work was as committed as anyone's. Each school year brought new adaptive challenges for me. I found myself inventing and searching out new ways to absorb, digest and learn the school curriculum assigned for each grade level. From September to June my time outside interacting with my peers after school shortened and lengthened with the season.

Sometime after I turned eight years old, I was told by my parents I was night blind and there wasn't any cure only hope. Being of a young age, understanding and acceptance was far beyond my knowledge. I was never told why I was night blind just that I was and it was something I would have to carry with me throughout my life. It was a heavy load for a young boy to carry but I like to believe they told me about my night blindness at that young tender age not to burden me but to allow me to grow and adapt much easier then if I was told later in life. They somehow knew the shock of knowing I had a vision problem could be easier handled then an adolescent or adult.

My father, a hard-working miner, decided to move his family closer to his work. It was a move I never forgot. I remember the trip from home in Bishop's Cove to Bell Island where my dad worked in the iron ore mines. It was late July 1959, everything was packed up and the house secured for the fall and winter. I don't recall who helped move our belongings but I do remember the car and boat ride to Bell Island. The drive there took more than an hour before we had to catch a ferry boat from Portugal Cove to Bell Island. It was my first time on a ferry boat, a voyage of 20 minutes; all the family went out on deck to enjoy the bright sunshine and warm salty July winds. My sister Greta two years younger than me wasn't impressed with the boat ride and had to be comforted by our mother. It didn't take long from where the boat docked at a place called the beach to drive to our new place of residence in Lance Cove.

I was in new surroundings and when darkness fell that evening I felt alone and scared. Our mother sensed our fears and tried to comfort both me and my sister. Still, the unfamiliarity of our new surroundings played havoc with my emotions until sleep took control cleansing my mind of fearful thoughts. We started school that fall; I had hardly enough time to make any friends so I was to be a loner for a longer period of time than my older brother and sister. My problem again with making friends was restricted to daylight hours and not after dark. My older brother and sister didn't have that problem and fitted in nicely with their peer groups. On the other hand, here was myself and my younger sister restricted to playing with each other just to pass time.

In the first week after we arrived on the island, my father stood by my side and pointed to the waters off Lance Cove. He then told a story from World War Two. The story was about a German submarine which settled on the bottom just off Lance Cove and when they got the opportunity they came to periscope depth and torpedoed three iron ore ships sinking each one as well as destroying the main loading pier for loading iron ore. What was more surprising to me was the part of the story he told about his participation in that event. In his recollection of the story, he said he was a sailor in the British Navy assigned to a British Destroyer which hunted down the submarine and depth charged it from the waters of Conception Bay to the rocky shores near Bay Bulls NL. However, he wasn't sure if the depth charges sunk the submarine or not. My father had always been my hero and that story reinforced his stature as my hero. I was so fascinated about the story, I wanted to follow in his footsteps and join the Navy. However, I was so naive and couldn't assimilate the fact that my dreams of becoming a sailor would never come to reality.

Winter passed slowly as all winters do and soon spring was upon us. It took most of the winter at school to develop a small group of friends. I wasn't privy to my parents' plans as to how long we were to live on Bell Island so until it was necessary, I never felt the need to tell anyone that I couldn't see at night, so my secret was safe. Like all small children, I had lots of fun and was happy during my time on Bell Island. Oh, there were drawbacks from not seeing at night but I accepted that reality and moved forward with my life as normal as possible. I am not sure if any of the boys and girls I befriended while living on Bell Island knew of my affliction, but I am sure if they did I would have been a target for bullies.

Like all children, most of my time was spent in school. But, unlike most children, my day ended either immediately after school or shortly there after depending on the availability of light. During the week, playtime with my peers was either just before the school bell rang, at recess, during lunch, or after school. In that time, I fitted in all the necessary playtime to sustain my childhood happiness as best a possible. On weekends I played during Saturdays and did my school homework on Sundays. As usual, I was always in a catch-up mode with school homework. Of course, the reason was obvious to me, if not to others, I couldn't see well enough under the artificial light at night time. Therefore, weekday school homework suffered.

My parents weren't aware of the artificial light restrictions as it related to school homework. They knew I could see to move around under the artificial light conditions and figured I could function well enough to do my school homework; I don't know how long I kept them (pardon the pun) in the dark about it but it lasted many years. I guess they felt I was doing enough for my grades in school were always amongst the top of the class. However, not doing school homework at home was never a problem with my parents but it was a major problem with my teachers. On many occasions I was forced to do my assigned homework at school along with the daily assigned work during class. Then there were the times that certain teachers took other forms of action for failure to complete assigned homework.

As a young student still only eight years old, I wasn't familiar with corporal punishment as a deterrent against disobedience in school. I was soon to learn its accepted application as a form of punishment to keep students in line. I wasn't a bad student in class; on the contrary, I paid close attention and was very observant. I had to, if I wanted to excel in my school work, especially since doing school work at home was almost non-existent.

A teacher in those days was a respected person holding a respected position and to complain to one's parents about a teacher was unheard of. In all cases the student never had a chance whether they were in the right or in the wrong. In most cases, the student succumbs to not only discipline punishment from a teacher but also parental punishment from their parents, because the perception was that a teacher wouldn't punish a student unless they were misbehaving. Therefore, it was always assumed the student had done something wrong for a teacher to punish them. It was no different for me and if I got in trouble at school, I kept it to myself for fear of being punished not only by the teacher but also by my parents. Thus was a case I will never forget, even if I wanted to.

It was the spring of 1960 and I had not yet turned nine years old. The spring thaw had softened the ground and the lack of pavement displayed soft mud every-where. A person could sink ankle deep into the rich iron red soil of the island. We were always careful to walk in well traveled beaten down paths to keep from sink-ing into the mud. The area surrounding the school was completely covered with a heavy thick layer of rich red iron mud. It was perfect conditions for basing marbles off the school's rear concrete foundation. A small narrow but shallow babbling brook ran alongside the school was still frozen over. The rushing cold water un-derneath slowly undermined its icy cover. The end result was to deposit the broken ice fragments further down stream were the fresh and salt water met. Once in awhile large chunks of ice would break away from its banks edge and a torrent of water would flush them over onto the riverbank itself. It was the middle of the week, a typical day on Bell Island (also known as Wabanna). Cloudy, damp, foggy weather was usually the norm and it was no different that day. It was almost time to return to school after lunch and we still had enough time to play at least one game of basing marbles. The girls with their skipping ropes sought out mud-free areas to skip or have a game of hop scotch. The boys with their bag of marbles crowded behind the school by its concrete foundation measuring the distance their marble would have to travel to become a winner. The cold damp weather didn't bother us much; there were marbles to be won and the sticky mud ensured the marbles didn't role too far. Of course, during the process of basing marbles our hands got quite dirty, reddened with many layers of thick iron ore rich red clay mud. Before entering class, we all went to the washroom and cleaned our hands as best we could. However, the lack of soap and hot water often left our hands icy cold and ingrained with the red mud as we returned to the classroom. I wasn't no different than the remainder of the boys; my hands were just as cold and as clean as theirs.

After the resumption of class, Miss Monica Reese, our teacher, instructed the grade three class to get out their readers and open them to a certain story. The remaining grade four and five students were ordered to work on their previously assigned work.

With her attention still focused on the grade three class, she then selected several people to read aloud. It was part of our homework to read an assigned section from our reader and each day a selected group would read aloud that assigned section to the class. I would be third in the list to read. My arithmetic homework was done, my spelling was memorized, but my reading aloud was somewhat less impressive. Learning to read under the yellow glow of the light bulb, or the kerosene lamp was quite the task for me to accomplish. If the reading passage was short, I could possibly stumble through it given enough time. But this passage was long and getting through it would be quite difficult maybe even impossible for me. Ample time, lighting conditions and a vision problem would be my nemesis. I tried to focus but the words and letters kept appearing and disappearing, looking mostly like smudges on the bright sheets of white paper. I would be the laughing stock of the class stammering and stumbling over my words.

The classroom was comprised of three grade levels, grades three, our and five. It was evening now; the morning light had faded into oblivion and the evening light always was a little duller to me. I sat by the far wall off the classroom away from the direct natural light entering through a large bank of the window. Being by the far wall in the classroom I was shrouded in its darkest area. I had just come in from outside and my eyes hadn't even adjusted to the inside lighting conditions. Still, I thought everyone was the same and paid no attention to it. Little did I know the adjustment to the changing light conditions for the other students was instantly automatic. I always thought everyone was the same and we were learning on an equal level. The changing light of day, the extended time it took my eyes to adjust, the darkly painted classroom with its dark stained hardwood floors and the bright white reader pages with dark print was too much for me. I was stressed and confused all at once. All I could see were just dark markings on a page of snow-white paper; I couldn't see to read properly. I tried to read, yes, I remember I tried and I did get a few words over a lengthy period of time, an eternity for me. It was then I knew that I would never be able to read at a normal level given even the most perfect conditions.

The teacher halted my reading and came to her feet. The class went silent when she firmly gripped a wooden yardstick in her hand. The stick consumed about two and a half inches of space in with, a quarter inch thick and a full three feet long. Using it as a crutch she marched to my desk where I was sitting unsure of what was to come. The sound of her shoes clicked on the hardwood floor with each footstep. The yard stick rang louder with its echoing thud as it too hit the floor in tune with the steady rhythm of her footsteps.

The stick stopped at my desk and flew from the floor to land flatly on top of the desk with a loud snapping sound. I kept my head down and waited for whatever was to come. The yard stick lay silently on the desk marinating in the loosened wooden fibres between the yard stick and the desk top. My eyes were transfixed on the yardstick; it would soon be the instrument for my punishment.

My ears were alert as the piercing voice of Miss Reese questioned me why I couldn't read my assigned homework. "You were supposed to read that story last night, weren't you?" she questioned. "You knew you would be asked to read today, didn't you?" she questioned again. "You know I don't like it when homework isn't done," she asserted. I never had time to answer either question; it was all Miss Reese. "I will take no excuses for not doing homework," she stated. "What do you have to say for yourself?" came a direct question. Finally, a break in the piercing voice of Miss Reese, but what would I say?

My response came slowly with no excuses and no lies. I tilted my head upward and allowed my eyes to focus on hers. In them I saw no compassion just emptiness and a cold icy stare. I began with my reason as to why. "Miss Reese," I said in earnest, "I couldn't see to read the assigned homework last night; it all looked like smudged out words on the paper. I did the arithmetic, printed the four lines of copy and learned my spelling before supper," I said proudly. "After super I got out my reader and tried to read over the assigned reading but I couldn't see the words," I explained. Continuing, I said, "My mom read it for me and then I went to bed. Just now, the white pages on the reader seemed smudged to my eyes once again and I could only see certain words and recognized certain letters; I am sorry, Miss. Please let me try again," I pleaded.

Miss Reese snarled at me, "Don't tell me any lies. For telling me lies and not finishing your homework you must be punished." My eyes caught the sight of the yardstick as it rose to rest on her shoulder as if she was a soldier carrying a gun. She said, "Stand up and hold out your hands. There will be five straps on each hand as punishment. Five on the right hand for not doing your homework and five on the left hand for telling me lies." A wide grin came to her face and her eyes lit up in excitement. Standing on my feet with my hands out in front of me, I awaited my punishment.

Miss Reese was a tall thin woman towering above me a short chubby eight-year-old boy. I tried to look into some empty space between us but found I couldn't. My focus was still staring directly into her eyes. Suddenly there was a change in her eyes; it now reflected sheer delight. Her facial features brightened as well as the huge facial grin grew wider. Although a leather strap remained hidden in her desk, her preferred weapon of punishment was the yardstick. Then it begun; down came the yardstick with excessive force equally on each hand until the ten straps were complete. I held my ground and kept my tears inside as I gritted my teeth. I would not be a crybaby and belittle myself in front of the whole class room. Miss Reese had done a good job of doing that for me. I was about to sit down but Miss Reese snarled again.

"Your hands are filthy dirty," she said. I gazed at my painfully stinging bright red hands. The ingrained dirt in my hands was more defining underneath the reddened skin. The pain I felt in my hands was unbearable and I wanted to sit and suffer in silence. "Remain standing," she said, "hold out those hands again!" came the command. "Did you wash you hands before you came into class?" she questioned.

"Yes, Miss," I choked out.

"Why are they still dirty?" she asked.

"I don't know, Miss," came a snivelling whimper but still no tears.

"For having dirty hands in class," she said, "I must strap you again." Down came my tormentor five more times on each hand with equal punishing force. How I held back the tears and the need to cry out loud I don't know, but I did.

I thought it was over and turned towards my desk to sit as the punisher rested on her shoulder. Then her mouth opened and she said, "Follow me." A cold icy stare with an anxious delight solidified her gaze. I was beyond myself, where was she taking me and why? The twenty straps on my hands had done its damage. Blood was just underneath the skin ready to break through; the pain was more than a little boy should have to tolerate, but I did.

I remember coming into class after washing my hands in the washroom with no soap available and only cold water to rinse the dirt off them. They were cold but the strapping heated them quite quickly. I thought the cold running water might ease the pain and give me some relief. As instructed, I followed Miss Reese out through the classroom door to the main entrance leading outside. The washroom was directly across where we stood but Miss Reese turned her attention to the out-side door. My thoughts went blank. Where she was going to take me, I didn't know. She then opened the door and walked out with me behind her. Her footsteps headed towards the little babbling brook running continuously alongside the school. Miss Reese stopped by the brook's muddy bank.

The punisher came from her shoulder and with several taps on the icy crust which covered the brook a hole was soon punched through to the rushing water underneath. Miss Reese turned to me and pointing the punisher towards me, or-dered me to kneel on the muddy riverbank and put my hands through the hole in the icy cold water. I did as I was asked; I saw the punisher waving up and down and I was never more scared in all my life.

My hands disappeared into the icy abyss and sank into the water below. I be-came dizzy, sick to the stomach and threatened to pass out but I remained stead-fastly strong and defiant against the will of the teacher. One can only imagine the levels of pain I felt.

"Scrub your hands," she said. After five minutes of scrubbing, she asked to see them. "Not clean enough yet," she said as I held them out for her to see, then without warning the punisher bit into my hands again for another five equal straps on each one. "Now," she said sharply, "put your hands into the water and don't re-move them until I tell you."

Another five minuets passed and finally she said, "Remove them and follow me back to school."

"Look at you," she said, "your hands are still filthy and your clothes just as dirty. Make sure," she said, "when you come to school tomorrow your hands are clean and you wear clean clothes and your homework is completed. When you get

14

in class go to the corner and there is where you will stay until school is out." With a poke from the punisher she urged me on. Blood was dripping from open wounds in my hands; the flesh was broken in several places and I suffered in silence tremendously.

The class was silent all that afternoon and kept their heads down trying to avoid the evil eye of Miss Reese. I sat facing the corner not venturing to turn my head; my thoughts were those of what I would tell my mother.

In those days a teacher was supreme and if a student was punished for something in school, then in most cases if the parent found out they would inflict their own form of punishment at home. I was suffering too much to be punished at home so a simple lie formulated in my head. I was given the ultimate beating and survived. Not only did I survive but defied the urge to cry profusely. My inability to read clearly had shamed me in class and the teacher's defaming words belittled me in front of my peers. I felt very small and wanted to hide in a corner. I got my corner, but not the way I wanted too.

However, it was a corner of pride. Through the pulsating pain, I felt admiring eyes focused on me as I remained silent staring at a blank wall in front of me. When the school bell rang to mark the end of classes for the day, I scurried from my seat of pain to the refreshing air outside and hurried home.

That evening when I got home my mom asked me why I was so full of mud and what happened to my hands. I lied saying I was running and fell catching myself with my hands. She accepted my response and lovingly washed my hands and dressed me in warm dry clean clothes. That night I went to sleep on a tear-stained pillow. The day's punishment was too much and my body automatically sought a release of emotions. The pain was still unbearable, however, the silent tears I cried that night helped tremendously. The following morning the pain had subsided but my hands were very stiff and the hot water in the wash pan brought back the stinging sensation during the morning wash and for a short period after. Thank goodness it didn't last any longer. I dreaded going back to school but knew I wouldn't be allowed to stay home.

At the school yard I was met by my friends as they in turn one by one wanted to know how I was and how much did it hurt. They grinned and laughed and stayed around me all day. I had cemented a friendship with many of them who otherwise didn't know I existed until I took a severe beating and didn't bat an eyelash. I had gained their respect and admiration.

In school the atmosphere was different as Miss Reese continued to pick on me often sitting me in a corner and/or strapping me for the least little thing. Each time I bit my lip and didn't give in to the tears she so wanted to see come from me. She was relentless in her will to maintain her absolute power even to the point where she wouldn't allow me to go to the washroom. It finally ended after my older brother Leslie who was in grade five finally told my parents the teacher was picking on me. Which often resulted in a strapping for no apparent reason in his mind. My brother never knew why the teacher was hard on me and therefore couldn't tell my parents why the teacher was punishing me. He only knew that I was one of her main targets when it came to dishing out punishment. My father saw Miss Reese that weekend after which I was left alone. The teacher from hell, as nicknamed by her students, remained cold and dominating as she focused her attentions on other classmates. It would be a very long time before I told my dad the true story of what was going on but I remained silent forever keeping that knowledge from my mother.

The end of the school year was a welcome sight especially when my grades although low were still high enough to be promoted to the next grade level. I guess it was Miss Reese's way punishing me once again. The one drawback was the knowledge the next two grade levels at the school in Lance Cove, Bell Island would be taught by Miss Reese, the teacher from hell. However, the summer had arrived and I would enjoy it leaving the trouble of school behind for at least a little while. The final reprieve came when my parents decided to move back home to Bishops Cove and leave Bell Island behind. Most importantly I would probably never again enter a classroom where Miss Reese taught.

## Chapter 2

# Beginning to Adapt

As usual, summer always comes to an end all to soon. The time for fun and games became restricted as school time would soon consume most of the day. Labour Day marked the end of our summer vacation and the beginning of a new school year. Soon the classrooms would be filled with rejuvenated eager students. It was grade four for me and a new school with a new beginning. As the sun crossed the equator on its journey south, I became another year older for my birthday fell on the 21st of September. If this school year was like the last school year, I would need to find new ways of adapting to the pending increase of school work at a new grade level. Besides being a year older, with a new beginning, I attended a new school at a higher-grade level and it made me feel good. Of course, with this new beginning came new adaptations which I had to figure out if I was to be successful. Still, I would not be denied the joys of growing up while projecting a certain normality to all my friends, classmates and playmates.

The teacher was Mr. Jackie Barrett, a tall man with a broad frame. He was a fair man who shied away from physical punishment as a disciplinary deterrent for the most part. On rare occasions, corporal punishment became necessary and was administered for the benefit of classroom order.

The time I spent with Mr. Barrett was quite productive for me. I utilized what adaptive skills I had learned and invented more. Thank God, I was blessed with a great memory and could retain a major portion of what I read, what I heard, and what I saw.

Things seemed to settle down for me. School work became less of a challenge as the changes I made to home learning seemed to work. Thank God Mr. Barrett didn't find it necessary for any of his students to read out loud. However, I didn't always follow my own adaptions and from time to time I fell victim to the mundane forum of school. Not that it was boring but I found it difficult to challenge myself early in the adaptive process. The marks on my report cards often reflected my lack of concentration on self-applied discipline. Of course, fun and games took precedence over school and the overpowering urge to ignore school was always there. Still, I managed to maintain an acceptable level of grading on my report cards. I often placed in the top ten of my class and my teachers often remarked I could improve and do better. If they only knew what challenges I faced in reality!

They perhaps saw in me something I couldn't see in myself. I worked extremely hard for my grades and couldn't see myself improving, after all I saw other students socializing more than me and they still maintained good grades. So, I questioned myself why should I neglect what social life I had and bury myself in school learning. Other times I often wondered to myself, was I less intelligent than them. What I should have known was that the key to their success wasn't more intelligence or more studying but the ability to learn without adaptation.

They weren't restricted by an impaired sight problem; they could read faster and see clearer. Whereas I had to read slowly focusing on one word at a time. The adaptive techniques I had incorporated in my learning process allowed me to study but were time consuming and often I couldn't finish my studying due to the excess consumption of time and eye strain.

My schooling continued as I moved from grade level to grade level always trying to improve my marks. Not one of my teachers knew of my eye problem so I never became a teacher's pet so to speak. As I moved up to higher grade levels, my marks increased with a renewed vigor in wanting to learn more. My marks were more often at the top of the class. It seemed I enjoyed the challenge of competition and the feeling it gave me when I posted higher marks than the best students in the class.

Mr. Barrett was well organized and stuck to his lesson plan throughout the school year. His ability to convey the assigned curriculum for grade four was quite skillful. Most of the work was completed in class with only minor homework assignments during the weekdays but weekends were different; they consisted of an increased level of homework assignments. It was then I formulated a solid basis for my educational growth.

Mr. Barrett's classroom contained three grade levels. Grades four, five and six. The time I spent with Mr. Barrett was quite productive for me. The weekday assigned homework being quite minimal allowed me the necessary time to cultivate existing adaptive skills as well as develop new ones. I could easily utilize my adaptive skills when doing homework after school during daylight hours. I also added early weekend mornings to study any assigned reading material, given that my eyesight was less stressed in mornings light. Of course, any unfinished homework material was also done at that time. My ongoing adaptation to help with schooling wasn't restricted to that venue. As part of growing up, I was continually integrating all my adaption skills in everything I did as part of my adaptive growth.

Soon the month of September became a month of the past. The upcoming months of fall and winter shortened as darkness encroached on the availability of daylight hour. In a continuous loop, the evening daylight shrank and expanded through the seasons but remained unchanged from year to year. As I grew older, the downgrading of my vision became an ongoing challenge. The presence of shortened daylight not only impacted my schoolwork but my life itself fell victim to an unseen disability. A disability no one knew I had unless I told them. After school was becoming more difficult for me to function well enough to do homework of good quality. I found it took me a longer time to complete my homework; something had changed and I didn't know what it was. I racked my brains to find solutions to my dilemma; my only solution seemed to be outside intervention.

Mr. Barrett was an excellent teacher; I couldn't blame him for my troubles when it came to completing my homework, nor did I. Still, I persevered unwilling to disclose my disability and allow outside intervention. I knew there wasn't anything else I could do myself to maintain adaption in an ever-changing environment. Internally I knew I needed help and finally I allowed a compromise between my pride and guarded secret. I would solicit outside help without them knowing of my disability.

It was late fall and the lack of evening light began to stress my ability to cope and learn at that time so I decided to manipulate outside intervention.

All too often my desk was at the rear of the classroom by a windowless wall. Personally, I felt comfortable there; it was a great place to hide my affliction but not a great place for adaption. So, I told Mr. Barrett that I found it hard to see the chalkboard from where I was sitting. Of course, this wasn't a lie and so I felt good about asking the question. His initial fix was to move my desk up front closer to the chalkboard; it was a major improvement for me and so I settled in nicely. This of course was the beginning of my manipulative ability to achieve adaption where needed without giving away my most valued secret. As I have said earlier, despite my disability, I was still able to maintain an acceptable level of learning while retaining my precious pride and guarded secret through adaptive intervention. Still adaption can only do so much for after school homework was always an ongoing challenge despite all my adaptions. I hadn't found a way to adapt to the fading evening light and later the yellow cast of an incandescent light bulb.

My dad's job as a miner on Bell Island caused him to be away all week long and only home on the weekends. His help with homework was almost non-existent. The weekends he did get home were filled with too many other things necessary for him to do before he returned to work. My mother tried to help as best as she could, but with a new baby and four of us in school she could never provide enough time to help with our homework and thus we were left to our own devices and self-learning. However, in the case of my younger sister and myself, she tried to spend more time with us but it too would never be enough. Still, I found what little help she gave was indeed invaluable to me. It helped me tremendously as I laid the corner stone and foundation to the building blocks of learning given the barriers of a sighted disability.

Although she knew both my sister and myself were night blind, it was her motherly instinct to notice it was I who was having the most trouble studying at home. This realization led her to make my father aware of the problem. It didn't occur to them that the yellow incident light bulb was the problem. So the solution for them was simple; an appointment would be made with an eye specialist to see if glasses could help me. Because there wasn't an eye specialist in our area, an appointment was made by our family doctor to see one in St. John's. When the time came, Dad took time off work, and both he and Mom accompanied me to St. John's for the appointment.

The first eye exam is still fresh in my mind. I can remember the name of the street where the doctor's office was located. It was called Duckworth Street. Dad told me the doctor I was going to see was Dr. McNicholas, a very gentle and mild man. Inside the building a large waiting room with lots of empty chairs along the walls awaited us. A large desk was off to the right as we entered. At the desk sat a smiling young lady, who immediately directed a question in our direction. "May I help you?" she asked. Mom took me towards a chair while Dad went to the desk and the awaiting secretary. Shortly after he returned and sat beside us while we waited to be called in.

20

People of all ages went into the inner sanctum as their names were called. My turn would come soon and I was scared. It must have showed for my parents assured me I would be fine. I was glad they were there to protect and comfort me. Then a name rang out; it was mine and it meant I had to go inside. My mom and dad stood and together with me we headed for the inner office. Dr. McNicholas greeted us with a smile as he closed the door and exchanged pleasantries with my parents. I paid no attention to their conversation as my focus was on what he might do to examine my eyes. I was instructed by the doctor to set in a large chair by his desk. My mom and dad stood up by the door. I noticed on the opposite wall from me was a large white chart hanging on that wall. The chart contained several lines of lettering, all printed in black. At the very top of the chart the lettering began with very large letters, but as I scanned down the chart each line of lettering became smaller and smaller until the lettering seemed to become just a black line across the chart.

Suddenly with a flip of a switch the lights went out; terror hit me hard as I saw a small bright light heading towards my face. "Don't be alarmed," came the soft-spoken voice of the doctor. "I am only going to look into your eyes with my flashlight," he said. "It is going to be bright," he continued, "but only for a very short period of time." The light was indeed bright. It hurt terrible and I wanted to close my eyes but his thumb and forefinger held my eyelids open until he was finished. Then the lights came back on and all I could see was a black circle in the center of each eye. What had he done, I thought, would I always be like this? However, to my surprise, the black circle soon faded into the clarity of vision. I could see again and as I thought much better than before. Had he fixed my eyes? Would I now have normal vision? Could I do everything all my friends did? Oh joy, I felt really good that Mom and Dad brought me here.

My hyped-up celebration was soon interrupted. The doctor instructed me to read from the large chart directly opposite me on the far wall. The first line contained one large single letter. The next line contained two letters but was smaller in size than the letter on the first line. From there each line of lettering continued to get smaller in size than the previous lines.

I started to read, beginning with the first line and proceeded to each line as directed. As the print got smaller, it became more difficult to see the letters clearly and finally recognition of what was there became impossible. I gave up saying I couldn't read any more. Parts of letters were missing and the remaining parts of the letters disappeared and reappeared at random. Of course, I didn't convey this to the doctor. He didn't ask. At that point he placed a pair of empty glass frames over my eyes. "I will now check further," he indicated to my parents who seemed very interested and yet concerned.

Once the empty glass frames were in place, they were filled with lenses. My eyes tried to focus with each different glass lens being inserted. Lens after lens were continually being inserted and removed. Each time I was asked to read the eye chart if I could; he wanted to know if the lenses made a difference. Finally, the right selection of lenses was found which allowed me, in his opinion, to read a little better. To me, I didn't see any significant change but only a minute clarity of what I could see.

The importance of getting measured for the right size of glass frames was mundane to me but necessary if I were to wear any glasses. My first visit to Dr. McNicholas had little impact on my life. However, a second visit with him many years later impacted me greatly.

My glasses arrived in the mail a couple of weeks later. They were of small wire frames with earpieces that wrapped around my ears and dug into the back of my earlobes. The fit was very uncomfortable which was a major factor in me only wearing them occasionally and finally not at all. I only wore the glasses for less than a year and only at home. I didn't want to disappoint my parents first and I didn't want my peers to make fun of me. I was in a difficult predicament but the passing of time and my unwillingness to wear my glasses soon won over my parents. They soon realized it was useless to try and force me to wear the glasses. Soon they no longer asked me why I wasn't wearing my glasses. I was happy for I still maintained my independence and my peers were unaware that I had any.

I was certain glasses didn't increase my vision for I was still night blind and reading remained a huge stumbling block. Therefore, the choice not to wear glasses was not only based on peer pressure and personal preference but the lack of vision improvement that the doctor assured me and my parents would occur.

I continued to adapt and change with every new grade level in school without the aid of glasses. I even excelled in school beyond many of my schoolmates. I often placed in the top five of my class. My success came from having a great memory during oral instruction but reading subjects were my most difficult. My grades in those subjects were adequate; they were barely above a passing level.

School was only one aspect of my upbringing; socializing with my friends and peers was no less important. I cherished those days as I tried to fit in with other students. However, after school, on weekends and holidays, such as Christmas, Easter, or summer break, I was restricted to daylight hours only to go out and mingle with my friends. Once daylight succumbed to the shadows of twilight, darkness soon followed and proudly enshrouded the night sky. It was then I became a shut-in protected by four walls and artificial lighting.

I lived in a small rural community far away from any city lights. The amenities taken for granted in a city such as streetlights, paved roads, inside plumbing, public and transportation etc. were non-existent where I lived. Due to the lack of these amenities, I remained a shut-in until I was well in my teens. For instance, the lack of outside street lighting meant I couldn't go out alone after dark. Toilet facilities were outside in an outhouse quite a distance away from the comfort of our house. To travel to the outhouse at night alone for a young boy who couldn't see in the dark was frightening. Therefore the use of that facility was mainly restricted to daylight hours at least for me. As a backup, chamber pots and slop pails were utilized at night if needed.

Of course, flashlights were available if needed. However, the narrow beam of its projected light lit up only a small circle; total darkness existed outside that small circle. There wasn't any fading from the bright light to the shadows of twilight and into total darkness. The flashlight only lit one spot of light ahead of me. Between myself and that spot of light ahead, darkness existed. It was in that area I was uncomfortable and unfamiliar in where I was treading. Even if I shined the flashlight down at my feet I would have to step from the light into darkness and I wasn't comfortable with that either. A flashlight for me was useless. Dark adaptation seemed impossible for me. Still, being bored at night was never an issue. There were games of cards, and board games for entertainment. Radio filled in the gap somewhat but when television came along my nights became more full and less boring. Meanwhile my friends explored and enjoyed the world of darkness, a world I had yet to explore. The mundane years of preteens passed; I forever marked and retained the significant memories, which became the building blocks of my future.

My early teen years saw life for me fall into a regular routine. I was getting older and adaptation evolved with that maturity. I no longer struggled to understand why it was more difficult and different for me than my peers. Acceptance of the way I was and how I lived life came with maturity and the more I matured the more I became comfortable with who I was and what my limitations were. My focus was no longer on why I couldn't do the things other children did but rather to focus on the things I could do. In this way integration of being with my peers was possible.

The life of a full-blown teenager has its highs and lows. Physically I grew plumper than most kids my age. Looking back, I blame my overweight physique as a lack of extracurricular activity which my peers so richly enjoyed while I remained a shut-in. Intellectually I maintained an acceptable level of growth on par with my peers.

My teenage years also saw a new school in a larger community with many more students. I would make lifelong friends and be challenged by would-be foes. It was junior high and I was soon to know the reality of life outside the protective dome of a small community. I was a protected segregated shut-in for all my young years and now I faced the unexpected challenges integration brought.

It was a new school and a new teacher. A teacher of strict discipline that was very good at his craft, both maintaining order and discipline while teaching. The class contained some fifty plus students. Mr. William Greeley, my new teacher, had his own way of segregating the brightest students from the average and below average achievers.

The daylight from a huge bank of windows allowed the bright sunshine to project its brightest warming rays of light on the closest two rows of desks. The sunshine was constant as it rose in the east and sank in the west. The only reprieve from its heat and direct sunlight was when it was at its apex in the sky. Of course, that would soon change as fall and winter settled in and the sun settled lower in the sky and shone directly across the classroom to the far wall. Mr. Greeley filled the first two rows of desks by the windows with the brightest students. The middle two rows of desks contained the average level students, while the remaining two rows of desks closest to the door and far wall contained the under achievers.

Prior to the start of the new school year, Mr. Greeley reviewed all the previous report cards from each student he would be teaching. His method was simple; he would arrange his class to reflect the intellectually superior students and segregate them from those who would need his help most.

My grades were stellar from the previous year and of course I got a window seat. I sat near the back of the classroom eager to start the new school year. With the exception of just a few close friends, Mr. Greeley and the remainder of the class had no knowledge of my disability. It would remain a secret for as long as possible. That first year in junior high took a major toil on me as my disability reared its ugly head. It's impact on my life and schooling became an everlasting challenge.

The bright light streaming through the windows in the closeness affected my studies greatly. The blinding glare of light reflected on the white paper and the black lettering became unreadable. The bright light affected my eyes as dark spots blotted out my vision when trying to read the chalkboard or even seeing the faces of my fellow students. My grades fell drastically. Mr. Greeley felt the outside distractions of being too close to the window impacted my attention and therefore my school work. His remedy to correct my perceived problem was simple. So in keeping with his system of an organized classroom he made a change; just before Christmas break he moved me from the first row of desks by the windows to the second row of desks. However, I still remained at the rear of the classroom far away from the chalkboard and still impacted by the sun's light. It was an improvement but not enough and far too late for my grades fell to failing levels. Thank goodness for Christmas break and the relief all the stress associated with schooling as it related to my disability.

The introduction of a new and larger school, the expanded enrollment of students, would be the basis of my coming out. I would join the outside world unprepared and naive. I was not so naive as to not protect my secret. No one would know my disability existed and that would be fine with me. Of course, bullying existed and as a new student in a much larger school I understood I would be a target. Because I didn't participate in many activities or socialize much, I was considered different. I was mostly a loner and for the bullies I was easy prey. I tried ignoring them at first but it only got worse as insults and character assignation soon fell to challenges of physical confrontation if I didn't do their bidding. At first, I complied thinking I had made new friends. However, I soon felt the heavy strain of being pushed around, laughed at and demoralized. It was then I welcomed the comfort of darkness as the outside world was shut out and I was protected from its ugliness.

Still, I couldn't live my life inside a two-story house forever. I was growing up. The urge to learn and achieve life's goals became overpowering. I would have to find a way to become part of the outside society. After all, I didn't think I was any different than those of my age. It was in those first three months before Christmas break that I found my inner strength. I would choose not to be bullied no matter what and strive to be accepted as an equal amongst my peers. It took a while of refusal to partake in being pushed around and bullied. I also had to re-establish my credibility as an equal and not to be branded a coward. It took several physical altercations of never backing down against bullies to remedy the situation. My secret was safe; I was and would never be bullied because of my disability. Still, I was a loner with only a very small circle of trusted friends to socialize with.

Christmas break was over and the return to school went without any incident. Mr. Greeley soon moved me into his centre row of desks, stating the grades on my midterm report card reflected his decision. It was his hopes my grades would improve with the move; they didn't. Mr. Greeley wasn't aware of my disability and I wasn't about to tell him. I would have to find a way to improve my grades myself.

I recognized the problem myself at start of school in the fall. The bright sunlight affected my sight greatly and caused blind spots and focusing problems. Also, my seat was close to the rear of the classroom, a distance too far from the chalkboard for my eyes to assimilate, digest and recognize—literally to sum it up, I was blind.

The move may have been considered a demotion in intellectual status by my classmates but it was a welcome change for me. The cool comfort of the shadows became my friend for the brilliant sunlight no longer blinded me. I decided then to always ensure I was sitting in a place where the light of day never affected me again.

So the remainder of my school years saw me in the classroom far away from the brilliant light other classmates so richly enjoyed and I finished junior high school on a high note amongst the top five average placements in my class. However, high school was somewhat different. I was getting older and maturity was just around the corner.

Peer pressure, to become one of the boys, played havoc with my existing station in life. I neglected my studies and fell from top marks to average and below. I wanted to be part of the larger group of students, those who were carefree and seemed to be quite happier. I wanted so much to be accepted by my peers. Even if it meant the sacrifice of my grades, then so be it.

Still, I elected to maintain the secrecy of my sighted impediment. I had fears of being labelled and I knew what that meant. Teenagers can be cruel and heartless when it comes to labelling. Let there be no doubt, I would be bullied and ostracized. I would be made fun of and not be welcomed as an equal peer with classmates and newfound friends alike. Also because of peer pressure my lifelong childhood friends would have to make choices and the thought of having to lose their friendship cut deep into my very being. Only a chosen few knew of my affliction and I didn't have any plans to change that. Those chosen few were my most trusted and true friends who would not abandon me or divulge any knowledge of my personal demon; my sighted impediment.

I was fortunate in that my sighted impediment was easy to hide. However, I felt the pain and hurt of others who had a functional impediment, which could not be hidden easy. Impediments such as mobility, deafness, Tourette's and stammering of speech were but a few that would absorb the full brunt of bulling, degrading and ostracizing at every opportunity. I often wondered how they coped? At least their impediments were out in the open while mine was still hidden. Was coping with my functional impediment more challenging and stressful than that of others who were disadvantaged? To this day I have yet to finalize an answer to that question.

Being young and now more carefree and of course less restricted at home, I lived like most teenagers my age, taking it one day at a time. Of course, I still had barriers to climb and obstacles to overcome without giving away my most inner secret.

Time slipped by through high school and I adapted to the ever-changing lifestyle of an adolescent, not yet matured but still in my teenager years. Because of my restricted lifestyle and parental protection, I was no doubt far behind the adolescent development than my peers. This of course was also a challenge for me; it took all my skills, adaptive practices and a willingness to succeed. The free-dom of a huge world I was introduced to during high school provided a pathway to maturity. Upon graduation I elected to take a break from schooling. I knew I wanted to do something special for myself and for others, but the taste of the un-restricted spaces in an evolving world was very alluring. Temptation was too great to ignore so for a short while at least I took the time to explore it. Although, I did promise myself I would return to my studies and enroll into a university where I would focus on a degree in social work. It would be a challenge, but no harder than the hurdles life had forced me to overcome thus far.

Up to that point in my life, my main focus on dealing with a functional im-pediment was not solely or collectively centred on my home and social life but mainly on my educational schooling. Of course, high school was no different when it came to self-accommodation, or adaptation to be creative in absorbing, digesting and retaining the necessary information required to move ahead in school than it was in primary, elementary and junior high. I needed a much-deserved break and so I took the time to experience life outside school.

My growth, socially, outside of school, from childhood through puberty and into manhood went from a protective shut-in state into a self-defined choice of knowing it was I who was in control. The world was evolving more and more. Mobility for me became a little easier to access; streetlights lit up the night sky. My friends got vehicles and when I accompanied them, the safety of being inside a vehicle was very comforting. Still, there were drawbacks to my newfound free-dom, i.e. streetlights often burnt out leaving areas of complete darkness until re-placement lights were installed which often took a month or more. Also, not all communities had streetlights and of course inside a vehicle apart from the dash lights I was always in the dark. Therefore, only my most trusted friends and fam-ily were my chauffeurs. This option was not always available to me as my friends as well as family members had their own priorities. In those times I was left to make a choice to either walk in the darkness under the dimly lit streetlights or stay a shut-in.

The knowledge I was restricted to a marginal independence outside due to limitations haunted my soul. However, being a shut-in was much easier and less restrictive than facing the unknown in the outside darkness. At least my limitations seemed to be far less and I enjoyed the mobility of independence inside as I could see very plainly in a well-lit room. The only eye-related stress I had to cope with was school homework. I was never disoriented or confused, even when the lights were out, for I had formed a mental map of our house in the dark.

My parents were always great company and of course I had my younger sister to play with. My older siblings would join us in play whenever they were home at night. Yes, it was a comfortable life being a shut-in, protected and shielded from the outside world. There was security, love, compassion and understanding which only a family can give. However, there were things even here I had to adapt to. Because from time-to-time things got changed around, I had to make mental notes of where everything was in case the lights did go out.

There were fourteen steps leading upstairs and I counted each one every time I was in the dark. In the dark my ears became my eyes for I had to listen for every sound of my family moving around. In that way I knew where they were at all times.

Often, they would move a chair or something else that would be left directly in my path. Most of the time my ears would alert of an object being moved and I would visualize its new place of residence. This of course from time to time would lead to a trip and fall, but other times I was able to navigate around the relocated object. It soon became apparent I was not the only one who had to adapt; my whole family soon realized they too needed to practice adaptation as well. Tidiness was a necessity; obstruction was to be kept out of the way at all times. Because my sister and I were night blind, watchful eyes were to be focused on us in the dark to ensure we were always safe. Conversation was a must, no matter how mundane it seemed. This, of course, would aid in maintaining a calming effect, offsetting stress and disorientation. It also brought the family closer together in all aspects of family life. I always knew I could depend upon my family no matter what.

I was totally independent at home during the night time but longed for that same independence outside. I was totally independent during day light hours outside. However, I was not independent outside in the dark—a feeling I wanted so much to experience. To that end I needed and would challenge myself to achieve that notion.

Somewhere, between birth and teenage years, I acknowledged I was different than my peers. The difference was a marked restriction in sight. It would be described later as a disability, one that had forced me to fabricate my own special way of living. Education would always be a significant challenge. However, education wasn't my only challenge.

With the unimpeded growth to maturity, I soon discovered the stimulating hormones of puberty to be quite overpowering. Through my early teen years and even into my mid teens I was still a shut-in at night time. My parents were still very much protective and quite unwilling to allow me to be out at night.

My body began to take a manly shape and my voice became heavier and fuller. My physical stature soon left my childhood behind as my shoulders widened and muscles became harder and larger. I grew at an alarming rate. I also noticed I wasn't the only one who was growing up. Both my male and female peers seemed to turn the corner of puberty at the same time I did. There was one significant difference: a barrier of darkness separated my peers from myself. They were out experiencing their newfound attraction to the opposite sex. Of course, for the majority of my peers this type of activity occurred mostly at night under the shroud of darkness; Mother Nature had planed it that way.

Being a shut-in at night wasn't the right place for a maturing teenager; I wasn't privy to the outside activities of my peers. That would change somewhat as I struggled to find out who I was and who I wanted to be. Daylight was my realm and the awkwardness of being comfortable with my female friends became a barrier for me. It was difficult to hide facial expressions and physical gestures during daylight hours.

Meanwhile, darkness for my peers provided a shroud for any embarrassing situations. During this period of my life, I shunned away from groups of people that included females. I also shunned away from conversations with male peers on the subject. Because I could not completely absorb the transition through puberty as my peers did, part of my social life with my peers was missing, and therefore affected my transition through puberty.

I was a shut-in, discounted from my peers without any reprieve. Not only did I stay in at night but I also didn't attend dances, parties or social events including just going out to the local snack bar or hangouts. My only excursions out would be to tag along with my parents as they visited grandparents, or other family members and their friends. So, the question was, how could I start a relationship of any sort with anyone?

The answer would be quite difficult for a non-shut-in to comprehend and so I accepted my fate. I would spend the majority of my adolescent years peeping through the windowpane out into the dark. All my friends were dating and partaking in adult chores. Often their chores took them well into darkness. I felt jealous of their added responsibilities; they were becoming men. I could only dream and wish some day I too would achieve that same fullness of responsibilities.

For a long time when it came to girls, I didn't think I had anything to offer them to gain their affections, or friendship. So, I remained focused on keeping close to home. When my dad was home, I would spend my daylight hours with him, helping in whatever way I could in an effort to mimic the responsibilities my friends had taken on. Yes, there it was, I was indeed restricted not only to daylight hours but also to the responsibilities of achieving manhood. I was only an adolescent in training with no responsibilities at all.

The result was plain; I would suffer in silence without anyone knowing what it was like to be me. Internal tears are the most difficult to control because they are unseen. However, the burden of being night blind and sheltered by protective parents in a shut-in environment no doubt played havoc with my emotions. This was something I wanted to keep as a guarded secret even from my few trusted friends.

The need to be more like my peers weighed heavy on my conscience; I struggled to find some sort of an adaptation to aid me in my quest. My parents suggested

I use a flashlight when outside; the use of a flashlight was uncool and would draw too much attention; that type of attention I didn't want. Also, the light a flashlight dispersed was insufficient for me to be adequately mobile. For me the beam of light was too narrow and not wide enough to cover a large enough area for me to be comfortably mobile. With a lack of outside night time accommodations my fifteenth birthday came and went; I was still restricted to the safety of my house after dark. It was difficult to maintain a balance of being one of the crowds, without actually being one out and about with them constantly, including at night. Since the first time I remember being out as darkness overtook daylight and I was afraid, stranded, confused, disoriented and lost. My parents took careful precautions to see it never happened again. But it did, not too often; still when it did, I would be caught up in my worst nightmare.

I lived in a rural fishing community on the north shore of Conception Bay, Newfoundland and Labrador. My uncles on mother's side of the family had taken up fishing for a living. I spend many a daylight hour around the shoreline playing and enjoying the sport and fun of shoreline fishing. Often, most of my friends would go out in boat fishing with the dads, uncles and older brothers. The fishing day would start early before daylight or late in the evening just before dark. All too often the evening fishing trips would end well after dark. I would often see the excitement in my friends' eyes as they told their stories of their fishing adventures. Soon they were allowed to go out fishing themselves with their friends excluding me of course; I was a liability and a huge responsibility. How I longed to experience just once some of the excitement of fishing from a boat as my friends did.

Like all my wants that were denied of me, I internally cried and accepted my fate. Still, fate sometimes surprise us and I was about to be surprised.

One late August evening in 1965, I was approached by my Uncle Tom to see if I wanted to go hand lining for Cod fish on the ledge. Now the ledge was a favourite fishing ground for fisherman in the area, especially popular for hand lining fish with line and bated hook. He told me to be at their fishing stage right after supper. I was so excited; my supper never had a chance to settle in my stomach before I was on my way to the stage head. In no time both Uncle Tom and Uncle Joe, mom's other brother, appeared. Uncle Joe asked if I was ready to go out. Boy, was I ever ready, for me it was a dream come true? Uncle Tom said, "We were going over to the ledge and jig some fish. Are you excited?" The ledge was just a short southeast boat ride across the bay from their stage. Its location was significant because a huge shoal directly off Bay Roberts point contained the feeding grounds of many schools of Cod fish. The outboard motor came to life and started to purr at the pull of its rip cord. Sitting on the taught of a small plank boat, off we went for an evening fishing. It would be a short trip; home before dark was the promise. The ride was short; the smell of the fresh salt air still lingers in my nostrils. The seagulls followed us to our destination. Patiently they soared above awaiting scraps of fish to fill their bellies. The boats carved its way through a gentle lop on the heavily tinted blue waters of Conception Bay.

In no time flat we were at our fishing station. Uncle Tom beckoned me to take the steering arm of the outboard motor and keep the stem of the boat pointed towards Mad Rock which was near the headland at the mouth of Bay Roberts harbour. Uncle Joe already had his fish line out; by the time Uncle Tom and I had changed places, Uncle Joe was pulling in a fish.

As the evening passed, their catch increased significantly. I didn't even get a chance to wet a line let alone catch a fish. All Uncle Tom and Uncle Joe would say was to keep the boat pointed in the right direction we are in a big school of fish. The gentle lops soon became rolling swells and the heavily tinted blue salt water changed its color to glossy black. Gone was the brilliant blue sky; gone was the blood red sunset; gone was my sight.

Daylight disappeared giving way to a nightmare for one scared young boy. Still my uncles fished on and continually urged me to keep the boat headed in the right direction. It was then I yelled to them, "I can't see the land any more!" The boat was twisting and turning in the swelling seas. Reluctantly they pulled in their lines. I could hear their grumbles under their breath; why did we take him along? Although I couldn't see a thing, Uncle Tom sat by me and took the tiller in his hand. Then with one mighty pull on the rip cord the outboard motor snarled loudly. In no time we were headed across the bay towards their stage with a boatload of fish.

The boat sat low in the water with its gunnels only inches above the crest of the waves. The outboard motor hummed continually but our forward pace was extremely slow. I knew this because I could feel the forward push of the boat as it butted the swelling waves to cut a path through. The sound of seagulls was gone, leaving only the sounds of each breaking wave that left white caps afloat. I knew there were white caps for with the heavy wind they were always present in the daylight.

# Chapter 3

# A Horrifying Experience

Soon the mounting wind made its presence known as loose clothing flapped freely. I couldn't see, but I could feel and hear. I felt the role and the continuous jutting of the boat as the sea rebelled against it forward thrust. I felt the wind weep cold salt spray all over me soaking my clothing and chilling my bones. I also felt the intangible fear and panic build up inside me. It was then I felt something different, a sense of knowing something was wrong. It was an uneasy feeling emitting from my two uncles even though they were silent. I could hear the waves as they hit the boat leaping over each other when the opportunity presented itself. I could hear the wind howl as it swooped down over the salty water tying knots into the head of each wave. Then there was the roar of the sea crashing into the land wash off in a distance. Some cod fish were still alive and flipped frantically around in the bottom of the boat as salty overspray formed a pool for them to waddle in. Even though every sound seemed magnified ten-fold, I could still hear my own heart beat. All my senses were on high alert but were of no comfort to me. I was in a small boat and only time, faith, luck and the skill of my uncles' seamanship would see us through. This was one of the most horrifying feelings I have ever had in my life. I was no longer a small child crying in the dark outside my grandmother's house. I was instead a teenager facing the fear of uncertainty and life itself.

As the fear of uncertainty swelled me up, I developed a pounding headache which blinded my thoughts. My body began to shiver uncontrollably; I felt as if I was freezing. I questioned my sanity; was I was frozen with fear, or was I feeling the effects of hypothermia? I am not sure, but not for the familiar voice of Uncle Joe speaking, I probably would have digressed into a state of hysteria. "Thank

God," he said, "the stage head is straight ahead." With that Uncle Tom put the motor in neutral and let the forward motion take us to the stage head where Uncle Joe tied up the boat. It was then I heard an angry voice pierce the darkness.

My dad was waiting for us and he was not too pleased. His words were very clear as he directed his anger to both my uncles. "You know he can't see in the dark, yet you kept him out here until now endangering his safety. We were worried sick about him his mother and I. Now help him up over the stage head to me. I will talk to you later." Their excuses and reasons why they were so late fell on deaf ears. He would have none of their excuses; they were responsible men and should have known better. My dad, a veteran of World War Two, was a well-respected man in the community and both my uncles knew he meant what he said. Strong hands grabbed mine as Uncle Tom spoke, "Stand up and I will put your hand on the ladder of the stage head." I did as he asked and he placed my hand on the ladder. Now he said, "Climb up the ladder." No sooner had I put my hand on the ladder I felt my dad's hands grab mine and he said, "You are ok, I won't let you go." In no time he lifted me up to the top of the stage head. I couldn't stand up; it seemed I had lost all my strength. I couldn't see where I was or which direction to move in. I mustered enough strength to crawl on my hands and knees even at times on my belly until I was off the wooden stage unto the solid rock of the land wash. My dad had me all the way with a firm grip on the back of my shirt. My memory of this place from daylight guided me as I crawled across the rocks up a steep embankment and then unto the grass of our potato garden. I had crawled some 150 feet over a wooden stage, over both sharp and smooth rocks up a steep rocky clay embankment and still I had about 400 feet up the steep incline of our potato garden to my mother. My mother was waiting at the top with a flashlight shining down at me. I saw the light and crawled in that direction. My dad spoke again. "You are ok now, just keep heading towards your mother and the light. I need to go back and talk with your uncles." I looked up at the light and told Dad I was fine and not to worry. His massive callous-hardened hand let go of me and I heard his footsteps fade as he headed back to the land wash.

I felt the shivering chills ease off as I continually crawled up through the heavy grass and over the clay beds of potato stalks. My heavy pounding headache and shivers were still strong, but the closer I got to my mother I began to feel warmer inside. I still couldn't stand but knew if I could, I would be stumbling all over the place from loss of physical strength and disorientation, so I continued to crawl.

The internal tears soon overwhelmed me and turned outward as they began to fell freely from under my eyelids to the ground. It was a silent weep but would convert into a loud uncontrollable outburst once inside the privacy and security of our house.

My mother hadn't moved with the flashlight pointed directly on me. Suddenly she left her position in the gateway of the garden and scrambled to meet me, as I got closer. With her help I was able to stand and together we headed across the main road towards our house. It felt so good to have her arms around me, comforting me as only a mother can. As we left the garden and my terrible ordeal behind, I could hear the clear sharp words of my father as he gave my uncles a piece of his mind.

Soon inside the house, my mother helped me to the couch and let me set down in silence. It was then the containment of all my emotions overflowed into a hysterical outburst. My mother was silent allowing me to vent all my emotions until I could no longer cry. A cup of hot tea was provided for me, which I drank eagerly. The hot tea warmed my inside and helped to calm me down. Under the comforting words of my mother, I felt much better. It was then I thanked God for the understanding, patience and unconditional love of my mother. Being a strong woman, I knew I could always draw my strength from her especially in the safe secure environment of our home. The knowledge that I was home, out of danger and safe, allowed me time to digest the terrible experience I had gone through.

I was glad my older brother and sister weren't present at my outburst; I looked up to them as being strong and I didn't want them to think I was weak. My younger sister and brother were both in bed unaware of what had happened, a secret I would keep for many years.

I felt ashamed at my emotional outburst in front of my mother, but she assured me it was our secret. No one else would ever know. She remained true to her word.

My father still hadn't returned; my mother said he had to feed the animals before he came in for the night. Suddenly tiredness hit me hard, so I told my mother I was going to bed. She asked one more time if I was all right. My answer came as a fabrication of the truth; I didn't want her to worry and so I said yes, I am fine. I gathered my thoughts as I headed for the stairs and my bedroom. Lying in the darkness of my bedroom I tried to sort out what had happened to me. I could hear my parents talk downstairs. My father's words to my mother were very quiet whispers but yet deafening, "He is becoming a man; he will be all right." I needed to put everything behind me if I were to move on and so I blotted out their voices. I then concentrated on taking the good experience in consideration leaving the bad behind. How would I explain my fishing trip to my friends? How could I move forward with my life after an experience like that? It was then my father's words to my mother echoed loudly in my head. Yes, I was becoming a man. Childhood would soon be totally left behind. I decided to be stronger and face life's challenges no matter how difficult it would be. With a promise to myself not to break down any more but accept whatever fate the future held for me, I sought the comfort of sleep. However, sleep didn't come immediately; my mind was still overactive. I had just come through the most terrible ordeal of my adolescent life and still I yearned to go out at night. I guessed to be a man the call of Mother Nature had to be answered as well. I thought on that notion until sleep finally filled my eyes; the morning's light gave me new energy and strength to fulfill that dream. I felt it in my heart the opportunity to move forward would present itself and so I waited patiently. When it came, I would have to take full advantage.

The year was 1965 and the community adjacent to where I lived became incorporated into a town. They immediately started to implement the benefits of that incorporation. One of its first implementations was the installation of outdoor street lighting on the wire poles. With this implementation, every second pole fell victim to an attached streetlight illuminating a large area around its base. With my first experience of the street lighting, I found it was enough light for me to see and become better mobile within that defined area. However, as the lighting was on every second pole, there was a defined space where darkness prevailed. For me, it would be a few extra steps through the darkness each time before I would be back into the next lit area again. The presence of these dark voids posed only a small problem for me except at the end of that town's boundary where the street lighting ended. I lived a short five-minute walk from the boundary of that town and I still would have to deal with the extended dark void which existed between my home and the boundary of Upper Island Cove. It was there in that dark void I would still need supportive assistance and/or adaptation if I were to go out at night to a snack bar.

The town of Upper Island Cove was a larger community compared to the community of Bishop's Cove where I lived and therefore it contained a population base large enough to sustain its incorporated status. Because Upper Island Cove was a much larger town it contained all the amenities required to sustain its population including snack bars for the teenagers to hang out in.

When I became a teenager, I felt the itch to go out at night but was restricted due to my functional disability. When the Town of Upper Island Cove finished installing street lighting, I saw an opportunity to scratch that itch. First, I had my parents to deal with for I still had to gain their trust and permission to go out. Thank goodness my dad was liberal minded and more forward thinking than my mother who was very protective over me. The memories of my disastrous fishing trip were still fresh in her mind. She didn't have any intentions of seeing her boy hurt like that again. It was my dad who saw the benefits in my integration into the nightlife of a teenager, so he sided with me in helping to comfort my mother's fears. Of course, there would be rules and I would have to adhere to them without question. I not only needed the support of my parents but also my friends as well, so I negotiated an unconditional arrangement between my trusted friends and myself; there would be no strings attached only true friendship. They would be my guide in the area of darkness between my house and the beginning of the streetlights. My parents were agreeable to this conception and felt some ease of comfort in knowing I would be safe. This meant I would have to leave and return with one of my friends every time I was out. Which included weekends during the school year or vacations and any school breaks. I was elated, overjoyed, and still scared too death of the unknown which awaited me.

It was time for me to step into a new realm of reality. One I knew I would have to adapt to if I wanted to be one of the crowds. I would have to overcome new fears and build up my confidence in being out in the dark. Most importantly, I would have to retain my newfound freedom without revealing my secret, if I wanted to be accepted as one of the crowd. The perception I projected as a normal person was of the utmost importance to me. If my secret were to be known I would become a target for every bully and fun maker around. My life would be destroyed; I would not be able to cope. What would I do? If I stayed inside, it would be the same as a sentence of incarceration for life.

It was with this knowledge I decided it was time to test the waters of freedom; at the very least I needed to try. Leslie Peddle, my cousin and close friend, came for me that first Friday night. Yes, Friday night had come and so did a newfound freedom; it was the beginning of a new chapter in my life. We stepped into the darkness of night under a dimly lit porch light. I glanced up at the light for an instant; it seemed to beckon me to stay under its warm glow. I shrugged off the feeling as my eyes tried to penetrate the darkness outside its comforting glow. No matter how hard I tried, there was no success.

I knew it wouldn't be easy, for all my senses seemed to heighten under the stimulation of fear and wanting. I made a mental note of everything I experienced, such as sounds, smell, and touch. Most importantly, I could sense where I was without having to see. I have always had this sense or feeling of knowing especially when I was in the dark. It seemed I always knew if an object was in my path or near me. It didn't matter if the object was living or non-living, its presence seemed to be always known to me. So armed with my other senses, my friend and I ventured out into the abyss of darkness. Fear was within me but I dared not let it show or take control. I trusted my friend completely. So, I drew strength from his experience and confidence in the dark. From this basis I would build my own experiences and confidence in the dark. Then hopefully some day I would venture out into the darkness of night alone by myself knowing full well I was restricted but yet fully confident in my ability to do so.

It was a new learning curve for me. I had to find ways to adapt in the darkness if I were to become a creature of the night. As we stepped down off the porch steps, collective memories became one of my most important senses. I would remember everything that night and then draw from it when needed to again. The utilization of this sense had one drawback; it was dependent upon everything remaining the same.

It was the fall and a chill was in the air. The dark atmosphere of the air held quite a different feeling then daylight. I would always remember that feeling; it was one of a peaceful calmness, almost soothing yet mysterious and alluring. Deep beyond the illuminated area of the porch light we waded into uncharted territory, for me, complete darkness. Our yard extended out about 70 feet to a large wooden closed gate. I knew the gate was there because I saw it every day in the daylight hours. Now under the camouflage of darkness I had no idea how close we were to it. Suddenly, I got a feeling that something was very close to me. Even though my companion was very close, I knew it wasn't him. I marvelled at this sense of knowing. It was then I knew deep inside it would never fail me. It was then my companion spoke to me, "The gate is here." He opened the gate for us to go through. I stayed close to my companion touching him from time to time and I listened to his footsteps as they impacted the cold hard ground. I could hear his breathing and the rustle of his clothing. This helped keep me close to him and walking in the same direction, otherwise I would have been disoriented and lost. Other sounds were quite distinguishable as well such as the rustle of leaves on the trees; the sound of the wind itself as a gentle breeze freshened into a snarly growl for short periods of time.

I wanted to be independent as much as possible and so I swallowed every bit of information that presented itself to me. Even though I trusted my companion totally, I still needed to remind him to keep an eye on me from time to time because it was dark and not daylight. With his watchful eye on me, it would be easy to find my own way in the darkness through his corrective assertions. I didn't want him to link up with me in any way just be there as a verbal guide. I felt that any linkage would be a crutch and that to me would defeat the purpose of self-independence in the dark. Unknown to him, his voice became a great comforter; it was the non-physical linkage I needed. In no time my confidence grew in my ability to follow him all because of a conversation between two friends. This too would allow me to know where he was at all times and would alert me if I strayed from his close company. Navigating through the gate was a breeze as I visualized myself walking through it in the daylight. In no time we were on the road heading for the local snack bar as it was called.

It was my first night out. I was elated, full of happy and joyful emotions. It would be a most memorable adventure; one I would never forget. I could hardly contain my thoughts; there were questions to be answered; the who's, the what's, the where's, the when's, the why's, and the how's. I wondered if in time if those questions would be answered; I had a strong feeling they would be. I questioned my companion constantly as we strolled along if only to keep close to him and stay safe. His answers to my questions may have been mundane to him, but for me they were extremely valuable. My curiosity seemed endless, but in time only the experience of being out at night would satisfy my appetite to learn more.

The main focus at that time was to get through the dark area from my house to the beginning of the streetlights. It was a five-minute walk during daylight hours. I imagined it would be a little longer in the darkness given the fact it was my first time out in darkness. I walked slowly quite unsure of where my feet were landing.

I couldn't help myself from focusing on every bit of light escaping from behind blinds and curtains, or even the flooding of a small area around a porch door of nearby houses. It was an attraction and a distraction for my eyes, both at the same time. It offered me nothing so it seemed at that time. Later, I acknowledged it did help to navigate my way. However, its beckoning beam of light kept drawing me towards it. I needed to overcome that urge, for walking towards those lights wasn't where I wanted to go.

Being functionally restricted means just that; I had a sighted impairment which restricted my movements in the darkness as well as limiting my daylight vision. However, I was still functional despite those restrictions. My companion had good sight and could function very well in the dark. In other words, he had a good functional ability to see in the dark. I on the other hand had a good functional inability to deal with it in the dark. There it was, I had a functional inability or for a better word I was functionally disabled which caused my night blindness; I was unable to see in the dark. Therefore, my inability to function visually worked exceptionally well in restricting my ability to see in the dark as well as in daylight limitations. Thank goodness for my other senses which helped to overcome my functional disability. Memorization plus my cognizant awareness of where I was at any given time became my constant companion.

During the daylight hours, I noticed, on a dirt gravel road, there were smooth foot like paths. These paths were the result of tire wear from the wheels of vehicles on the dirt and gravel road bed. In doing so they dispersed small stone to the centre and sides of the road respectively leaving mounds of loose stone along the sides and centre of the road. If I walked on the right side of the road, I would walk in the smooth path closest to the shoulder on the right and vice versa for the left side of the road. If a vehicle came along, I would step into the mound of crushed stone and then unto the shoulder of the road depending upon which side of the road I was on.

Also, if I was on the road in total darkness and I ventured from the smooth path I would know immediately. My brain would alert me I had strayed into the mounds of crushed stone on either side of me and therefore off track. I would immediately make a correction and return to the smooth path. In that way, I would not walk over the edge of the road and I could navigate fairly easily going forward.

Still, there were unforeseen potholes I could step into and often I did just that. Many a time I turned an ankle or got my feet wet if they contained water. Then of course there was winter to contend with. Snow and ice covered the roads and I had to change my adaptability for those winter conditions. In that case, I always walked closest to the side of the road where the snow was ploughed up. If necessary I could step into a snow bank on the side of the road to avoid traffic. If the roads weren't ploughed then mobility for me was restricted and I would not go out; I didn't have any adaptive way of coping with those conditions.

The adaptability to become mobile at night evolved more and more each time I was out. Along with my adaptability came confidence in myself and my ability to be independent at night. At the very least I was getting from where I was to where I wanted to be. Which was of course either from home to the snack bar or visa versa. I also knew my limits and constantly tried to exceed them whenever possible. The reasoning to push myself beyond my limits was quite simple. I needed to challenge and test my adaptions in the dark to see if or where changes had to be made. However, expanding my limits would take time—an acceptance I had to bear alone.

Unless accompanied by a companion, I never went anywhere outside the streetlight area except the one stretch of road from the end of the streetlights to where I lived. Being quite familiar with that area from daylight experiences, I became quite confident at night also.

I remember that first year of being out at night quite vividly. It was a huge learning curve for me in adaptation and self-accommodation. I utilized all my other senses and more, to make the transition from a shut-in to a person of some nightly independence.

Although darkness for me was a significant barrier to overcome, I continually adapted until that barrier was no longer a major problem.

Yes, I was night blind but not totally blind. What light was around me in the dark I would utilize its alluring attraction as part of the adaption process. It allowed me to be able to know where I was in familiar surroundings. Whether it was artificial light or natural light I found a way to utilize its beckoning glow and navigate through the darkness; they were, to me, points of reference like navigation points on a compass.

It was a short distance for a round trip between home and the local snack bar. Along the way, another friend of ours, Wallace William joined us. I was quite familiar with that area in the daytime but soon through support, adaptation and confidence I became quite familiar with it in the dark as well.

There were places when the shroud of darkness was complete away from any source of artificial light. In those places the natural light of the moon and stars provided a dim illumination that I needed to navigate. However, I couldn't depend entirely upon following the light of the moon or stars. The atmosphere conditions were different every night and the light penetration ranged from good to bad. Thus, I really couldn't depend upon this source of light solely to be useful. It was however quite useful in conjunction with other adaptive techniques.

It wasn't easy for me to adapt to being out at night, but through perseverance and sheer will I did. I learned mostly by trial and error. I took risks way beyond my level of confidence, hoping for positive outcomes. Sometimes the outcomes were quite unexpected while other times they were exactly what I expected. I was stepping into the unknown every night I went out taking risks, building my confidence, knowing full well it would be a lifelong learning curve for me.

In those early days of dark adaption, it soon became apparent most of my fears for the unknown quickly dissipated. It seemed the shroud of complete darkness was never total but rather incomplete; it seemed the composition of darkness was rather thin for through my adaptions I could punch holes in its very fabric. Although sometimes heavy cloud cover threatened to rebuke my reasoning on that matter, yet natural or artificial light always found a way through, thus providing enough light to paint a tinted glare of transparency through the darkness which spread over the landscape.

To explain the joyful emotions, I felt being outside at night would be limitless, however, I didn't dwell on that singularity. It was enough for me to know I could move around comfortably, especially since I had built up enough confidence to do so. For me the nightlight or lack thereof was always a challenge but for the most part it became routine. On the nights when the moon wasn't in bloom and the stars weren't twinkling, I utilized what artificial light that was available. In the winter, because there was mostly a blanket of snow on the ground I felt more comfortable being out at night. Any light artificial or natural would always be magnified in its reflection on the snow to illuminate the landscape in dust like conditions. This of course made it much easier for me as my eyes absorbed all of that illumination. Once the snow was gone so was this illumination and then I was forced to utilize other senses too be able too adapt to the change. The end result was significant in that I became more self-independent. Although I enjoyed the company of a companion in the dark much like a security blanket, I soon became totally independent with enough confidence to venture out at night myself. I no longer needed a companion as a crutch but companionship was always welcome as being my first and best option. I guess the darkness still cast a spell of fear over me.

Yes, when winter was gone and so was the snow. I wasn't about to give up my newfound freedom yet. As the snow disappeared, I found new life in utilizing some of the other senses which normal sighted people completely ignore or don't know they exist. My feet, ears, nose and most especially my self-awareness became my eyes. I was ready for whatever challenges came my way.

After the winter my navigation skills needed fine-tuning as it related to utilizing the gravel road to its fullest potential. In the spring, summer and fall the roads around where I lived were constructed of gravel and stone. The dump trucks would spread gravel and stone over the road occasionally. Then a grader would spread out and level off what the dump truck had left behind. During those times, gone were the smooth worn tire paths on the road. It would take a week or so for the traffic to displace some of the gravel and stone to reveal the smooth paths again. Although a newly graded gravel road meant my normal adaption ability for walking at night was obstructed for a while, however, I didn't despair for I knew it was only temporary. As it was for only a short period of time, I would always find ways around this obstruction. It was during those times a companion was most useful in conjunction with my other senses. If all else failed and I didn't have a companion or none of my other senses were sufficient then I resorted to thinking outside the box. The solution I came up with seemed off the wall but quite valuable in times of need. In those times I would stand on the side of the road and wait for a vehicle to approach and pass by. While the vehicle was approaching, its headlights lit up the road in front of me and thus with the new found illumination I was able to move forward until the vehicle had passed by. One might have thought I would have stopped then but I didn't. There were the tail lights on those vehicles and as long as they remained visible I followed behind them. However, in time they would vanish and I would have to stop to wait for another vehicle. It was a slow and time-consuming process but trust me it worked. What was most helpful at that time was the ability to hitch a ride and in some cases, I was successful in getting a ride to my destination.

No matter what, I would not be denied the newfound freedom which lay before me. Who would have thought I could utilize this unique process as an adaptive tool to travel at night and feel confident in being successful?

My success of being out at night was restricted to a very small area covering a portion of the community in which I lived and the neighbouring community of Upper Island Cove. To go further, a field to other communities was my next goal. Some of these communities had paved roads which I would soon utilize to my advantage; I had a plan. Keeping to the right side of the road with one foot on the pavement and one foot on the shoulder, I would be able to maneuver fairly easily through the darkness.

The sounds of night became a welcome companion; I could tell how far away or close I was from their origin. This of course aided me greatly in knowing where I was.

Not all adaptations were of my own creation in helping to maintain as normal a lifestyle as possible; it seemed Mother Nature blessed me with something special, something extra in lieu of a functional disability. From time to time a four-legged animal such as a cow or a horse would be directly in my path blocking my way forward. Their presence would not be revealed to me until I got close enough to sense an awareness of their presence, sometimes almost too close. I always knew something was there in front of me. Of course, this would cause me to stop suddenly. I would listen, smell and if needed be, bend low to look up in an effort to see an outline of what it was against the backdrop of the darkened skyline. Yes, if you stoop low enough and look up carefully you can see where the sky and earth meet. The earth is much darker than the sky. I am not sure that humans can navigate by built in sonar like a bat flying at night, but I could avert a collision with an object because of this self-awareness. My sonar or sense of perception was very acute. So acute in fact that any object not alive gave me a cold numb feeling; objects such as parked vehicles and bicycles just to name a couple. If the object were alive, I would have a warm tingling feeling all over; objects such as a cow, a horse, a goat, etc., just to name a few examples. Cats and dogs were more active and could be easily identified through their unwillingness to stay in one place as well as their vocal expressions. I had learned a lot; still, there were more revelations for me to discover at night as I presented myself as a willing participant.

I soon discovered total night blindness was only temporary depending on certain conditions. The most important was the amount of time I spent in darkness. Conditions had to be right; there had to be enough artificial or natural light present for my eyes to adjust. Once adjusted, I could see quite clearly and the use of adaptations to get around was not needed. This I soon discovered was a natural occurrence; I became aware of it as I took more risks in going out at night and expanding the circumference of my restricted boundaries.

The bright light inside a snack bar was always a welcome site. I was beguiled and drawn towards the beckoning call uncontrollably. It became a safe haven for me as I left the darkness outside but there was drawback. This, of course, was not the place for my eyes to adjust. I soon found out that stepping from the darkness into a bright light destroyed any visual adjustments my eyes had made to the darkness. There was never a gradual change; it was always sudden and abrupt; the shock was too much for my eyes to handle. Of course, I didn't know at that time my eyes could adapt given time. My peers could step into bright light or into total darkness and not bat an eyelash. Their eyes would adjust within seconds. But not mine, which was the difference between my peers and myself. It was not possible for me to assimilate the change of lighting conditions as they did. One might think the almost instant change from daylight to darkness would allow for my eyes to adjust, but the plain fact was just that—a plain fact. There wasn't an instant change only a slow and frustrating adaption. Therefore, I elected to stay inside the snack bar until I left for home.

# Chapter 4

# Socializing with Restrictions

Life in a snack bar soon became mundane for I craved more. I had left the safety of my home as a shut-in for the sanctuary of a snack bar and the realization that I was a shut in there. Once inside the snack bar I left the world outside which was filled with darkness and mostly artificial light. I wanted so much to explore it, but there was the fear someone would find out about my night blindness. So, I never went outside only to go home or if my companion accompanied me, and then mostly only to get some fresh air. My friends' only obligations were to get me safely to the snack bar and back home again. In between while at the snack bar I was on my own left to my own devices. In essence as I have expressed earlier, I was still a shut-in. Most nights while at the snack bar, I stood alone; no one approached me to chat and I personally didn't feel comfortable in approaching other people. I am not totally sure why, but the constant fear of having to go outside to continue a conversation may have been the reason why.

Of course, I knew different; for deep inside I felt the pain of being alone. I really didn't know if I could adapt to that feeling. However, the feeling was for a time a bearable one because most of my peers were in and out of the snack bar on a continuous basis. The sight of their presence was enough for me to feel somewhat comfortable. As I monitored their comings and goings at will, I hoped someday I could do the same. There was some comfort in knowing I had achieved my goal of being out with my peers; to this end I applauded myself for that success. However, engaging at times in their conversations and nightly activities would be another challenge for the future.

My next mobility challenge was to attend a teenage dance as it was something

I was yet to experience. Maybe if I did attend one, I might shake off the feeling of wanting to be alone. In time, I reassured myself I would attend one but it became so alluring that I couldn't contain myself any longer. So, I caved into the thought of attending a teenage dance and awaited the first opportunity to do so. With the start of a new school year came the potential of a school dances; it would be a perfect place for me to attend my first dance and expand my adaption at night. The decision was made I would go and experience what everyone was so fired up about. I felt comfortable in taking that risk because there would be teachers present to supervise the proceedings. Of course, I would have to get to and from the dance. Once there, I would have to analyze the situation and decide what I needed to maintain a level of confidence in my ability to fit in unnoticed.

The dance was in a large vacant room at the junior high school in the community of Upper Island Cove. Of course, I could, by then, go there with my eyes closed so to speak, but the logistics of being in a closed room full of teenagers in total or near darkness wasn't so alluring. Still, the dance was new to me and to overcome the logistics of being there I needed a companion as a guide. Again, it fell to Leslie Peddle if he was going and willing to accompany me. I was restricted in the dark myself and a companionship staying by my side all night would be restricted as well. I hoped it wouldn't be too much for me to ask of him, for I don't know if I could have handled the rejection. However, one always knows what a true friend is and in Leslie Peddle I indeed had a true friend. Everything was arranged and when the time came, off we went. It would be a night I would never forget.

The lights were on before the dance started and a local band was setting up. Lots of people were arriving. Everyone was peering off with their friends. I, of course, had a male companion who promised me he would remain with me through the night. Soon the lights went out and only dim lighting remained. I was in shock; I couldn't see. I felt so scared but some relief came when my friend spoke to me asking me if I was ok. Before the lights went out, I noted I was in the middle of the room. It was then I lost complete sense of direction as fear took control. The music started and soon the dance floor became crowded with happy dancers. My friend must have realized I was in trouble and grabbed my arm. He said, "There are some empty chairs by the walls. Come on, let's sit down while we can." With that he dragged me through the crowd of dancers to the empty chairs. I was bumping into everyone and tripping over not only my feet but everyone else's as well.

It must have been difficult for my friend to guide me to a place of safety, but soon we were there. He placed my hand on an empty chair where I sat down. Once I was seated my mind wandered and I questioned my decision to attend this dance. It was all too much for me. I was in unfamiliar surroundings, totally blinded, imprisoned in darkness. I felt sick to the stomach and it would get worst.

Even though I had a companion I still felt so alone. Loneliness is a feeling I know quite well, one I never seemed to get used to.

My companion had eyes for a certain girl. Finally, he spied her with several friends nearby. He was itching to go ask her for a dance. The itch needed scratching so off he went but not before informing me he would be back. It was then I was truly alone. I could hear voices from all directions but I couldn't see anybody to match the voices with. Then, I heard my name as someone spoke to me. I wanted to engage in a conversation but it was totally dark and I couldn't look directly into that someone's eyes to respond to them. To me it was a strange voice. I didn't know who it was and I had no comprehension of where that person was. So, I didn't know where to turn and look to respond.

I felt so ashamed and embarrassed. I couldn't even understand what was being said, amidst the shuffling of feet, the music, the laughter and chatter. My response came as I shook my head from side to side pointing to my ears as if indicating that I couldn't hear what was said. I wasn't sure if my response worked or not, for the music, laughter, and chatter continued but the voice went silent. I hated myself for not being able to respond in voice form. It was then self pity began to fill my soul. The music stopped and the dancing of 200 plus feet fell silent leaving only the muffled sounds of idle chatter remaining. Within seconds of the break in music a familiar voice asked if I was all right. Not knowing where the voice came from I nodded my head up and down in response finally realizing it was my friend. However, self-pride forced me to hide my fears from him.

I was in a world of demons and darkness while he was in a world of happiness and joy. He then indicated he would be back later to check on me. It seemed the lure of female company was a stronger bond than that of a friend. Her name was Rosalind and I assumed they would be chatting with other people and dancing up a storm. I then questioned myself, why was I so head strong in wanting to be there? It seemed obvious I didn't belong.

What were my peers thinking of me and what were they saying about me? Here I was all alone on a chair with no one to talk too and my head hung low. I was in plain view of everyone, they could see me, but I couldn't see them. I must have stuck out like a sore thumb.

I suddenly found it very difficult and uncomfortable to socialize within large size gatherings. Then I realized I had that feeling many times before when I was within any size gathering; it was a feeling of insecurity one which would haunt me through life.

I must have been the only one in the dance hall with no partner. The music started again, 200 plus feet danced in rhythm, laughter bellowed from the crowd. Many voices exchanged idle nothings as a shroud of darkness continued to imprison me. What a sight I must have been for all the night sighted to look at? There was no smile, there was no laughter, there was only a saddened face of loneliness and despair with a total look of emptiness in my eyes. Internal tears saturated my heart. My burden was heavy and it would get heavier as I grew older.

I guess half an hour had gone by and I was almost in total meltdown. I wanted to scream, I wanted to cry. I wanted so much not to be there but rather to be home in the sanctuary of being a secure safe shut-in. At that moment I would give anything to be there; it was where I was safe and comfortable. The final barrier of my self-defense against a meltdown of emotions came when a female voice from the darkness spoke to me. I couldn't see her and didn't know if she was on my right or left side or even if she was directly in front of me, but I understood every word she said. She wanted to know if I would dance with her! Thank goodness I still had enough sense to respond. My response was simple. I shook my head from side to side and said I am quite dizzy, maybe later. A shuffle of two feet told me she was leaving. No doubt dejected, I thought. My burden grew heavier. Besides being ashamed and full of self-pity, I may have hurt someone who had conjured up enough nerve to ask me for a dance. My sorrow was heavy as I felt my heart breaking. I could only imagine how that girl felt. I couldn't hold it back any longer, tears oozed from underneath my eye lids and found their way down my cheeks leaving a salty taste on my lips before I could dry them up with my shirt sleeves. I had lost control over a promise I told myself I would never do but I couldn't keep that promise. Although it only lasted for a moment, there it was, a complete meltdown. It took all my will to recover and soon stoned faced I forced myself to regain control.

The friendly voice of my companion found my ears and once again asked me how I was doing. I wanted to tell him I had enough and was ready to go home, but

I didn't want to spoil his night. He was having a good time, and besides I had already hurt someone earlier; I didn't want to hurt him as well. He told me the girl he liked asked him to walk her home later. He wanted to know if I would wait for him outside of the school while he walked her home. What could I do, I needed his aid and if it meant I should wait then that was the way it would be. I nodded in agreement with his request and hoped the dance would be over soon. The dance was into its second hour even though it seemed like an eternity to me. It was then I suddenly noticed I could see people on the dance floor and as I focused on them the whole room lit up before my very eyes. Everything and everyone came to life through the dark. For all the time I had been sitting in near total darkness my prayers were answered. It was a complete turn around. I could get up and move around almost as if I was in daylight on a gray foggy day.

I remembered during my time at the snack bar there were times I thought I could see much better almost as if my eyes were adjusting somewhat.

Was it possible I had been miraculously cured of my night blindness? Oh, what joy, only a few seconds ago I was so depressed and distraught that I really didn't know how I was going to cope. My future seemed so bleak and lifeless, but things can change and how quickly the change had come.

The English dictionary does not have enough adjectives to explain how I was feeling at that time. There are some times in people's lives where their feelings are indescribable. It was the same with me; I too attained an indescribable feeling and then some. It was as if I was in a world of my own looking out and seeing everything. How long I was bewitched by all my feelings, I don't know, but a bright smile and a familiar voice peeked my attention. It was my younger sister, Greta; she too was at the dance. It seemed she had made similar arrangements as I did with our parents. However, in her case, she had been more open with her sight impediment and thus had a larger circle of friends than me. It seemed she had more persuasive powers over our parents than me and so she was allowed more freedom. However, I am sure she still had the same feelings that I had regarding our sighted impediment. It must not have been easy for her as well; I am sure she found her own way of coping.

Her voice was a comforter and it made me more relaxed. "I have been talking to someone who has her eye on you," she said. She chuckled a little and said, "She wants to meet you. Are you up for the challenge?" she added. I considered her proposition and thought it ok, even if it only could help fill the empty void left by my friend. At least I wouldn't be alone; besides I could now see and the thought of entertaining company might be fun. Still chuckling, Greta waved her hand and within a few seconds my admirer was standing in front of me. Greta introduced her as Margaret Drover and then with an even louder devilish chuckle she went her merry way. In all the commotion I forgot to ask Greta if she had experienced the sight changing adjustment to darkness as I had just experienced. The night would pass without me seeing her again and the subject never came up again until some years later.

As we stood alone, I was unsure of what to talk about but she spoke first. Immediately I recognized her voice as being the one I had heard twice before penetrating the dark silence shroud which surrounded me. "I see you are up and about!" came her statement. "If you are not too dizzy, what about that dance?" I had never danced before in any capacity let alone with a girl; everything was coming at me so fast. My answer came swiftly after my brain had processed the information. It was true I had turned her down twice before and now that I could see it would be wrong to do it again. Suddenly I realized I was there to experience the fun and enjoyment of a teenager. It was all I wanted to be no different than the surrounding crowd of fun-loving teenagers. Her face lit up as I extended my hand and motioned for us to join in the excitement of dancing. Dancing seemed easy; all one had to do was to move one's body to the rhythmic beat of the music. I nodded yes, let's join in. I found dancing came easy to me and I thoroughly enjoyed it especially after the dark bubble I was in had burst allowing me to experience the light.

Once the dance was over, I expected my dance partner to move on but to my surprise she didn't; the result was unexpected but welcomed for during the brief time we danced the feeling of being alone was gone. When the music started up again, it seemed to come natural as my hand reached out to her and we moved to the dance floor joining everyone else dancing to the music. It was a great feeling being part of the crowd and the company of a sweet girl beside me. The remainder of the night passed on as an emotional high for me lifted my spirits like never before.

The dance ended all too soon; my friend still hadn't returned and the doors were about to close. I then turned to my dance partner, whose face was still lit up with the brightness of a star. It was the brightest smile I had ever seen. Where it came from, I didn't know, but I told her I enjoyed her company and I also enjoyed dancing with her very much.

This was no lie; I totally enjoyed her company and the dancing attached to it. Idle conversation broke out between us as we strolled across the dance floor towards the exit. Margaret told me her name once again as if it was necessary to reaffirm my memory of who she was. "My name is Margaret Drover and I live just up the street!" she proudly exclaimed. I had told her my name earlier but also felt the need to reinforce her memory also. She then confessed she already knew my name from a mutual friend. Greta, I guessed, but I didn't say anything, allowing her to think she had a secret. She giggled and with a devilish grin said, "It's for me to know and you to find out." I of course was astounded at this revelation; being totally naive, I had totally ignored the importance and significance attached to her words and actions. She was flirting with me and I hadn't recognized it.

We left the dance floor and headed upstairs for the outside doors even before the lights were turned on, but I didn't care, I could see everything around me. We headed through the school doors outside into a world of darkness only a short time ago my eyes could never penetrate through. However, at that time I could see into the splendour of darkness perfectly. It was a cloudy night with no moon or stars to edge me forward. My perception and clarity of vision was totally unrestricted; this was what everyone else saw, eureka, I saw it too. Between every blink something new held my attention as my brain put it all into perspective. Everything was alive in my eyes; I didn't know where to look. I couldn't get enough of looking around. It was in that instant I noticed the concrete steps leading from the open doors down to the ground outside. I also noticed Margaret was still at my side reaching for the handrail to hold onto. I didn't need the handrail; it was the first time I felt totally independence as a person. My movements were athletic like; I guess I was showing off without knowing it.

Margaret was off to my right as she attempted to navigate down the steps. Her movements were measured and graceful as each step seemed a difficult task for her to accomplish. Human instinct took control off me for with my right hand I reached out and attached it to her left hand. Her eyes lifted to mine and she smiled. A smile I thought could be no brighter, etched itself into my memory forever. The warmth of her hand sent sensations through me. I was helping someone in the darkness and not someone helping me. This was a complete role reversal. It was an awesome feeling, one I wanted to relish forever and so it too became a solidified memory. Still, there was the tingling feeling of warmth all over me. It remained unbroken as we held hands all the way down the steps to the ground. Once on the ground and I knew Margaret had steadied herself, I released my hold of her hand. It was then the tingling warm feeling left me but not without a longing to re-attach my hand to hers once again, but I thought it otherwise. There were others around and what would they think. It was then I told Margaret I was going to wait for my friend to return so we could walk home together. Margaret then told me she had to be in right after the dance and so with another smile she touched my hand and headed for home leaving me with a warm tingling feeling again. After a few steps she turned and asked if I was going to the next school dance. I replied yes; it seemed my heart answered for me. I swear when she turned to head home again, I saw her skip like a little girl until she was out of sight.

Within a few moments of Margaret leaving, my friend returned and we headed home. I eagerly told him of all the events which I experienced while he was gone.

To start with, I told him about how horrible I felt for the first hour or so. Then, I told him about the miracle of being able to see. His response was normal in that he was glad I could see in the dark. He had questions I could not answer. One question in particular was obvious; it was concerning if my newfound night vision would be permanent. Or not.

Time would be the answer and it would come the next night I was out. I myself had the same questions and as I lay in bed my mind raced to supersonic speed trying to predict what the answer would be. I tried to relax but to no avail. I questioned myself, if in fact my night blindness had ended would I experience every thing a sighted person would? It was a great feeling; I would leave the memories of night blindness behind in the folds of time. If night blindness returned, I would be disappointed but capable of dealing with it. After all, through life's many challenges I adapted quickly to each one I faced. Then it dawned on me, from the time I realized I could see that night, my adaptive skills along with other senses had switched off and I was running solely on eyesight alone. I knew my acquired adaptive skills would be there but I questioned my other senses. Would they be as sharp as before? My thoughts were out of control. All types of questions with all types of possible solutions filled my head. My head hurt, I had a huge headache and I needed to settle down. I always found if I was stressing out I tried to think of something relaxing.

Up to then, all my thoughts were focused on how marvellous it was to actually see at night. To change my focus on something relaxing could be a problem given how hyper I was. Boy was I ever wrong, besides, the change to night vision and how wonderful it was, there was something else more relaxing that had happened to me. A girl had asked me for a dance and stayed with me for the remainder of the night dancing. Her smile put me at ease and I felt comfortable in her presence. I hadn't told her about my sight affliction at that time for my restrictions at night were limitless. As my focus turned away from the miracle of sight, I felt more relaxed and the remaining thoughts were on Margaret. I was quite pleased with myself in helping her down the steps. Then, there was the warm tingling feeling when for a brief time I held her hand. The throbbing in my head eased off as blood vessels shrank and returned to normal size. The final thoughts before I fell victim to sleep was the memory of a teenage girl joyfully skipping her way home with part of my heart, I am sure.

As dawn awakened the next morning so did I. I was refreshed yet very anxious for the daylight to wind down into dusk and finally darkness. It seemed to take forever for darkness to come, but it did. Disappointment engulfed me completely for the adjustment to darkness never came within the time of adjustment as it did with others. It would be a while before I knew how long it took for my eyes to adjust. I was left to wallow in my own self-pity. Self-pity is a dark lonely pit I knew too well. From as far back as I remember, I have always been continually trying to climb out of it. To this date it still haunts me. It seems I am always following the routine of adjusting and adapting to the dark of night.

I found my other senses were still intact and as sharp as ever. So my comfort level in the darkness remained unchanged and true to me. It would be several weeks before another teenage dance came around. I had promised Margaret I would go. Besides, I wanted to see if the miracle of sight would return to me again. Given the fact I would in near total darkness for an extended period of time. Besides, I promised myself I would be patient and wait regardless how stressful it would be for me considering how it was the last time. I hadn't seen Margaret out to any of the snack bars only at school. Still, when the time came, the main reason I would go would be to experience the night sight again. This would be my very own private experiment. It seems disappointment would befall me again. The impending dance that was to be held at the school was cancelled and not rescheduled. This news stressed me for I wanted so much to go given the importance it meant to me. My most trusted friends were the only ones who knew how much it meant to me for I never told anyone else including my parents. They suggested I go to a regular teenage dance in Bay Roberts at the old bowling alleys; it would be a great place to experience darkness and low light. I would know if my eyes adjusted to the darkness given time. The bowling alley was a large building and teenagers from all over Conception Bay North went there for the dance. It was the place to go for our generation; the thought of mixing with so many different teenagers both scared and excited me all the same time.

Fear was always my constant companion and the thought of unfamiliarity stressed me to the limit because I was never inside that building before. It would be up to me when I would go and that decision was difficult to make for it was outside of my comfort zone. I would be taking a major step forward and a huge risk. I really wasn't ready for that step yet and I knew it. Therefore, I made a conscious decision to remain within my comfort zone for a while longer.

The nights lengthened and soon darkness overtook a major portion of the daylight. Then fall disappeared into winter as the light of day shrank to its lowest point. The realm of darkness wouldn't last long for soon it too would start to shrink as daylight fought back to regain its superiority for the summer season. The new year slowly etched its way back to spring with increasing daylight hours creating an equilibrium of daylight and darkness. This equilibrium wouldn't last long for the power of daylight was too much for the darkness; in time it would ascend to its apex of mid summer. With the onslaught of summer there was no more long dark nights but rather extended daylight for a much longer period of time.

Although I loved winter's daylight activities, I enjoyed the longer days of summer much more. It gave me more freedom to be out longer with increased independence. I had expanded my zone of travel to a radius of approximately five to seven miles taking in another community. While Upper Island Cove was situated northeast of Bishops Cove, the community of Spaniards Bay lay in a southwest direction from my home. Spaniards Bay would be my next challenge as I expanded the radius of my nightly wondering.

Like Upper Island Cove, Spaniards Bay had several snack bars for teenagers to attend and hangout. In the beginning with the company of a trusted companion we frequented them several times together until I had a mental map of everything, then I would be on my own. I loved the freedom of independence and out on my own because, I hated having to impose on a friend's independence and private life just to satisfy my own wants and needs.

Spaniards Bay was within walking distance of home and so there was no reason why I couldn't go there. With all my nightly skills, I felt confident in my ability to go there alone if need be. Only after my friend moved on to other communities, outside my area of familiarity, did I avail of going it alone. By then, I could go alone at night within an expanded defined radius without any major problems. There was one snack bar that seemed to attract a large group of teenagers each night. That snack bar was situated on a street known as Pikes Avenue, likewise the same name as the snack bar (Pikes Snack Bar). It was there that I made several new friends both male and female alike. The comfort of mingling with my peers reinforced the good feelings of being out at night. Also, I was slowly emerging from my shell of wanting to be alone. However, I still maintained my most cherished secret; I was still unwilling to allow anyone else into my most private life.

On my many trips to Spaniards Bay while at Pikes Snack Bar I befriended a girl whom I spent a lot of time with. Because I maintained the major part of my time inside the snack bar for obvious reasons, however, I noted that she too had chosen to remain inside as well. It was this commonality that brought us together. Even though I was miles from home among my peers in a snack bar, I still felt like a shut-in. I wondered if that feeling would ever leave me as my thoughts centered on the girl who remained inside, maybe I postulated she too preferred the light over darkness. It was a postulation I would never get an answer to for she never offered any explanation and I never asked.

I had been going there for less than a month when one night she approached me inquiring where I was from. From that point on we hit it off. Her name was Karen Barrett and she lived just three houses from the snack bar, a note I filed away for future retrieval. I also made a note to survey the area around the snack bar and most especially her house during daylight hours. If only just to familiarize myself with the area in case I had to revisit it in the darkness, if I did, I would be ready. Karen was a typical teenager full of life and quite enjoyable to be around. She had a twin brother Keith who spent his time sampling all the snack bars in the area. Karen also had two sisters: Bonnie the oldest who was dating a friend of mine from Bishops Cove, John Williams, and a younger sister Christine who was dating a boy from Shearstown. Shearstown was outside my radius of travel at night and therefore, I didn't know him until Christine introduced him to me. The location of Shearstown was between Spaniards Bay and Bay Roberts both places I planned to familiarize myself with when I felt comfortable in expanding my range of travel.

School was drawing to a close and summer break was near. Like most junior high schools, the end of the school year would end with a school dance and

Spaniards Bay was no different. Karen asked if I would be interested in going, I wanted to say yes right then but thought otherwise. I needed time to think things through before I committed to anything. Before I left Upper Island Cove, my warm relationship with Margaret Drover came to an end; it was a mutual decision but difficult one for both of us to digest. She was satisfied in staying in Upper Island Cove whereas I wanted more.

The need to expand and develop adaption skills at night continually haunted my thoughts. So before I committed myself in going to a dance I wanted to be absolutely sure that I wanted a relationship with Karen. I told her I wasn't sure if I would be able to make it, but I would check it out and let her know the next day. She looked disappointed but reluctantly agreed to wait for my answer before she asked someone else. On my way home from Spaniards Bay later that night, I had time to analyze the potential opportunity offered to me. There would be obstacles I would encounter if I went to the dance; I had never been in that school let alone its auditorium. The thought of unfamiliarity threatened to impede my progress going forward. My head filled with an array of questions pertinent only towards whether I should or should not attend the dance.

My arrival home an hour later still left me undecided; before going in for the night I decided to focus on my first dance in Upper Island Cove. I was sure I would get my answer there.

# Chapter 5

# Confidence in the Light

The solitude of silence which comes before sleep is always the best time to think and plan. The following morning, I knew my answer and I would relay the answer to Karen that very night. It seemed the relationship with Margaret Drover wasn't that strong and the alluring chemistry between myself and Karen was indeed much stronger.

I would attend the dance on a Saturday night with Karen while all my true trusted friends would be at the bowling allies for that dance. I would be on my own. They had migrated to that dance a year or so earlier leaving me behind. It was heartbreaking for me as I was left alone mostly just to attend the snack bar by myself, which was now crowded with teenagers much younger than I. Still, I took it in stride and tried as best as I could to move forward. I was always a loner either by choice or under uncontrolled circumstances. So, my friends would not be with me at this dance and I would be left to my own devices. I knew I could walk to and from Spaniards Bay alone so that wouldn't be a problem or at least not a big problem. My next issue was to find a way to get into the dance before the light went out and to find a comfortable seat. Once I was there, I would remain seated until I either adjusted to the dim light or I broke down and told Karen I was night blind and needed her assistance. It was a hard pill to swallow but at least my experience at the dance in Upper Island Cove gave me much needed experience and confidence.

I felt ashamed at the thought of having to tell Karen I was night blind; my pride was in jeopardy. Would I be the laughing stock of Spaniards Bay if I allowed my inner most secret out? I wasn't sure. The risks were becoming huge as I faced every new challenge. I told myself that with huge risks comes huge rewards and so I resigned my fate to what will be will be. The trip to Spaniards Bay on Saturday night came much easier than I had expected.

My father in his wisdom wanted the same for me as my older brother and what the other boys my age had. So, a month prior to that Saturday dance during daylight hours only, he would take the time to teach me how to drive a car. I could see well enough to drive in daylight but not in the dark. His one condition for teaching me how to drive was never to try driving after dark if I couldn't see. It was an easy condition for me because I had sense enough to know it would be impossible and so the driving lessons continued. On the Saturday night I was to go to the dance, I told my parents I would be leaving for Spaniards Bay before dark. The reason being, I could walk there during daylight hours much faster than in the dark. My dad said he would take me there and I could drive while it was still daylight. I jumped on the opportunity and so while the sun remained in the sky, I drove to Spaniards Bay. I told my father I would be late getting home because there was a dance and for him and Mom not to worry. He said if I wanted him to pick me up later, he would do so. I didn't know how late I would be so I thanked him but declined the offer.

There was lots of time before the dance began, so while I waited around for the doors to open, I scanned all the area around the school to familiarize myself with the area. All that remained was to get into the school auditorium as soon as it opened. The lights would still be on and I would find a place most comfortable for myself.

When the doors opened, a handful of teenagers were lined up behind me but no sigh of Karen or her younger sister Christine. Her older sister Bonnie was dating my friend John Williams; they were no doubt at the bowling alley dance. Karen's twin brother Keith would no doubt be attending the dance but like Karen and Christine there was no sign of him.

I purchased my ticket and had my hand stamped in case I went out again. Once inside I found a perfect spot; it was next to the canteen where the light from the canteen lit up a small area. At least, I thought I would be able to see in that area once the lights were out.

Soon the lights were out and the band began to play. The auditorium had filled to capacity before the light went out. Karen found me right where I wanted to be. I had a seat for her and requested she sit for a while. Taking the seat, we chatted about nothing special, only the normal conversations of excited teenagers.

When the music started only a few people got out to dance; I wasn't ready yet. I was waiting for the change before I committed to dancing. I put off dancing with Karen for quite a while, even though she continually asked me to get up and dance. Soon other boys were coming around and taking her out to dance. It bothered me I couldn't get out to dance. As usual deep within internal tears stained my heart and self-pity crowded my emotions. I had learned early to accept my restrictions as part of who I was. Still, I knew I would never be able to control the hurting I felt caused by my functional restriction. Several other girls came by to see if I wanted to dance but my answer was the same; I would remain where I was until the change happened or I released my secret. Time went on and for me being at the dance was no fun. My eyes weren't adjusting like I hoped they would. After about an hour or so the band took a break and the lights came on. Through the dazzling lights teenagers flocked to the canteen for refreshments. I decided to get up and go to the canteen as well. I would buy a snack for Karen and myself in hopes it would smooth over my inability to dance with her. After I got our snacks, I turned to go to my seat. Someone else was sitting there and Karen was gone. Thank goodness the lights were still on and in no time I spied her at the far end of the auditorium. Several girls were chatting with her including her sister Christine; no doubt she was exclaiming her disgust of asking me to the dance. My intentions were to go and give her the snack and improvise my actions from there, and this I promptly did. I lost all thoughts about the safety and comfort of the brightly lit area around the canteen when the lights were out.

I found Karen still chatting with several friends as I passed her the snack. She smiled and thanked me as she continued her conversation. Finishing my snack, I walked to the garbage container and disposed of our garbage. I remember walking back to Karen and suggesting we should head back to where we were earlier. To my astonishment Karen agreed! The lights were still on as we started back but the light went off before we got there. Darkness overtook us. I stopped in my tracks; fear affected my senses as my breathing became rapid. My heart raced and pulse quickened; I was totally helpless. No one in the building knew I couldn't see in the dark. How was I to get to my sanctuary at the brightly lit area by the canteen.

Unable to move, I realized I was holding Karen's hand. It was then a feeling or relief settled into my soul as I stopped the urge to hyperventilate. The warm tingling sensation I had felt when I first held Margaret Drover's hand was much stronger and my heart beat quickened once again but not with fear; I knew Karen was someone special. It was then I thought I would humble myself to tell her my secret. Before I got the chance, the music started; it was a slow dance, a waltz. Thank goodness, I thought, as her arms found their way around my neck.

"We are on the dance floor now," she said, "you can't say no this time." Reluctantly I gave in and let her lead and automatically my eyes closed as I focused on the music. The urge to tell her suddenly wasn't so important, so I just let it fade away. Our dancing came natural as we fell into the rhythm of the music. My eyes remained closed for the duration of the dance. When I did open them there was still darkness, the music had stopped and our dancing had taken us further away from the brightly lit area around the canteen. I didn't know what to do except keep holding Karen's hand, which is what I wanted to do anyway. Karen remarked, "That wasn't so bad, was it?" Idle chatter filled the void of empty time in the darkness which threatened my very life as a teenager. Even before I spoke in response, the music come alive again; it too was a waltz and once again I closed my eyes and allowed Karen to lead.

Through the twisting and turning of the waltz, we ended up much closer to the canteen and the bright lit area. My eyes flicked open to see the canteen and the light it dispelled. Thank goodness, I thought. I could see the outline of dancers between the canteen and us. Karen was directly between the canteen light and myself. I figured if she stayed there, I would at least see her outline. Nothing was spoken between us as I was looking around to see if I could see anything else. Nothing was plainly visible to me but I hoped and prayed for a change soon. However, I remarked to myself there seemed to be a small visual change in my night vision for things seemed to appear from out of no where. It was then I knew my eyes were adjusting to the conditions of the dim lit dance hall and as a result I felt my confidence rise.

The band changed the tempo of the music to a fast dance. This time I would lead and keep facing the canteen and its beckoning light. Thus, I was able to keep Karen between the emitting light of the canteen and myself. I could at least see the outline of her physical form; it was enough for me to focus on. The outline of a physical form against the backdrop of a bright light was a new adaptive adjustment for me. Although similar to the backdrop of the skyline and the ground when trying to find out what was in front of me. It was different in that I could follow a physical form anywhere as long as I kept that physical form between myself and the light.

There it was I had identified another skill for future use. If I could keep Karen between the emitting light and myself during a dance, things would be fine, I thought. The music remained at an upbeat tempo with back-to-back fast dances. It wasn't enough time to head for the light or clear my mind as to what I would do. It seemed my vision wouldn't get any better and sooner or later keeping Karen between myself and the light would pose a problem.

I was once again debating if I would tell Karen about my night blindness. The dancing continued; it was one fast dance after another and then a slow dance. I was coping but barely; my one reprieve was to remain on the dance floor. Once again during the slow dance I let Karen lead as I closed my eyes and floated with the movements. When I opened them after that waltz, everything was in plain sight; this was my second eureka moment. I could see again and like before in Upper Island Cove words could not describe my overjoyed emotions. I packed away my secret for another time and from that point on we had a good time. No one was the wiser that I had a sight problem. My secret was still safe. I would only tell Karen if needed, of this I would remain steadfast.

The walk home was lonely as I didn't have any companion to share my happiness with, but thank goodness I finally had sight to see where I was going. Like before I pondered on the happenings that transpired over the night. I tried to understand more about myself and how my eyes adapted to the darkness. It would be years before I would be informed of how my eyes worked and so I would remain in the dark not understanding until then.

To be totally integrated into the teenage society I needed to test the murky waters a bit more. I wanted so much to be one of the crowds, but the sad fact was plain; I was still a loner who was unable to assimilate my feelings of insecurity.

The enlarged bubble of my nightlife remained within the boundaries of that five-to-seven-mile radius for a while longer. I was very comfortable inside that bubble especially while Karen remained there with me.

Two years later, unforeseen circumstances forced me to move forward without Karen; she had chosen to move on leaving me behind. My time in Spaniards Bay had come to a close. Karen and I went our separate ways for teenager relationships are very fragile at best; sometimes they end all too soon and so it was with Karen and myself. It was then after constant urging from several of my friends that I decided to consider attending a dance at the bowling alleys in Bay Roberts.

Bay Roberts was outside my five-to-seven-mile comfort zone. If I went to

Bay Roberts to the dance, I would be entering a new unfamiliar territory and expanding my nightly world. I knew it would take me time to get comfortable with the area and I would have to adjust but I was ready. A lot had changed in the time I spent in Spaniards Bay. Most of my friends had a driver's license and a vehicle or access to one. This of course caused me to be somewhat jealous and envious of them. I constantly had to battle self-pity; no one ever knew how much I suffered in silence due to my functional restriction.

Mobility over longer distances was no longer a major problem for me. Although I never took advantage of my friend's access to vehicles, I was often asked to join them on outings both day and night. The luxury of being in a vehicle greatly reduced the need to adapt outside. I was picked up and dropped off at home. I never had to leave the vehicle if I didn't want to. The dash lights in the vehicle greatly improved my comfort and vision within the vehicle. Things were changing for me no doubt for the better, I thought. A careful review of all my adaptive tools, senses and expanding zone of comfort weighed heavy on any future decision making with respect to night outings. My next most important decision of attending a dance in Bay Roberts continued to occupy my mind. I knew I would be able to get to and from the dance with a companion. I knew it was going to be stressful with my fears of not seeing in the darkness. I also knew I would be mingling through a large crowd of teenagers which gave me a scary feeling of helplessness. To that end, I wasn't sure I would be able to contain unwanted emotions.

Saturday night came on too soon; I wanted so much to get it over with. I was beginning to doubt my decision yet deep inside I knew if I turned back then I would never try again.

A car ride to Bay Roberts sealed my faith and I had to make the best of it. The bowling alleys dance was no different than the other dances. There were several exceptions to contend with; the crowd was larger and the lights were dimmer. There wouldn't be any chaperone to maintain order but instead burly bouncers for crowd control. I wouldn't want to be alone if a fight started and I was in the middle of it. I always instructed my companion to get me to a place where I could sit in comfort. Most likely it would be near the main entrance to the building.

Because the lights were dimmer, my eyes could adjust quicker and I would be able to move around sooner, at least I hoped so. Just because I had a ride to the dance didn't mean that same person would be available to give me a ride home. I always had to ensure I had a way to get home, as it was almost too far to walk but, if necessary, I could walk it.

It was evident to me I still had huge problems to solve even through I was proud of all my successes. However, my perception of feeling almost normal gave me a natural high and with it came the feeling of fitting in with the crowd. The dance at the bowling alleys in Bay Roberts was a phenomenal success. I didn't dance much but had a great time.

When I could see plainly, I stood close by the band and watched them play. It was there while watching them play I learned how to play the guitar. I had been trying to learn over the years but failed to do so until then. No doubt about it, this was the place to be as a teenager. It was a teenagers' paradise. All the fun and excitement a teenager could imagine and devour. I knew what to expect with respect to adapting to the dark environment inside. Once I had a place of safety to curl up in, I would remain there until I was mobile.

My companion would go on his way leaving the sound of music as my only companion. Of course, people would speak to me but mostly they were strangers and I didn't mind ignoring them too much. Sometimes when a familiar voice spoke to me, I would draw on past experiences on how to deal with it. Although mingling with the crowd at dances was somewhat stressful, I for the most part totally enjoyed myself.

The worries of fitting in no longer haunted me much. I felt more comfortable with myself and my ability to adapt and fit in. Still, I would remain vigilant too never letting my guard down. I knew there would be times I would encounter fear and extreme risk moving forward.

High school was fast drawing to a close as I was in my last year. Graduation was near and so was the high school prom. Before the school year end, I attended our graduating prom confident yet alert and aware. It was what I expected. There too were the same problems of adapting to the dark. It took time but my eyes absorbed the dim light slowly adapting. Although the venue was different, I had the ability to remain focused and confident in everything working out. However, I soon realized I had more problems other then just adapting to darkness. Most of the students attending the graduation were well known to me: classmates, friends and acquaintants. To this end I didn't feel totally comfortable even in their presence. Although a large crowd at the bowling alleys dance didn't seem to bother me, being at the graduation dance was different. These were students who were closer to me and therefore the need to protect my secret seemed most important. I didn't want to be treated different or looked upon as a sub-standard person.

My mind wondered and I reflected back to years earlier when I encountered the same feelings during the first two dances I attended. At that time, I discounted it as the fear of the darkness and my inability to cope. I thought I had conquered it by the time I attended the bowling alleys dance. I was comfortable at the bowling alleys and nothing seemed out of place. I asked myself what was the difference here. I was wrong in assuming I had conquered all my fears as I analyzed my inner soul. The night continued without me ever having one dance; I was a loner with nobody to comfort me. This was supposed to be the best night of my teenage years, leaving high school and moving forward with life but it was the worst dance I had ever attended.

The feeling was one of loneliness and rejection. Self-evaluation told me I really couldn't initiate a conversation or communicate with my peers comfortably due to the fear of releasing my innermost secret of a functional impairment. It was obvious I was the one standing or setting alone not partaking in anything. Because of my functional restriction, I had created my own private space; to allow anyone in would be unthinkable. There were couples and groups of various sizes paired off socializing. I was the one alone. I wasn't part of any social group or conversation. This was something I would have to work on if I wanted full integration into the mainstream society.

My fear of circulating within large groups was real and I didn't know if I could change.

A transition was taking place. I had matured from child to adolescent and was finally knocking on the door of manhood. My body had entered the final stages of physical growth. Educational schooling and methodical reasoning sharpened my intellect. My brain was able to accept, retain and assimilate more information than ever. I was fast becoming a man, but I wasn't quite there yet. Childhood and adolescent schooling were behind me. Decisions had to be made regarding the directions I would take to step into the future. I questioned myself and pondered my choices. Should I go to college and study a trade? A job as a trade's person would provide a secure income for my future. Should I go to university and focus on an intellectual career in the academics? The thought of starting my own business became a fleeting thought but for only as short time, as I didn't have any skills or training to be successful in business. Finally, should I bypass any further schooling and seek unskilled employment? The thought of becoming a sailor like my father was in his early life wasn't feasible either. I had a functional disability and therefore was not eligible to join the military. This to me was discriminatory in that the military didn't represent the entire population only the functionally abled body and then that too was restricted somewhat. The decision I would make would be mine and mine alone. My future was in my own hands.

Being a restricted shut-in all my life forced me to adapt. I had left every stage of my life in an incomplete state. Self-determination with an ever-expanding confidence in my own abilities became a powerful force in my efforts to find some sort of completeness for my life. I had taken small steps towards a life of independence. Of course, independence for me depended on an ability to adapt, accommodate and knowing the limits of the life I was living. Thus, independence for me was not total because there would always be restrictive limitations known only to me. I was getting older and with it came the wisdom of maturity, understanding and acceptance. All of which remained my constant companions as I developed into the person I would become.

I always had the urge to look into the future, but knew it was impossible. If a person with 20/20 unimpaired vision couldn't see the future then what chance had I. However, I realized the past is a product of the future and as such, I could build on it. Unlike me the future has no restrictions; there would always be an infinite number of outcomes. As humans we strive for certain defined outcomes we wish to achieve. Of course, I wanted to be like everyone else but that wasn't possible because of my ever-degrading functional disability. The main outcome I wanted to achieve was to be accepted as an equal by my peers knowing full well my functional disability was with me forever. Was it a fantasy for me to think otherwise considering my functional restrictions and its direct effect on me?

The normal change from adolescence to maturity comes only when a person is ready both physically and mentally for the change. For me, that change was abnormal; yes, my physical body changed; yes, there were emotional and chemical changes within me; however, for me, the abnormality was in my ability to adapt and adjust because of my functional disability; I wasn't complete. I was always playing catch up in everything while my peers moved on. It seemed to me I was always behind no matter how hard I tried. Soon the group of friends I kept company with was always much younger than myself. I acknowledged the fact everyone is different but there is a level of acceptability and tolerance within their differences. It's when the tolerance and differences fall outside the level of acceptability that problems arise. That was the category I fit into; still, the change to maturity did occur and I adapted with it much later than my peers.

It had taken all my preteen and teen years with continuous adaptation against an ever-changing environment for me to become extremely adaptable and comfortable at night. The fear of darkness or of things unseen no longer haunted me, yet I still had fear of my own safety and security at night. I was taking more risks and reaping the rewards but I also knew I had found a balance between my restrictions and my limitations. I was ready to experience a limited nightlife going forward. I still would be a shut-in at times but it no longer bothered me as much as it did; left behind was depression and frustration.

I often wondered why I wanted to go out at night, for at home I was safe, secure and comfortable. Still, I continued to pose that question to myself—why? Was it because of adolescent development? Was it because of a subconscious decision to overcome my fear of darkness and the terrors awaiting me there? Was it because I wanted to be like all my peers? Was it because I felt a sense of loss by missing out on something? Was it because I was growing up and my male hormones were urging me out? Was it because I wanted to experience what all males my age was experiencing? My questions seemed endless. But still, I was a shut-in. Yes, I was safe and secure but I wasn't alive. I only existed and that bothered me greatly. I don't have a direct answer as to why I wanted to conquer the darkness; it may have been all the reasons I have stated or something different. Whatever the reason, I met the challenge of going out at night and I have never regretted that decision.

With my newly found freedom at night, I awkwardly blended in with the crowd despite the insecure feelings. I still maintained my secret of night blindness from all except those whom I had total trust in.

The teenage years were soon to be behind me and I began to think of my sight impairment as more and more of a functional disability. I was 18 and had achieved much for a person with a functional disability with its attached restrictions and limitations. Although night blind, I managed quite well in the dark given the abilities of self-adaption. I even passed a driver's license test and acquired a driver's license. I should note, I did not disclose my functional disability to the testers. I am sure if I told them I would not be allowed to hold a driver's license. So, I remained tight lipped and kept my secret. Internally I promised myself I would not go beyond my own limitations, which meant no night time driving unless I could see, which was most unlikely. I felt this decision was solid for I had no intentions to drive in the dark. The key word for me was limitations. I would not break my promise pending the expansion and contraction of my eyesight limitations. Besides, I promised my father I wouldn't drive at night if I couldn't see in the dark and I would never break a promise to my father. Given my functional disability, I was quite satisfied driving during daylight hours only. I still had good daylight vision, but my driving time was still restricted for it depended upon the availability of my father's vehicle to drive.

I didn't own a vehicle, but as a new driver this of course was a buffer zone for me, in that I had to gain approval from my father to drive. I was not only restricted by my functional disability but by the availability of a vehicle. With those restrictions I would never have total independence driving. Even if the conditions were right for me to drive a vehicle would have to be available. I was even more restricted during winter with shortened daylight and snow blindness caused by the snow-covered ground. Dark cloudy rainy days were never a good time for me to drive as well; the reduced light also reduced my sight. I considered myself a responsible driver for I only drove during those restricted days when it was absolutely necessary. I was proud of myself and the commitments I made regarding driving, even with all the restrictions I was happy to be a driver. I was self-policing myself and my functional disability was still solidly locked away in secret.

I was no longer a total shut-in at least during daylight hours. I could go miles away from home without worrying about the restrictions caused by my functional disability. Along with the newfound independence of driving I was also looking forward to a career and someday, total self-independence out on my own. Time waits for no one and a decision on what I would strive to achieve loomed large in my mind. I knew I needed an income to support myself. My parents had financially supported my siblings and myself up to that point in my life. Like my older siblings, Dorothy and Leslie, I needed more and so the burden of supporting myself became mine and so became the need of a vehicle to be more mobile.

As I have stated earlier, I lived in a rural area and when a person lives in a rural area there isn't any public transportation to depend upon for mobility. Therefore, the logic of owning my own vehicle for mobility reasons was a solid one. I also needed to decide if I would train as a professional or trades person or even forget about training at all and look for unskilled work. The door to manhood was open and stepping through would open up new challenges for me as well. Ready or not, I needed to step forward and meet all the challenges head on.

When Dorothy got married both she and her husband George Adams moved to Toronto for work. My older brother of two years, Leslie, followed them shortly after seeking work as well. After I finished high school, I carefully weighted my options and in turn decided to follow their lead. My reasoning was sound; I would take some time and experience the outside world first before I made any major decisions about my future aspirations.

I had come a long way; the apron strings my mother once kept tightly tied around me were left behind. It was a difficult decision for my parents to let me go out on my own but a necessary one. If I ever was to become a man, I needed to be able to make my own decisions and so I stepped through the threshold into the unknowns of adulthood and a world of total self-independence.

Living in a big city became a valuable experience for me; I marvelled at everything. There was public transportation of all sorts, buses, subway trains, streetcars and taxicabs. Mobility was not a problem at all; I didn't need any assistance. Street lighting was everywhere and so darkness would only be a problem if I went into an area of total darkness. The streets were laid out on a grid of north and south, east and west. All one had to know was the compass and getting lost was never a problem. I knew the compass well because it was part of our island culture. Besides, my father had been a sailor in the British Navy during World War 2, and as such he taught us how to read the compass saying it was an important tool in life's journey. Concrete sidewalks provided safety from traffic while walking especially in the dark. It was a place I finally felt what I considered total freedom; for me there would be no more shut-in blues. I found it very easy to adapt to city living. I didn't need to utilize as much of my adaptive skills to get around and to integrated myself into city life at all. I had the freedom of going almost everywhere without assistance. It seemed my functional disability wasn't a major problem compared to living in a rural area.

I found work, which I enjoyed doing, but soon realized my sight limitations would restrict me somewhat while being employed. This stressed me out because I needed to be able to drive the company vehicle not only in daylight but also at night. There was no way around or adapting to this situation so I resigned my position and sought other employment. This was the first obstruction I encountered in city life. I found employment in a factory, which seemed to work well at first but soon turned sour. A factory works continually 24/7 with no stop. It takes three different work shifts to complete a 24-hour workday. At first, I was on day shift; this was fine until I got changed to night shift then the problems started. Getting to and from work was fine; public transportation was easy and comfortable to use. Working inside in a well-lit area wasn't a problem either. The problem occurred once a week when the factory shut down for maintenance. There was outside work to be done in the dark and the use of a flashlight was needed. I talked my way out of those duties for a while but my supervisor was getting impatient and demanded I do the work I was assigned or be fired. Again, the functional restriction of my sight became my downfall. It took a couple of months before my turn to go outside came around again and so to conceal my secret I submitted my resignation before that day came. It soon became apparent; I would have to seek work that would be adaptable to my functional disability. However, thank goodness, the big city offered employment opportunities of all sorts.

Socializing was quite adaptable as I was the one who determined the outcomes. However, employment was the opposite, I had no control of what was required of me and therefore less adaptable.

I saved some money from my employment and decided to return home. Once home, I would consider future options regarding employment solutions. That spring, not yet 19 years of age, I applied to a college for a course in clerk accounting. I was accepted into the program for the fall semester. I chose this course because I was good with math, also the work would be in an office with good lighting. Satisfied with my decision, I awaited the first day of class.

September came and I was ready. The registrar's office told me I would have to pay a tuition fee before the end of the month. However, the text I needed for the course would have to be paid for immediately. As this was the first day of orientation, I decided to buy my books later in the week. I attended several classes and got to meet several students. Some of these students were former school friends of mine. At lunchtime we chatted about the course load and how exciting it was going to be getting some skilled training which would lead to employment opportunities. However, at evening break my excitement and enthusiasm came to an abrupt end. I was informed by several of my previous schoolmates they were sponsored into the course through a federal government program. The only cost to them would be their lunches and travel expenses. However, some of these expenses would be covered as well. I was astonished, for I in turn would have to pay the

71

full cost of the course, which included tuition, text, and other fees. This of course was on top of the cost for lunches, boarding and travel expenses. I was furious at the notion my friends were getting a free education while I had to pay the full cost. The next day I went to the local federal government office and inquired about the program. The answer I got wasn't the one I was looking for. They first told me all the seats they had sponsored were taken. I tried arguing my position a little more. My position was clear; I was already accepted by the college with a confirmed seat. All they would have to do was to sponsor that seat as well. The answer was still no, it couldn't be done as they only had funding enough to sponsor a marked number of seats and all those seats were filled. It was my first rejection but not my last.

This rejection forced me to analyze my predicament from an adult perspective. It was true the cost of the two-year course would be my burden and mine alone. I didn't have any grants, sponsorship, or student loans in place. All my savings and then some would be needed for the first year alone. I would have to find future funding for the second year. Then there was the cost of travel to and from the campus in Carbonear, if I chose to use that option. My other option was to find a boarding house in Carbonear, then there was the cost of meals and boarding plus possibly a short vehicle ride as well. The winter was coming and with it—shortened daylight. I would have to cope with darkness as well. I couldn't drive in the dark and I would be alone with no security companionship to guide me. I would be in unfamiliar surroundings all alone; the risk would be great. I felt less confident in my ability to take on such a challenge. Carbonear was still a rural town, with only minimum street lighting and no public transportation. There was only one taxi service, so the cost and availability would always be a problem. So, it didn't matter if I was sponsored or if I covered all the cost myself; my functional disability presented a problem I didn't foresee initially when I applied. I may have been overconfident for I guess I thought I was the same as everyone else free and independent. This was a lesson I wouldn't forget not ever.

I left the college and the possibility of a career behind before I even got started. The one bright spot for this lesson was that I hadn't spent any money learning it. I followed up with the registrar's office before the end of orientation week to withdraw from the program.

# Chapter 6

# A Blind Date

As with every obstacle I encounter, a complete analysis was necessary to formulate an informed opinion for adjustments. With respect to my career choices, I discovered I hadn't made a good decision. In fact, my decision to attend college was solid and yet flawed. It was the cost of which got me thinking. Still, I deduced that a college or university program was best for me. I neglected to include my functional disability. My adaption to my functional disability was so complete that I forgot about it. Therefore, when I decided to attend college, I didn't include it in my plans. The neglect of not including it into my career training plans cost me another year of waiting. I would not make the same mistake ever again.

After leaving the college behind, I made plans to return to Toronto for work. Construction work was out of the question due to the shortened hours of daylight in the fall and winter. It would have to be inside work like a factory job in a well-lit area at all times. I was confident I could secure a job like that. However, the pay would be of minimum wage value.

Before leaving for Toronto, I examined the possibility of applying to university. I could select my course schedule to coincide with daylight hours. The university was in the city of St. John's, which was and still is Newfoundland and Labrador's capital city. There would be ample street lighting; I could find a boarding house within walking distance. Even if the boarding house was not close enough to walk, there was public transportation. It was a system of regular bus stops with scheduled stops several times an hour during the day. There would also be student loans and grants to help support the cost. There was a bus system running daily from home to St. John's with a daily return schedule. I could take a bus home and back on weekends. The course load would be rigid but more flexible. I already had adaptive classroom skills and a great memory. I knew there would be glitches in my plan and I accepted that notion. After all there would be times I would have to adapt to certain situations; this wasn't new for me. I also realized there would be times my adaptive skills were of no use to me. All in all, I surmised the glitches I expected to encounter would be at an acceptable level and only minor at that.

Indeed, this was the path I needed to take. It seemed I had included everything in my decision-making process including my functional disability. All that remained was to apply and await a reply of decline or acceptance. I submitted my application with hopes to start at the beginning of the winter session in January. In the mean time, I needed an income to support myself. I couldn't and wouldn't depend on my parents to support me. I felt good about my plans and so I headed for Toronto. I intended to return home by Christmas and enter university shortly thereafter pending acceptance.

The first part of my plan worked out fine as I did secure suitable work in Toronto. I stayed only a few short months before returning home as planned. Once home I would apply for student loans and seek a boarding house.

I arrived home just in time to receive a rejection letter from Memorial University for the winter's semester. However, an attached notice informed me if I wished to attend Memorial University then they were still accepting applications for the next fall enrollment. This rejection wasn't so bad; it gave me more time to plan for my future. It was a future I envisioned with dreams of success in every aspect of life.

I set aside my plans to apply for a student loan until later before the fall semester. The same plans were stayed with respect to finding a boarding house. I needed to decide what I would do for the remainder of the next nine months before the fall semester. I had come a long way and was confident I would go much further, all I had to do was apply myself that much more.

I quit my job in Toronto to return home and enroll at university. However, I hadn't planned on being rejected for the winter semester. I carefully considered the options that lay before me. I could return to Toronto and seek work, but it was winter and work would be hard to find as factory production slowed down in the winter and most people working there tend to remain in their positions until after winter breaks. So, a trip to Toronto for work wasn't feasible. Going to university was out of the question due to a letter of rejection. Finding work at home would be difficult even at the best of times and now during winter it would be almost impossible. However, I remained confident and would try and find work at home. There was one other option I had to consider—unemployment insurance. I had enough insurable workweeks to apply. I would have to apply regardless in case I couldn't find any work.

I still needed an income to sustain myself and unemployment insurance would do that so I applied for it as a bridge to another job or until I was enrolled into university. Sometimes faith surprises us and it surprised me for shortly after Christmas a friend of mine, Randell Smith, informed me he had spoken to his dad about considering me for a job. His father, Jack Smith, was a skilled trades person currently employed as a site supervisor on a major construction site. I commonly called him Uncle Jack not that he was my uncle but I was taught to show respect for my elders at a young age. Also, Uncle Jack was a long-time friend of my father and a cousin of my mother, so I was well known to him.

The short month of February was nearly over when I was called to Uncle Jack's house. Uncle Jack informed me I was to start work at the Oil Refinery site near Come By Chance, Newfoundland and Labrador. I would be hired and trained as an office clerk with work to start the first week of March. Uncle Jack had thought it through; he knew of my functional disability and so he secured a job for me in the office where the lighting would be constant. I thanked both Randell and Uncle Jack for their support and confidence in me. I knew what I had to do next. I needed a ride to and from the work site on a daily basis.

This wasn't a problem as a lot of construction workers from my area were being hired to start work that same time. They would be seeking passengers to accompany them to work thus helping to reduce their fuel costs in commuting to work.

The shrinkage of daylight had hit bottom in mid-December and then the light of day began to expand. The beginning of March would see daylight exceed beyond 5 p.m. Daily work hours would begin at 8 a.m. and finish at 5 p.m. I would be fine with that work schedule given the amount of daylight available. Darkness would not impede my working performance. I had sufficient sight to work comfortably during those hours. All in all it was a win-win situation for me. I would have employment income enough to support myself until university started.

The duration of the job was of an indeterminate nature possibly leading into a life long career. I made the decision to accept the job on the premise if I enjoyed the work and it was of a long-term nature leading to a career then I would not continue my dream of attending Memorial University of Newfoundland and Labrador. If this job weren't to my liking and not of a long-term nature with no career potential, then I would continue to pursue the yniversity dream. I would know this from my first day of work at the proposed Come By Chance Oil Refinery construction site.

During the first week of March in 1971, I secured a passage to and from work with a heavy equipment operator who had just been hired as well. His vehicle was large enough to take seven people. My first day at work consisted of meeting with the Human Resource personnel from my new employer, Procon Industries from Des Plaines, Illinois USA. They outlined my wages, benefits and work schedule. I was then informed the position I was to be hired for was already taken and so I was considered for a position as first year's Carpenter Apprentice. I was disappointed in the change of the work positions but I was accustomed to change and so I accepted, besides I needed the income. My uncles on my mother's side were highly skilled carpenters, and being their nephew, I was, of course, well schooled in the workings of wood construction. Therefore, I didn't have any problem doing what was required of me. Still my knowledge was basic in the carpenter trade and I welcomed the opportunity to learn more. However, the notion that I would retain an indeterminate position in the office was gone. I felt somewhat hurt at that realization. I no longer could plan on a career with the oil refinery. I found out a week later that politics exists everywhere and thus it was so here. It seems another supervisor had more connections then Uncle Jack, which left me out in the cold so to speak.

I elected to take the job even though I knew it would only be for a few months, until I had conformation I was accepted to Memorial University. If I weren't accepted then I would pursue my job as Carpenter Apprentice until the dust of fall darkened my eyesight. Then I would have to make a decision. Internally I questioned my thoughts: Why was it so difficult for me to move forward? It seemed I never got any lasting breaks at all. Even though I was completely careful with my decision-making regarding a career, I still managed to hit a stone wall.

I thanked my lucky stars I still had an active social life, one I had worked so hard to achieve. However, I still had to concede the fact my social life may not have been as flavourful or colourful as most of my friends but I was comfortable with it and that was all that mattered. I was barely 20, not old enough to drink legally but still I attended taverns and bars. I guess I looked old enough for I was never challenged on my age or asked to produce an ID. I was not a drinker; in fact, I detested the taste of liquor and reluctantly sipped on beer just to pass myself. What really got me into attending taverns and bars came as a result of commuting to and from work. It started when at the end of every workweek on Fridays, our carload of passengers wanted to stop and quench their thirst before heading home. This became a weekly ritual for most every carload of workers at week's end. It took about an hour extra to get home on Friday nights after those whose thirst needed quenching was satisfied.

I of course, being the youngest, had to tag along and thus my introduction to taverns, booze and bars. Little did I know my friends were experiencing this rebel act against the established drinking laws long before I did. Even though I accompanied my co-workers every Friday evening, I was never comfortable in frequenting taverns and bars. The main reason why was of course a sight-oriented reason. Most of the taverns and bars were very dimly lit and therefore my eyes couldn't adjust quickly enough to feel confident in being there. There were tables and chairs everywhere and for me it was an obstacle course for sure. If I happened to trip or stumble over one of these obstacles, I could fall and worse hurt myself. Also, if I tripped there was the possibility of these obstacles threatening to expose my most guarded secret. Not one of the men knew I was night blind. I choose to keep it that way.

To overcome these obstacles, I needed to adapt so I let everyone else enter the tavern first. Then I would follow using my heightened sense of hearing and what little light was available. Although, they didn't know it they in effect were blazing a trail for me. I could easily follow them by listing for their footsteps, voices, grunts, laughter and their physical form framed against the light emitting from the bar as they excitedly headed towards it. I of course joined in not to be branded an outcast. Using the same approach of entering the tavern, I followed my fellow companions to a table of their choice after being served at the bar. That is where I would stay until it was time to leave. I didn't drink much as it was the start of a weekend; I needed to be good and fresh if I wanted to go out socializing with my friends.

There was one very close friend, Harrison Smith, with whom I was spending a lot of time; for some unknown reason we got along really great. He knew of my functional disability but never once considered me any less than an equal. Harrison had a vehicle and would pick me up every weekend to go out; only our gas consumption restricted our range of socializing. We went from town to town sampling the nightlife and what it offered. It was a joyous time to be out and about on the weekends; we made many friends both male and female. Of course, the female friendship was the one we most cherished. We dated, went to dances, snack bars, taverns and did most everything young people do. When Sunday night came, I dreaded going home early but I had an early rise Monday morning for work which forced me to do so. I was having so much fun I forgot about my career and my future plans for at least a short period of time.

Life was good. I had a job I could work at, while learning a trade in doing so. Although the job would be of a short-term nature, it helped me to intermingle with people of all ages. What I took from this job was not only the training and experience in carpentry but also growth in maturity as well. I was moving forward in life, having overcome the difficult challenges I encountered through childhood and adolescence. My functional disability seemed never to be an impediment. I knew my limits and if I couldn't adapt or adjust I never went beyond them. Most of my friends had vehicles either their own or the use of their parents. I too had a driver's license and from time to time used my father's vehicle in the daylight hours only. Night driving was off limits and I followed that fact almost to the letter. However, there were few times I did drive at night. In those cases my eyes had completely adjusted to the dark and it was mostly of an emergency nature. I never made it a common practice. In fact, one could count the fingers of one hand to arrive at the number of times I drove at night.

Socializing had taken me many places, but the need to expand further burned within me. The main objective of course was to meet and court females in an attempt to identify possible long-term relationships. This process had played out several times in the past but in the end the chemistry was wrong. I needed someone with whom I could discuss my inner most secrets with, a person I could depend upon totally. This person would have to be a compassionate caring person, who would stand by me through all, including the need for physical guidance during my time of blindness at night. This person would have to understand what it meant to be faced with a functional disability. To me it seemed most of the girls I met didn't fall into the category I had defined for myself. Love, marriage, and a family seemed to be an objective I wanted but would never achieve. After all, I questioned myself, what girl would fall in love and take on the liability of possibly caring for a person with a functional disability?

I didn't have any extended educational training for a career; I didn't have a job that offered security. I would be subjected to minimum wage no matter what job I worked at. At that time as far as employers were concerned, people with functional disabilities never existed. There weren't any inclusion programs for people with functional disabilities at least not any I knew off. Thus, the result was plain to see; the existing work force remained taboo for an identified functional disabled person. There was no access, equal rights, accommodation, and accessibility for the functionally disabled. So, what did I have to offer in turn for a long-term meaningful relationship? The reality was nothing and I knew it. I lived in a world of survival of the fittest and I didn't fall into that category. I would have to settle for less or so I thought. My parents often told me there is always someone out there for everyone and I was someone who fell into the group of everyone. So, I remained somewhat positive to that end.

It was mid-March, and my job was working out well. I could cope and do my share of work with ease. I enjoyed the work as a carpenter and it wasn't taxing on my eyesight. Darkness was never a problem as I only worked in daylight hours. My social life or should I say my nightlife was reduced to weekends only because of work commitments. Weeknights were out of the question as I found myself too tired to get up fresh for work the next day. Not soon after I started work a very close friend approached me with a proposition.

It seemed he was going steady with a girl in St. John's. Of course, the ride to St. John's took about an hour and then another hour to return home. It was a lonely ride for him both ways. His girlfriend suggested he get a buddy to commute back and forth with. This would keep him company as well as offset the cost of fuel. She in turn would set up a blind date for his buddy and hope that things would work out. Then if things worked out all would be solved. It would be a win-win situation for both couples. My friend thought of me because I wasn't seeing anyone. So from that point on he focused on talking me into accepting his proposition. In the meantime, his girlfriend had to talk a friend of hers into dating a complete stranger on a blind date. I remember it well. It was a Friday night; I was home long enough to get something to eat, clean and freshen up before I went out. I didn't have any intentions of going anywhere special that night but out I was going anyway.

Saturday night was the best night; there would be dances and other things on the go. Besides, I would be well rested on Saturday night. So, for Friday night I would take it easy and go with the flow. Dressed and ready to leave for a night out my friend came by. I was surprised, as I thought he would be on his way to St. John's to see his girlfriend. So, I questioned him, why was he still home and not gone to see his girlfriend? His answer came quick as the car started to move forward. I was startled at his reply; it seemed he wanted to know if I would go on a blind date with a girl that his girlfriend, Debbie Dyson, had made arrangements with. He had never met her himself and couldn't offer much more on what to expect. I didn't know what to say. He needed my answer then and there as he was about to leave to go to St. John's. Would I say yes? I never had time to consider all the options available to me. In fact, I couldn't even consider the implications of my functional disability into the decision-making process. To him it was simple, either yes or no but to me it was complicated and yet, I didn't want to let a friend down. This was a true friend. He had supported me many times in the learning curve of adaptation at night. His word was his solid bond. I could trust him completely. I noted to him if I did say yes, I would only be available on weekends and not weekdays. He was in agreement and noted saying, you might not even like the girl. In fact, he continued, she might not even like you and in that case, it would only be for one night. With my stomach in knots, not knowing what to say, I blurted out yes let's go for it.

The next hour or so was full of chatter on every subject imaginable; the time went quickly for what seemed like just a few minutes was in fact more than an hour. We arrived at our destination. It was at the old original nursing residence on Forest Road near the then General hospital in St. John's. A few toots on the car's horn brought many a girl to the windows looking out. An excited voice from one of those windows shouted down at us, "Give us a few minutes and we will be down."

It was true, I would be meeting someone and going out on a date, not just any date but a blind date. My friend pointed out the door they would be emerging from. He suggested I should keep an eye on that door for they would soon open it. The area around the entrance was well lit; I could see very clearly. I couldn't help myself; excitement was almost too much.

My eyes focused directly on the exit door and I waited for my first glimpse of the girl I was about to meet. I was beside myself, in a trance. Only the impatience of my friend saying what's taking them so long brought me back to reality. Then suddenly the door flew open and out stepped two girls. I had never seen either one of them before; I didn't even know which one was my friend's steady girlfriend and which one was my date. As the girls approached the car, my friend said to me it's time, you go into the back seat. I opened the door and stepped out; as I did one of the girls slid past me into the front seat. I turned towards the back door of the car and opened it allowing the other girl access to the back seat. I introduced myself with a normal greeting and slid into the car by her side. Her response came quickly. "Hi, Jim, my name is Valerie Lambert." With that a small hand found mine and a gentle squeeze ignited something special inside me. I had warm tingling feelings from holding hands with a girl before, however, this was different. I felt shivers all through my body. She released my hand as I was settling into the seat. Immediately the realization of my functional disability hit me hard. The back seat of the car was dark and with no dash lights to create enough light for my eyes to focus, I was struggling to see. The only type of illumination available came through the windows of the car from atop the wire pole lights.

What did Valerie look like? How was she dressed? Was she tall or short? Was she small or big? These were questions I couldn't answer at least at that point. I felt angry inside and silently cursed my functional disability for its inability to function normally. I struggled to find answers. Then my other senses kicked in, bending around and bypassing my eyes. I smelled the sweet and alluring perfume she wore. Her feminine voice was soft and low. It was kind of timid yet strong. She spoke with conviction; one could plainly see she was a passionate person. Her personal aura which surrounded her projected an image of acceptance, compassion, understanding and an inner beauty unmatched by any female known to me thus far. Indeed, my first impression of Valerie was one I so very much liked. The gentle squeeze of her hand told much; it amplified her bubbling personality and outgoing spirit.

I was extremely impressed and knew I needed to know more about Valerie. My only thought was, did she want to know more about me? As I sat beside her, I was choked for words and small talk eluded me. I was never a person to initiate a conversation and so I allowed her to talk openly. From time to time, I managed a response to her questions. I am sure my face was frozen into a broad smile all that night.

My smile was real and genuine; however, the anger I felt inside wasn't directed at anyone except myself. I wanted to see more and know more. Yet I had taken the first few minutes of our meeting as far as possible in formulating a mental picture of Valerie, one that would remain vivid through out my life. I hadn't paid much attention to the conversation in the front seat between my friend and his girlfriend until I felt the car move. We were on our way for a night on the town. My heart beat with excitement; I was crossing new bounders.

The streetlights lit up the inside of the car like flashes of strove lights. Every bright flash of light forced me to look directly at Valerie. I couldn't help myself. In no time, I recognized her facial features as being small and very striking in beauty. Her physique was of a petite nature defining her beauty even more. The color of her hair and eyes were still beyond my capabilities of identifying at that time. However, by night's end I knew Valerie was someone very special and I also knew I wanted to see her again. I didn't know how she felt about knowing me or if she wanted to see me again but I hoped she would. Before the curfew at the nursing residence expired, we had both girls back to register in. I had asked Valerie if she wanted to go out again the next night; her answer was yes. Her one condition was attached to the reality of her friend and my friend going out as well. Her answer caused me to get angry at myself again. Little did she know I had to depend on someone else to get to see her again. I felt the self-pity swell up inside me but managed to keep it in check as so often I did; I would suffer in silence once again.

On our way home, my friend questioned me as to what I thought of Valerie; my answer came quickly. I told him I was very impressed and I hoped he was going in again the next night, because I had arranged another date with Valerie. He said yes of course. I still had secrets to tell Valerie and worried much about her response. However, Saturday night was less than 24 hours away and I would get my answer then.

Plans were made to attend a dance at the Bella Vesta a popular club on Saturday night. It would be before then I planned that I would tell Valerie about my functional disability and hoped she would understand with acceptance. It was the first time I wanted to tell anyone outright about my functional disability; if she was as understanding and compassionate as I thought she would be, I would have no worries.

As usual the relaxing time before sleep came was always a time of reflection for me and so I focused on what had transpired since leaving work that evening. It wasn't planned; it just happened. A night out with some of my friends was all I expected, but how things can change and this time it was definitely for the better.

I would tell Valerie about my functional disability; it was then up to her on how things would go. I had nothing to lose. The risk was great, but for me it was worth it if things worked out favourably for me.

Sleep came with thoughts of Valerie on my mind. I could hardly wait to see her again.

The next morning, I got up early. My internal time clock was accustomed to the early rise because of work. Still, I was good and fresh and the day passed quickly as I prepared my self for my date with Valerie. My friend picked me up early and confirmed that we would attend a dance at one of the night clubs in town. I agreed immediately. I knew my friend would be aware of my functional disability and not allow me to fall into any problematic situation. I also knew I would tell Valerie of my functional disability and prayed she was the person I thought she would be. If I was right, it would mean that the someone I was searching for existed and hopefully would become a major part of my life.

The excitement mounted within me as we approached the parking lot at the nursing residence. Like the night before, there were several girls at the windows looking out awaiting arrival of their boyfriends; I thought no doubt among those were Valerie and her friend. In no time they were in the car beside us. This was the time I would tell Valerie about my functional disability.

It was agreed by the four of us to stop by the local A&W drive in for a burger and fries first. This stop would take up some time before we went to the dance. While we waited for our burgers, we chatted openly about each other. She told me she was from a small community in Trinity Bay called Little Hearts Ease. She also told me she moved away from her home town at a very young age.

Instantly I thought, she well represented the name of her community. She was a petite girl with an outstanding personality, one which put me at total ease and comfort. There was no doubt she would always be in my heart. She was extremely beautiful outside with an inner beauty to match. On our first date I hadn't seen her plainly but formulated a vision of her. She was exactly as I had envisioned her to be. I told her my story finishing up with my most guarded secret. My explanation was as complete as possible; I didn't want any misunderstandings as to who I was, and how I coped with a functional disability.

I couldn't tell if her facial demeanour had changed due to the darkness in the car. However, I did feel the warmth of her small hand slide into mine and squeeze so tenderly. In that instant I knew Valerie was someone really special. She would always be my rock in good times as well as bad times. It takes a special person to show compassion, support, and understand the inabilities of others. With Valerie there was that and much more. She reaffirmed a firm commitment to me, through the tone of her voice, the touch of her hand and her compassionate eyes, which so beautifully adorned her petite but striking beautiful face. Her smile was both compelling and accepting as she looked beyond my functional disability into my heart. That is where she found the true me and only time would tell if she was willing to stay.

Of course, our friends, who were sitting in the front seat, had their own conversation and were oblivious to us. However, from time to time they fell silent allowing that special moment between Valerie and me to transpire uninterrupted. In telling Valerie my secret, I knew her friend would have to know as well, if we were to be double dating, going places and shearing each others company. I felt comfortable with this knowledge as well. It was a necessity to move forward. Valerie's friend acknowledged the importance of what I told them and so we became fast friends. Out of respect for Valerie, myself and our friendship she never mentioned my functional disability to anyone. Later we went to the dance and as we exited the car Valerie held my hand never to let go but to guide me along. I felt so proud of her, I allowed her to guide me along. Once inside we found a table with four chairs. Not once did I trip or stumble over anything. My guide knew exactly what to do. When dancing time was needed, she would take my hand and lead me to the floor. I didn't need anymore help than what she gave. She became my eyes until my eyes adjusted and my focus became much clearer. My eyes framed a picture of beauty as I stared into the sparkling eyes of Valerie. I felt so alive, so happy, so comfortable with her. It was then I knew for sure I had found that someone special I was searching for. That night I recognized Valerie was the one true person who would respect me for who I was no matter what. At least I had myself convinced she was.

Their curfew to sign in at he nursing residence was at eleven o'clock sharp and the house mother of the residence was very strict to that end. Before we said good night, Valerie asked me if I wanted to go out again next weekend. Of course, I did and I told her so. For me love at first sight was definitely a yes. However, an ongoing long-term relationship would be a true test for both of us.

Time slipped by as spring gave way to summer. I was still working at Come By Chance and the relationship between Valerie and myself blossomed beyond our wildest dreams. So much so, we dated not only on weekends but also a couple of nights during the week. Being young I could manage less sleep and still do a day's work. However, by mid-June my friend and his girlfriend parted ways not because they wanted to, but because her training took her to another part off the province for an extended period of time. Too far for a budding relationship to exist especially since he still had a job to go to and so he couldn't join her. For a short time, letters between them were exchanged but they soon stopped. My friend told me she had broken off their relationship and urged him to move on. He had no idea as to why she had made that decision but it devastated him. I knew this to be true for he always confided in me. This of course affected both Valerie and myself. However, through adaption and acceptance we managed to find a way to continue our relationship.

I couldn't drive at night and Valerie didn't have a driver's license thus our dates were reduced to weekends again. There was a bus service from St. John's to home every day and so Friday evening before the last bus left St. John's, Valerie would ride to my home and then return on the last bus leaving Sunday evening. We would have all weekend together; at home I was mobile and so we went out as young couples do. I had friends at home who we could share time and go places with, so our social life was still active but not as complete. My parents had met Valerie early in our relationship and their approval was immediate; Valerie in turn responded in kind. I was happy for there became a strong bond which cemented a place in our family. In those few months, a budding relationship between Valerie and myself became a solid bond as I planned to propose to Valerie and ask her to accept my engagement ring.

Even though my social life had solidified into a long-term relationship, my educational training and career path was yet to be determined. In early July I applied for university and later received notification of acceptance. I was determined to work until late August and resign my carpenter's apprentice position at that time. I secured a boarding house within walking distance of the university and if needed, I could also use city bus transportation. The university campus was well lit outside and underground tunnels interconnected the campus, thus the need to go outside was greatly reduced. I also would have a greater opportunity to spend more time with Valerie during the weeknights, depending on my workload. All in all, I was well pleased with my decision to attend university. My intent was to study for a degree in social work as I was interested in that field. The time came to resign my position at Come by Chance and register at Memorial University. That day would be the beginning of a normal career like my peers had achieved or were striving for. I would have something that would bring some sort of a normalcy in my life. I would be able to sustain a lifestyle similar to my peers and enjoy all the benefits they would soon achieve. Yes, it was a warm feeling to know an education would propel me into the future with so much to look forward to. It was a bold ambition, but one which I felt was attainable.

# Chapter 7

# A Major Meltdown

The transition from work to university went smoothly; not everything centred around my functional disability. Still, I was ready, with all my adaptive skills as I focused on the next step in my life. It would be hard work but I was up to the challenge. Adapting to lighting along with note taking in lectures would be of a minimal impact as I had a great memory for retaining information. I would jot down specific topics, key words and fill in the notes from memory, when I was in a room where the lighting was conducive for seeing better. My first semester went fine, but not as well as I would have liked.

It was doing assignments and constant night time studying which took a toll on me. I didn't have the necessary skills for doing assignments and studying for long periods of time so I struggled to get through. It wasn't like high school where I did most of my work during school hours and teachers were always present to assist if needed. My school nights, back then, were mostly free of school work yet here I had to rely on my own steadfast will and try to suffer through with no assistance. During that time I wasn't so sure I was ready for a university education. I found the constant reading and writing at night became a stumbling block for me.

The onus was on me as self-motivation became an issue. I knew I could handle the course curriculum if my functional disability didn't exist or if outside intervention existed. I had the determination to see it through but the unforeseen nightly studying created a problem. I didn't have any alternative adaptive skill to address that problem. After fifteen minutes of reading, I would consistently lose sight then I needed a break of about an hour to recover and adjust to reading or writing again. Because I didn't have any adaptive skills to combat that problem, stress became a major factor and I didn't know how to cope. In the past I had found ways to over-come my functional disability and yet I was totally unable to solve the problem before me.

After starting my second semester, I couldn't see myself continuing if things remained the same. The only options I had were to seek advice from my facility adviser or pay for tutors to help with studying. Paying for a tutor to help understand the course content in aid of maintaining good grades was acceptable, but that wasn't my problem. My comprehension of the course content wasn't in jeopardy; it was my sight impeding my progress. I also knew of tutors who would do assignments and write exams for a fee; this wasn't ethical and I was much too proud to utilize this illegal practice. It was cheating and I wasn't about to do that. I was taught to be honest and fair by my parents and I wouldn't stray from their teachings.

The only option left for me was to seek help. I arranged a meeting with my facility adviser and sat with him for about an hour or more. Reluctantly, I gave him a complete description of my eye condition. He had only one possible solution and suggested I avail of it. His solution was to take a speed-reading course in an attempt to increase my reading ability. In effect if I could read faster them, I could consume more in the fifteen minutes my eyes afforded me before they went berserk. His idea sounded fine but would it work, only time would tell.

Eagerly, I enrolled into the speed-reading course. However, after one session, I knew it was a complete failure. My eyes couldn't focus and follow the flashing words quickly enough. My eyes went berserk and I couldn't continue; it was a wasted effort but a lesson well learned. I followed up with my facility adviser who didn't have any further suggestions or advice on the matter. He then suggested tu-tors, but I felt the cost would be too much for my budget. If it was to help with one assignment or provide notes for an exam it may have been fine, but I would have to use a tutor for the whole semester on every course, which wasn't reasonably sen-sible. His only reply after that was for me to try and cope as much as possible in hope for good results. Given he was an educated professional I accepted his advise, not knowing there may have been other outside help which I could avail off.

This was the second semester and the course load was much heavier and un-like high school the professors gave their lectures and never offered any individual help to students. Things weren't looking good for me but I tried to remain positive if only to combat depressive emotions. Although my facility adviser failed in his attempt to assist me, I somehow knew it wasn't over. I knew, however, there may be other options but I would have to find them so I forged on alone struggling with stress and inner pain. The sad fact was plain; I had hit a stumbling block, and try as I might, I couldn't find an answer. It all came to a boiling point two weeks prior to the end of the second semesters and final exams were coming.

I had taken the advice of my facility advisor and forged on but I found studying more and more difficult as I was trying to cram for the finals. What was a good fifteen minutes of studying before my eyes gave out had reduced to a total of five minutes? I spent extremely late nights trying to get the minimum amount of studying done and my grades weren't what they should be and I was afraid I would fail. I carried this burden myself not telling anyone including my parents, as well as my friends and most especially Valerie. What could they do? I would have to find my way through myself and so I spared them the pain and hurt I felt myself. After all it was our nightly phone calls, occasional meetings and weekend together that helped keep my sanity and reduce my stress. If she was aware, she would be concerned and I didn't want her to worry about me. It was my problem and I was the one who needed to find a solution.

I had my eyes tested for glasses years prior but never ever used them for any length of time. In fact, I really didn't find them of any major benefit to me at that time. However, I was much older and maybe, just maybe glasses could help. I made an appointment with an optometrist named Dr. McNicholas, for an eye examination. Prior to attending the appointment, I felt good about the decision to get my eyes tested. I really believed it would improve my vision enough for me to continue studying and finish the university semester on a positive note.

I had made the appointment for Friday evening after classes. I was finished classes at 1:00 p.m. I would see Dr. McNicholas at 2:00 p.m. and catch the bus home at 4:00 p.m. to go home for the weekend. If all went well, I would have my glasses in a week and I would study hard and long for the finals.

I arrived at Dr. McNicholas's office and waited my turn to see him. In no time I was called into the inner examining room. An eye chart with various size of lettering hung on the opposite wall from where I was setting. The exam commenced with the lights out as a bright hand held light shone in my eyes, one eye at a time. The doctor remained quiet as he turned the lights back on. He then fitted what seemed like an oversize pair of glass frames on my face. The frame was constructed in a way that he could interchange many lenses to test my reading ability. Through the testing of each lens and his continued question 'is that better or worse,' my response was the same. I didn't find much of an improvement at all. It wasn't enough to make a significant change in my reading ability. What was most significant was the change in my ability to see clearly for in no time the lettering became black lines and my sight became fuzzy even with glasses. Soon the testing stopped and Dr. McNicholas spoke to me. He asked if I ever had my eyes tested before; I confirmed I did when I was much younger but even then I didn't find the prescribed glasses of any use and so I disregarded them.

It was then I informed him I couldn't see in the dark for as long as I could remember. Continuing, I told him that bright light also affected my vision most especially in school. I also told him while reading and writing words, the letters would become black lines or dark smudges on white paper. Sometimes when reading, the words would overlap as well and become jumbled together. My eyes as well couldn't focus and follow a line of reading to the next line below. In those cases, I found I would have to blink to clear my vision, wait a moment or so before I could continue. He listened with deep intensity and paused for a while before asking me what I was currently doing.

My answer came quickly, hoping he had some kind of remedy or cure for my condition. I told him I was a student at Memorial University and was preparing for final exams. I also told him of the time constraints on my vision to allow me to read only for five minutes at a time. Then I would have to rest for an hour before I began again. I told him I had tried speed-reading but didn't find it any good. I told him the cost for tutors was too expensive and I had exhausted all the adaptive skills I had learned through my life but with no success. Finally, I was hoping an eye examination and prescription glasses would be the solution. His facial expression hadn't changed much since the time I first met him a few minutes earlier.

Speaking in a low voice he said ,"I have nothing to offer you. Your eyes are as good as they are going to be. My advice to you is plain; you drop out of university and find suitable work for yourself." There it was! My answer! It was the second time I was told there was no plausible solution to my dilemma. He was a professional optometrist and presumable a well-respected one in the field of eye examination. So once again I accepted a professional's advise not knowing if anything else was available to assist me. I was just a naive student, looking for a way forward to achieve a career goal. Emptiness filled my soul. I felt as if I went through a tree shredder; my life and dreams were ripped to pieces. I left his office completely numb and dumbfounded; it would be no doubt one of the lowest points in my life, if not the lowest.

My adult life was only beginning and already my dreams of a successful career were shattered. Where I found the strength to carry on, I don't know. But I took a step back as I always did and analyzed all my options no matter how small or trivial they were. In no time I found myself at the bus stop awaiting a bus to go home. The bus wouldn't be there for another two hours or more. I was lost deep in thought and emotional stress but I felt relieved for I needed some private time alone to think and work things out in my mind. My parents would be disappointed but through their love would support me in whatever way was necessary. They would comfort me and shield me from the outside world until I was ready to face it again.

Within two hours Valerie would arrive; it was her intent to accompany me home for the weekend as per normal. I struggled with the thought of how disappointed she would be. How would I tell her, better still how could I tell her I was a failure? There were no ladders of opportunity left for me to climb, no pathways to success. I had experienced and examined them all. I concluded there was nothing left to step up to and so I wept in silence alone and distraught. I was numb both inside and out. My life for all intents and purpose had reached an apex; there was nowhere else for me to go.

As I sat on the cold cement side walk, the pan handlers and homeless people passed me by sometimes stopping to beg. A cold realization forced me to acknowledge the fact if I had nothing for myself then what did I have for them. My mind wasn't cohesive; it didn't gel together and parts of it flew off in all directions. As I watched the homeless people pass by, I wondered if that would be my fate as well and if I would become part off their ranks. I finally managed to shake off that thought and focused on what little light was left in my life—the love, compassion and undying support of Valerie. Through her, I hoped, I might regain enough strength to carry on, but to what end I didn't know. If anyone could empower me it would be her. I loved her so much and right then needed her total support in every way. Even though I hated the word crutch, I needed one and so I sat and stewed in my own sorrows and self-pity. It was no doubt I was a pitiful sight; I was in a bleak hole both dark and deep, without any substance. If I were to climb out it would have to be soon.

Hours passed in what seemed like an eternity; the comprehension of time didn't seem important to me. With my head still hung low, I felt a tug on my hair. It didn't startle me for I was still numb all over. Looking up I saw Valerie, smiling with a devilish grin attached. In that moment I felt a warm surge of relief fill my soul. I stood up and gave her the biggest hug I had ever given her. She saw my tear-stained cheeks and empty eyes. Instantly, she asked me what was wrong. I was still confused and unable to unscramble the details of events that had brought me to that state. Instead of telling her then, I openly cried and choked out a response that I would tell her once we were on the bus in the warmth and I had regained some composure. I would tell her everything including the fact that I felt better because she was there with me. I asked for her to be patient with me until I sorted things out in my mind first. She wanted to know if there was a problem with our relationship. I answered no, it has all to do with me and me alone. She wasn't satisfied and kept questioning me but I held my ground and remained tight lipped.

A few minutes passed and the bus arrived; we were the first ones inside the bus and headed for the back, a place where we would be secluded and have some privacy. I felt the heat immediately as it started to warm me up. Valerie still held my hand and when we sat down she snuggled into my shoulder. Her soft voice broke down my defences and as I began my explanation of why I was feeling so low, the numbness began to leave me. Valerie remained silent allowing me to fully exhale the explanation underlining the circumferences leading up to my emotional meltdown. Words came from my mouth at an alarming rate. With each word I spoke, I felt a heavy weight lifted off my shoulders. However, I was still vulnerable but felt positive support emitting from Valerie. My personal dream of having a career may have ended, and I couldn't help but wonder, would our relationship also end as well? After all, besides being a disabled burden, I had nothing to offer in return for her love. That thought sent shivers through my body.

There was little doubt my station in life had made a complete 360-degree change. Less than a year earlier, I was working and making good wages, but that was gone along with my career goals.

With the depressed economy, work of any sort was scarce even for a normal person let alone a person with a functional disability with no training, experience or trade. Under the direction and advice of a professional, I no longer would pursue a university education; it was no longer feasible for me and so with thorough bitter distaste I forever left behind my dream of a successful career.

Although I had the unconditional support, compassion, love and understanding from a very special person in Valerie, the question for me—was it enough? I continued to question my way forward—had I reached a dead end, or was there a path forward for me to follow? What could I do? For the first time in my life I couldn't find any answers. My only thought was to accept all the support offered to me by both Valerie and my family. This I thought would allow me to heal no matter how long it took. I stayed home the remainder of that spring and soon my collective thoughts gelled together and I began to think clearly again. However, it still hurt to know my friends would continue on with their education into the summer semester and beyond. With my mind clear, I realized acceptance was needed if I were to move on even if it left a bitter taste of being envious of their ongoing successes.

The one thing I hated most was the part my functional disability played in destroying my life. Thank goodness for unemployment insurance to help carry me through. I had enough insurable hours to register and draw an income until I found suitable work or was forced to seek alternative financial help—welfare, a dirty word. Valerie was away at work all week and all my friends were either working or getting an education. It was an extremely lonely time for me. Then things began to look up somewhat at least on a social basis.

My close friend stopped by to inform me his ex-girlfriend contacted him and was returning to St. John's for more training. He was overjoyed at that prospect for it meant they were about to start seeing each other again. This also meant I would be seeing Valerie on a regular basis including weekdays again. It also meant the four of us would be going to dances, taking sight seeing trips as well as just hanging out and enjoying life. At that juncture in my life reuniting with some close friends was something I needed and needed badly. I began to feel much better about myself and so I accepted the new reality of adult living without a formal education.

Before moving on, I took a look back at how I arrived at that point. It is said that hindsight is 20/20; I say the past is nothing but a product of the future. The present is forever creating one's future and that future would determine my past which I hoped would be more fruitful than the past I had previously created.

Still, the past which I had created had left me with a better understanding of how life works. I knew then I would have to remain more patient, more accepting, remain more focused and maintain a positive attitude no matter what life brings. It was with these enhanced abilities I would be sure to create a new future and thus produce a past I would be proud off. Even though the future is never completely known to anyone, there is a choice; one can choose to follow. In my case it would be my own defined path hoping the end result would be what I had envisioned. In the past, I had chosen a path that led to a dead end; it wasn't what I had envisioned or wanted in my life at all. My mistake was simple; I was trying to be the same as all my peers in every way. But in reality, the sad fact was, I was different. I had a functional disability which restricted my every move. I could not follow their path to success. I had to choose a path of my own. I was unique and to follow someone's chosen path wasn't going to work for me and so through this realization my life began anew. It was time for me to create a new future. I would accept my fate and walk a path in another direction. It would be a path of my own choosing specifically designed by me and for me, where the outcome would be much different and brighter.

I have always thought of myself as being a forward-thinking person and so the ability to adapt to change was not uncommon for me. I had to identify and develop new future goals for a career suitable to my own uniqueness. However, before I did I had to focus on the most important thing in my life. With this new resurgence in my life, it was time to reaffirm my commitment to the love of my life, Valerie.

June passed into July and the month of August began with good weather, hot days and lots of sunshine. I loved the sunshine! It uplifted me and made me feel good in all ways. Whereas the short dull cloudy days of winter bore heavy on my emotions and drained my spirits. My unemployment insurance had carried me through as I looked for work. I managed to find several meaningless jobs at labour work paying a little more than minimum wage, not suitable for my expectations but acceptable given my circumstances. Although these jobs weren't quite suitable for my own uniqueness, they were necessary if I was to be self-sustaining. I thanked my parents for teaching me good money management and saved as much money as I could. My friend and his girlfriend's relationship was flourishing so much so they got engaged in late spring. However, sad news soon befell my friend; his girlfriend's refresher course was near completion. This meant she would soon have to return to her home and workplace. It became definite the first week of August when she notified us she would leave St. John's the first week of September. I felt sad for my friend for a long distance relationships hardly ever worked.

Valerie and I were going steady, and our love grew enormously. The fact was,

I could do so much more with her by my side. I felt a great relief for my dependency on her was never taken for granted. She constantly reinforced me with her faith and confidence in my abilities, always projecting a positive outlook in whatever I did. She would say, I knew you could do it if you tried. It was mid-August 1972; a decision day had arrived.

My friend and his girlfriend would accompany Valerie and myself to a dance at a local night club known as the Pirates Cave. The music was great, the atmosphere was relaxing and when my eyes adjusted to the darkness, we danced continually. It was during a slow dance, while we were in a close embrace, I felt the time was right. I whispered in her ear words of love followed by a simple question, "I love you! Would you give me the honour of marring me?" It was a simple proposal of marriage from a simple man.

Valerie's eyes lit up. She was so excited, her answer came quickly and it was a definite yes. The dance hadn't stopped but we did; it was a moment of stillness and privacy. In essence, we were trapped in space and time just the two of us, just as it should be for young love. In that time I produced and placed an engagement ring on her finger with a promise to always love her. Her eyes sparkled like the diamond ring she now so proudly wears. We remained there for what seemed an eternity just absorbing the importance of the moment and all it represented. A final kiss of love sealed the moment forever and released us from our trance. Our friends joined us on the dance floor sharing in our happiness with words of congratulations. We danced until closing time.

That night was unforgettable in so many ways. My true love I adored had agreed to share her life with me. It was a night my vision had enhanced and adapted much quicker than usual as if a miracle had occurred just for that night. I can only attribute it to the release of the chemical reaction in a person's body that creates emotional happiness. Everything was so sharp and defined. There was only one drawback; my friend's girlfriend had to return to St. John's that night to start work the next day. Unfortunately, it was extremely late and Valerie decided she would stay home at my parents' house while I accompanied my friend and his girlfriend to St. John's. It would be a lonely drive home for him and I agreed to go with them.

My emotional high stayed with me as we headed towards St. John's. He had worked that day and tiredness was draining his energy. My company would help keep him alert during the long drive. We had enjoyed the night dancing and chatting. Alcohol wasn't a necessity to have fun and enjoy oneself on a night out.

Besides, for me being night blind was my impairment and to allow alcohol to further impair me was self-defeating especially on that very special night. I wanted to be clear and focused. My friend on the other hand had different reasons for not drinking; he was driving and therefore needed to maintain a clear focus as well. However, we did partake in a couple of social beers during conversation at the table. Most of the time we were out dancing to the music.

Besides, my friend working that day he also had driven to St. Johns to pick up his girlfriend. She had to work the next day and so she needed to return to the nursing residence after the dance.

The night went much too fast; we all totally enjoyed it to the fullest. Valerie was much surprised and loved all the attention I gave her. As the night came to a close, I fulfilled my promise to my friend and his girlfriend by accompanying them back to town; of course it was with some reluctance I did so. Due to the fact it would be very late when I got back home, I told Valerie not to wait up for me. We dropped Valerie off at my home and continued on our way. My friend had only driven a few miles when he exclaimed he was sleepy and asked me if I could see well enough to drive. My friend had confidence in my adaptive abilities and knew I wouldn't lie to him under any circumstance, especially regarding my night blindness. I told him I could see extremely well. It was a clear bright night and my eyes were already adjusted to the dark from being in the dim light of the bar. Also, I wasn't tired and not impaired by alcohol. After checking all my facilities, I gave him a positive response and told him I would give it a try. However, I had one request in support off my decision to drive his car. I requested his girlfriend remain awake and be a co-pilot. If I strayed too far to the right or left of the driving lane, she was to alert me immediately. Both my friend and his girlfriend supported that idea with a definite yes. With that my friend stopped the car and we switched places. In no time my friend was asleep and both his girlfriend and myself were left to carry on.

Everything was in my favour, the beautiful night, the adaptation of my eyes to the darkness, the self-confidence within me and the emotional high of knowing I was achieving another milestone.

I was proud of myself I drove the car perfectly; it was so exciting. It was a different feeling to drive at night. The headlights cleared a pathway ahead through the dark abyss. Each rotation of the tires propelled us into the lighted driving lane ahead. Then the cloak darkness immediately filled the vacuum of space we had left behind. The only visible light behind us was the hint of a red glare from our taillights in the darkness. I wasn't naïve; I immediately knew it was the adaptation of my eyes to the darkness which allowed me to see at night and to take advantage of the car's headlights to drive, otherwise it would not have been possible.

Still, things were definitely looking up for me. I was entering a new phase of my life. My childhood, adolescent and teenage years were long gone as maturity began to mould my life's journey. That night was a very special night for me. First and foremost the woman I loved accepted my proposal of marriage. Secondly, I had driven a car for the first time at night. It was no doubt the highest emotional feeling I had ever known or felt outside of the love I felt for Valerie. Still, I felt the need to reflect on my past achievements and marvelled at how much I had achieved given a functional disability continually impeding my progress.

However, the ride to St. John's was not without incident. We had about fifteen miles left to go when the car's engine shut off. With my friend now awake, both him and I checked underneath the hood and saw a blood red engine; it seemed the water pump failed and the engine seized solid. It was a terrible thing for my friend to lose the engine in his car. I felt bad for him, however we still needed to get to St. John's and drop off his girlfriend. Within minutes things changed; it seemed luck was with us as we flagged down a car. The driver was courteous enough to drop us off right at our destination. After leaving the nursing residence, my friend and I found a phone booth and called another friend to come pick us up. He arrived an hour or so later and we headed home.

It was daybreak when I returned home. I was still hyper from the night's events and wanted to share my story with Valerie. She was still asleep and I was overtired myself. So, I decided not to wake her but instead found the comfort of the bed sheets myself and somehow, I found the solitude of sleep. How long I slept I can't recall, but I was completely refreshed once awake. It didn't take long for the emotional high from the previous night to take center stage. It was the first time I could completely confide and share my most guarded secrets with someone. Valerie listened with high intensity and allowed me to expel all the details in living color. At that time the burden I carried alone for so long became a burden of two. This loving, caring, compassionate woman understood my plight and supported me through it all. I was certain Valerie would become not only my wife but my rock as well.

# Chapter 8

# Restricted Mobility with Happiness at Last

My friend once again fell victim the loss of a true love. His girlfriend returned to her home in another part of the province leaving him behind. He was alone again with an empty feeling which bore deep into his heart. I was saddened over his loss because of how it affected him. I also could not deny the effect his loss would have on both Valerie myself. We no longer had the opportunities to go out as much; my functional disability once again restricted not only my mobility but Valerie's as well. Her commitment to me was solid and she stuck by my side through thick and thin. The normalcy Valerie and I enjoyed no longer existed in our relationship. However, I noted not once did she complain; we were once again restricted to weekends together because of her work commitments and my inability to travel at night.

Mobility was an issue for weekends as well; if we wanted to go out, we were restricted to the availability of my parents' vehicle and of course this would only be during daylight hours. My father must have seen the hurt and wanting in my eyes. All my friends both male and female alike had attained or would soon attain a vehicle of their own. The sky was the limit for them when it came to freedom of movement and independence both day and night. He knew the independence they had over me and so before summer's end, he shopped around for a vehicle to fit my budget. Of course, this was unknown to me; in his own way he knew what was necessary and he didn't want to disappoint me if he failed to find a vehicle. I guess he took up the search when I mentioned several times in passing conversation of how wonderful it would be if I had my own vehicle. I wasn't actively looking for a vehicle myself mainly because I wasn't mobile enough to look and I didn't want to burden anyone else. Also, I guess I was still somewhat dependent upon my parents for the use of their vehicle. I guess I was taking it for granted as long as I could use their vehicle, I didn't need one of my own. In some way, I believe, I was still seeking approval to drive. I felt they trusted my judgment and knew when I could drive or when I couldn't; their blessing meant everything to me.

I wasn't aware of what my father was doing until one day I got the surprise of my life. After work that day he approached me and told me he saw a car for sale that he thought would fit my budget. It seems the car was in good shape and worked really well. It also was within my budget if I wanted to buy it.

My father was a very astute man and knew what I could afford in the way of a vehicle. To his credit he had found a vehicle well within my budget; the next move was up to me. My spirits were immediately lifted. Here was the opportunity at least for total daytime mobility leading to freedom and independence. Finally I could go places I couldn't go before without asking permission, or having to ask for the use of my parents' vehicle. Of course, there was still the restriction of driving only in daylight; if I wanted to go at night I would still need to find alternate arrangements. However, for me it was a boost in my confidence and another step towards my vision of complete self-independence. Internally, I thanked my parents for their trust and support in my decision making when it came to my limitations and restrictions; I would not betray their trust.

With the purchase of a car I would definitely experience the freedom and independence within my restricted limitations. Of course my friends were not as restricted as me and they still held the upper hand on freedom and independence. That thought burned deep in my soul; what I had was enough to satisfy my needs and at the time it's what mattered most. To my joy I saw in real time the shrinkage of my restricted limitations. I no longer was restricted to walking; I had wheels and could come and go at will if only in the light of day. When Valerie came on weekends, we were no longer restricted to home and the charity of my parents for the use of their vehicle. I wanted to teach Valerie how to drive which would give us even more mobility especially at night but she declined noting that she was comfortable with the way things were.

The summer solstice would mark the decline of summer and allow for the intrusion of fall. It would also mark my 21st birthday. Even though in that time I had faced many failures, by the same token, I had achieved much and there would be much more to achieve. It seemed I always had to remind myself of my successes and failures going forward, while my friends just moved forward with success after success never falling back with failures.

I searched for work but to no avail. I had very little to offer any potential employer; my skills were limited to my physical abilities and intelligence. Also because of night blindness I was restricted to daylight hours of work only and any job I got would have to be close within the proximity of home. It wasn't logical for me to take a work position any distance from home unless I got a passage with someone else. In any case I would have to be home before darkness fell. The other choice I had was to move to St. John's where work would be more plentiful and public transportation was available. However, due to being unskilled, I would be paid a very low wage thus making it impossible for me to afford a boarding house, save money and still support myself. Clearly this was not the best option.

My other option was to once again move to Toronto and live with my sister while working. I considered this as well and ruled it out also. The plain truth was simple; I didn't want to be away from Valerie. I realized then that I depended upon her a lot and that dependency was growing in leaps and bounds to the point of being an addiction. Other than my family there was no one else I could trust and depend upon. So, I remained home hoping I would secure work there. It was not an easy choice; I was making reactive decisions and hoping for the best possible outcomes. I had lived a structured life; for whatever reason I began creating my future day by day with no defined plan or path to follow.

The winter passed slowly with no work in sight. I felt heavy in my heart with disappointment and frustration. Valerie was keenly aware of my struggle and assisted me financially when I needed it. I reluctantly accepted it only after she insisted. She would say, if we were going to be married then the financial burden was hers as well as mine. I knew she was right, but it didn't cure the feeling of being somewhat less than a man who was expected to be the breadwinner. I looked at my father who worked hard to support his family and I wanted so much to be like him.

It troubled me greatly for not bearing the burden of financial support for both of us; it was a new feeling for me, one which existed because of my functional disability. The stress that came with the feelings of my inability to secure work seemed to affect my eyes, for I noticed a small change in my sight but only for a short period of time until my eyes adapted and the feeling was gone but the reduction in sight remained. In the past if something went wrong, it only affected me and me alone. With Valerie in my life, if something went wrong it affects both of us. This realization flooded me with new emotions. Having to deal with those emotions was more difficult for me than in the past; I was older and bore more responsibility. From that point on I would have to incorporate Valerie into my decision making process. She was now a part of me and what affected me would also affect her. Still, I was the one with the limitations and restrictions; there would be times in life's challenges when the burdens would be mine and mine alone. I would have to endure them myself and find my own way forward.

Life is forever evolving and so my focus on the future became our focus. We planned our wedding for the following summer. September 1st, 1973 would be the date. Valerie also chose to submit her resignation a month before our wedding, a decision I am sure she didn't make lightly.

An enormous amount of energy went into the planning of our wedding. Valerie needed to commit full time on our wedding plans, thus part of the reason for submitting her resignation from her job; the other reason was to commit herself to being by my side whenever I needed her support. Although I was restricted in what I could do to help, Valerie seemed satisfied with my efforts. The logistics of planning a wedding are quite challenging; Valerie was up to that challenge as she took the lead. It was a beautiful wedding; most importantly what made it beautiful was the stunning beauty of the most wonderful person I had just married. The wedding was all we expected it to be and then some. That night as I declared my love to her, I once again prayed silently for our future together to be filled with complete happiness. In my prayers I also prayed that my functional disability would not cause the kind of struggles, hardship and problems I had encountered in the past.

With our wedding behind us, we were both starting anew. Valerie had resigned from her work to maintain our home. Valerie and I decided to move to St. John's and begin our life together there; we would be independent and it would be easier for me to find work.

I found work in a department store as a security officer; things were looking up for us. We found an apartment nearby which was within our budget and so we moved in. Commuting to and from work wasn't a problem. I could walk on fine days; on wet days or in the short days of winter I could take the public transportation. The use of a car wasn't a necessity and so it remained parked unless we went home on weekends to visit.

Adjusting to city life wasn't too difficult at all. What was most challenging was the instability of a job. Work was never of a long-term nature and people were being hired and fired at will. There was no security and therefore no way to plan for future growth. I didn't have any training or skills to offer any potential employer. Therefore, I became one of those who was hired and laid off at a moment's notice. This was not for me. I had responsibilities and I needed to plan for the future. Valerie and I both wanted children and thus the reason why we needed more. This meant I needed to secure a full-time job with long-term security.

We struggled through the winter and when spring arrived we had enough. What work was available wasn't suitable for a married couple and so we considered all possibilities. Due to being unskilled and functionally disabled, I was even more restricted in attaining work; no employer wanted a person with a disability. We both agreed to leave the city behind and move back to my hometown. It wasn't an easy decision, but a necessary one. At home we would have more support and friends to depend upon. Work would be scarce but at least if successful it would be for a long-term nature. Within a month after the move, I secured a job at a car dealership; a lot man was the title. The pay wasn't great but better than what I had earned in St. John's, and we were able to save money towards the construction of a new house.

We moved in with my parents, who welcomed us with open arms. My two sisters and older brother were gone to Toronto for work leaving a large two-story house almost empty. The one exception was my younger brother Edward who was still in school. The large two-story house gave us plenty of room: enough to ensure we had privacy and independence when we needed it.

Things were looking up. I had found a secure job, we had total privacy and independence and our next plan was to build our own house. My parents gave us a building lot next to them. I guess they saw the validity in having us close by. They could help us if we needed it and in time, we would be there to support them. Within two years, the land was cleared and prepared for construction. I was managing really well; my adaptive skills were second nature and a sense of normalcy at least for me existed. The hiring of a contractor or even a local carpenter was not possible due to the lack of contractors in the area and to get an unemployed carpenter was quite impossible; everybody was working, and besides the financial cost would impact our budget greatly. The economy was on the upswing again which meant my position would be more secure as more people were buying cars. However, in rural areas, most everybody built their own house and so I too took on the challenge, not knowing if I could do it.

As usual I always met a challenge head on and it was no different building my own house. I could utilize the expertise of my uncle's advice if needed or if I got stuck, I could also use my adaptive devices to guide me along. I did have some carpenter training as a result from working at Come By Chance on the construction of the oil refinery and so I put it to good use. My understanding math and training would guide me through. Along with my father and brother we cut enough logs for the framing and sheeting of the exterior walls. A local saw mill sawed all the lumber we needed from the logs we cut. The result was a major cost saving for our budget.

I welcomed and enjoyed the hard physical work attached to the construction phase of our house. My goal was to finish the house in three years of commitment.

I was proud of my goals and aspirations. I would build a house from start to finish. This would also include the plumbing and electrical. This would be one time my functional disability wouldn't restrict me. I would work within my own time frame and limitations. In this way I knew everything would work out fine.

However, during those three years, I also had to maintain a job and secure a living for my family.

The birth of our son came the week I started the construction of our house. Valerie became a stay home mom and I became the breadwinner, just like my dad. I felt so proud; we were a family for sure and when it came time to give our baby a name, Valerie honoured me by naming our son after my father and myself. His name would be James Scott Mercer; however, because my dad was named James and my name was James, there was confusion when we referred to our son by his name as well, so to overcome that problem we chose to call him by his second name, Scott. Of course I was concerned that he may have a sighted problem but continued monitoring by myself and Valerie would eventually ease our fears.

The construction of our house began in earnest as little by little it took shape. However, to maintain construction I needed a steady income.

I soon discovered once employed, staying employed would always cause problems for me and so it was with my job at the car dealership. It seemed the company's upper management had brought in an efficiency expert to curtail their expenses and streamline their business. There was always something new occurring which I had to adapt or adjust to and being laid off from a job was an adjustment I was used to, so I became part of that curtailment. Once again I found myself looking for work. For me it was a never-ending battle; I always had to be aware of everything. What I took from each job was experience and with that experience I could maintain my employability and still guard my most valued secret.

It finally occurred to me why I wanted to keep my functional disability a secret; I was ashamed that I was something less than others. I had guarded my secret all my life and to tell anyone was most difficult.

After leaving my job as a lot man, I took a job on the inside at a supermarket. My job at the supermarket was defined as long term with better pay. It was enough to maintain a decent living as well as provide extra for our house construction. Again I felt things were definitely looking up for Valerie and myself; it wasn't the career I longed for but it was work which made me feel useful again. My work colleagues didn't know anything about my functional disability, therefore that in itself would create a problem if they were to find out. So, I remained steadfast in keeping my secret, I just couldn't allow myself to tell anybody. The day-to-day minor challenges of adapting and adjusting to these challenges were for the most part insignificant, but from time to time something different would evolve and I would be in a bind to cope sufficiently, but cope I did.

My job description included loading and off loading freight, stocking shelves, helping customers, etc. There existed a chance for advancement there so I worked hard in an effort to attain that goal. Then new problems surfaced as I was asked to work overtime beyond daylight hours. Getting a ride home would always be a problem; carrying out groceries for customers in the dark became a nightmare, handling of stock in the dark and dim light of a warehouse became problematic as well. I often got my colleagues to change work schedules with me but was not always successful. On these times there was no choice but to work. I tried to stay in the lighted area as much as possible, but more often than not I was left powerless to adapt. In those times I became clumsy, stumbling and tripping over things. Thank goodness most of those times I was alone with the assigned task. On the times I wasn't alone, I often conned other people to do my work or would lie to them explaining away my reasons for stumbling or tripping. At those time I was so embarrassed for I never knew if they believed me or not. One can only imagine the many different excuses I used to cover my functional disability. I often wondered if they talked about me behind my back. Also, I often felt it was obvious to everyone I was different, but I dared not believe it. I knew I was different, so why wouldn't they—it was a feeling I really couldn't shake. Yet, I remained steadfast and silent about my functional disability. I felt that if my employer knew about my functional disability, I would lose my job and I needed my job, so I persevered as best I could under the pretense that I was normal.

Then came the need for glasses; it seemed that my visual acuity was somewhat impaired. I was prescribed glasses when I was young but I didn't find them of any significant value at that time mainly because my visual acuity wasn't impaired significantly. My thoughts reflected to the eye exam I had during my time at university when I saw Dr. McNicholas. As a matter of fact, he said my eyes were as good as they would ever be and I should move on with life. From that point on I lost complete confidence in eye doctors and to see once again left a sour taste in my mouth.

My visual acuity was very good or at least I thought it was. Still, I was corrected by my family, friends, colleagues and employer on minor mistakes made because of my vision. I was often told I needed glasses; I actually thought it wasn't my visual acuity which needed improving, rather it was the blindness which dwelt within my eyes that needed improving. I always found my daytime sight not to be a major impediment but the opposite existed at night caused by my functional disability. I believed it wasn't near-sightedness or far-sightedness that caused my eye problems. So, to ease everyone's wishes, I embraced the notion of making another appointment to get my eyes checked once again.

Visual acuity wasn't a part of my functional disability and for whatever reason I still couldn't accept the notion my daytime sight was failing. It was part of a normal sight which could be improved with the aid of glasses but past experiences had not proven their necessity. However, as I got older, sighted mistakes became more obvious to everyone including me; I didn't need anyone to remind me my daytime visual acuity had become more then just a minor impediment.

What was most significant was the continually degrading of my night blindness and the effects it had on my vision as a whole. Even though I had agreed to see an optometrist, I put it off for much longer than I probably should have. I guess the sting of hurt from Dr. McNicholas and his analysis remained bitter in my heart. I hated his analysis and advice; I was a proud person who could achieve anything and I would prove him wrong. He didn't provide me with any options or hope whatsoever, which left me with an empty void in my life. After all, he was the professional and I was just a naive student and it left me wondering who could I turn to if not a professional like him.

The year was 1977; it had come to a point where the changes in my daytime vision threatened to affect my employment.

I no longer could read clearly. The job required me to be able to read invoices, labeling, monthly statements and purchase orders, etc. I needed to see an optometrist about improving my daytime visual acuity. It was imperative for my reading ability be improved and if glasses were necessary then so be it. I caved in and made an appointment to see an optometrist in my area. Dr. Richardson had an office in the Bay Roberts mall which was about fifteen minutes drive from my hometown. The following day I took time off work and went to see Dr. Richardson. After testing my eyes for the normal defections in visual acuity, he prescribed suitable glasses to assist me in seeing more clearly. In conclusion he suggested I see an ophthalmologist for further evaluation of my eyes. He then informed me he saw something completely different in my eyes, something he had never seen before during his time as an optometrist. Although I had a distasteful encounter several years prior with Dr. McNicholas, I dreaded the thought of seeing someone else and told him so, but reluctantly, I agreed upon his continued urging. My agreement was based on his explanation and my understanding of the difference between an optometrist and ophthalmologist.

His office made an appointment with an ophthalmologist, Dr. Johnston, at the eye clinic at the Health Sciences Centre. The Health Sciences Centre was located in St. John's, the Capital City for the Province of Newfoundland and Labrador. After leaving Dr. Richardson's office I was very upbeat; Dr. Richardson was more transparent and compassionate. He provided me with more knowledge than anyone else had given me in the past, which of course not only headed into the future but also into a direction of hope. The prescribed eyeglasses helped greatly to clarify and improved my reading capability. The thought of seeing an ophthalmologist who might help me with my night vision clearly uplifted my spirits; I felt more confident and positive about my future. If there was a positive way to address my functional disability, I would be able to do so much more in every aspect of life; this gave me feelings of joy and hope.

The time had come. It was a sunny day in mid summer; I secured a day off work from my employer to go see Dr. Johnson. I took with me Valerie and Scott;

we would do some shopping and visit some relatives as well before my appointment. The appointment was scheduled for eleven o'clock in the morning; this gave me lots of daylight to drive to St. John's and return home. Thus, I would not be impaired by the onslaught of darkness.

I found a close parking spot near the main entrance and all three of us went inside the Health Science Centre to find the eye clinic. After locating the clinic, I registered and waited to see Dr. Johnson. It was only a short wait before I was called into an inner office. Dr. Johnson introduced himself as we shook hands. I took him to be at least ten to twelve years older then myself. He was of average height with a slim body. The distinctive sound of his voice echoed in my ear. I immediately stored it away for future retrieval if I ever had to identify him in the future. It seemed I was losing the capability of identifying people by sight and so was forced to rely on voice recognition.

He then directed me to an examination chair and proceeded to test my eyes for visual acuity first with my glasses on and then off. He concluded my glasses were exactly what I needed at that time. However, I felt somewhat disappointed until he picked up a hand-held bright light which he shined directly into my eyes. It looked like a small flash light about three inches long; it was a very small, slender cylinder with a protruding head on one end. It looked almost like a tire gauge except it had a bright narrow beam of light when turned on. He then proceeded to shine the light into each eye individually. His reaction wasn't in words but simple mumbles of human acknowledgement. I couldn't mark the measurement of time he spent looking into each eye; for it took him a while to examine each eye very slowly going back and forth from one eye to the other. Finally, he reclined back into his chair. I, of course, was blinded from the stressful direct light which had been shining in my eyes for a lengthy period of time. It would take time for my eyes to return to some sort of normalcy, so I just sat back and relaxed quietly until I could see clearly again. I noted to myself being blinded seemed to directly affect my vocal ability. I remained silent and just listened. I wasn't impaired by injury but rather by choice; this same effect seemed to be present if I was in darkness of night as well. I guess my adaptive senses took control when my eyes couldn't see.

After jotting down several notes on his note pad, he said, "I want to see you again this afternoon just after lunch." I was astonished at this revelation for I wasn't expecting to see him again let alone after lunch. He picked up a small bottle from his desk and turned to me. "I am going to put some drops in your eyes and after they take effect, I will see you again? Just come back here after lunch say about two hours' time and let my staff know you are here. They will call you in when I am free." This was the first time I had drops in my eyes and was ignorant of the effects they would have on me.

It was around noon when we left the hospital; we decided to go spend the two hours' wait with some relatives. The persons we were going to visit were about a fifteen-minute drive away in the neighbouring town of Mount Pearl. Once there we had some lunch, chatted and relaxed. It was after one o'clock in the afternoon when we headed back to the hospital and the eye clinic. Half way between Mount Pearl and St. John's, my eyes got funny, blurry, fuzzy and things began to look distorted. It was as if I was looking through a very thick drinking glass or soft drink bottle. I remember I was driving in a centre lane with traffic on both sides of me. I couldn't see clearly and I felt boxed in; fear bore into my very being as I felt something terrible would happen if things didn't change.

Aboard the vehicle with me were Valerie and our baby son Scott. I feared for their safety but kept my cool as I slowed down and tried to find a way to get off the street. It was of no use. I was completely boxed in and going straight ahead was my only option. I really didn't know how I was going to get off the road or to even get to my destination. I needed help and quickly; the safety of my family was at stake not to mention the danger I was to other motorists. I concluded the only solution was for Valerie to become my eyes; our safety would be in her ability to give directions and feedback on my driving. I asked her to keep me going straight and to let me know if I was too close to vehicles in front of me or those on either side. I knew my speed wasn't a problem; ever since attaining my licence I had been able to judge and maintain the speed limit. However, from time to time I asked Valerie haw fast I was going.

With this information I could make simple corrections either left or right and breaking when necessary. It wasn't the perfect solution to our predicament but rather a very risky one. I really had no choice, so immediately I switched on my emergency lights to alert other drivers to be aware of my vehicle. I don't know how we got to our destination but we did; I thanked God and Valerie for her astute attention to what needed to be done. Once out of the car I thanked our lucky stars and hoped my vision would clear before it was time to go home.

We went inside the hospital and headed directly to the eye clinic. My sight was completely disoriented and Valerie had to assist me in mobility. Valerie notified the eye clinic staff we had returned and within a few minutes I was directed to Dr. Johnson's office. With assistance I managed to get to his office stumbling and tripping over my own two feet. After being seated, Dr. Johnson once again looked into my eyes with his bright light, carefully noting his fascination of what he saw. "It's salt and pepper like," he noted. "It seems to be RP," he said, "but some of the characteristics are different. I need further testing before a diagnosis can be determined," he noted. "I will need to see you again. I have scheduled visual fields test this afternoon followed by a color test," he continued. "You should be finished within an hour or so. I will see you again within a year where further testing will be done; at that time I will have the results of today's test. Also, I want you to see a colleague of mine, a geneticist. All the appointments will be on the same day as you see me. My staff will contact you with the appointments," he concluded.

Before leaving his office, I told him I was driving and that I drove from Mount Pearl barely able to see with distorted vision. He seemed astonished at my remarks then he picked up his small handheld light and continued to check my eyes once again. When he was finished, he advised me not to drive for at least another two hours depending how clearly I could see and if I had the confidence to do so. He then scolded himself out loud and apologized for not advising me to refrain from driving until the effects of the drops wore off.

Immediately after leaving Dr. Johnson's office, his assistant led me to a small office where I sat in front of a huge concave dish almost like a large bell laying on its side. It was approximately three feet in diameter; the inside of the dish was lit up completely showing a white interior with one exception. That exception was in the centre of the dish where a small round orange coloured orifice lay. The dish to my perception was about sixteen inches deep from the outside rim of the circumference. The outside part of the bell-shaped dish had attachments all around it; those attachments were movable around the outside perimeter. Finally at the bottom edge of the outside circumference, an upright post with a chin rest stood which awaited its next appointment, namely me. A technician introduced herself and briefly described the test.

The lights would be turned off in the room. The only light would be the one inside the dish. Also, in the orifice of the dish there would be a tiny orange/red light. I was to focus my eyes on that light. One eye would be patched as the other eye was tested and then the patch eye and testing eye would be switched to complete testing of both eyes. I was to rest my chin on the chin rest and focus directly on the orange/red dot in the centre and then there would be flickers of small bright light appearing and disappearing in different quadrants of the dish's dome.

I was given a small handheld buzzer to push every time I saw a flickering light. With the lights turned off and my chin at rest, I focused my eye on the tiny orange/red dot. Each time I saw a tiny flickering light, I pushed the buzzer. The lights came from all over the place popping up everywhere and then disappearing as quickly as they appeared. It took approximately thirty minutes to conclude the test, fifteen minutes on each eye. It was difficult to keep my eyes focused as they tended to wander and focus on wherever the flickering lights appeared.

I was amazed the feeling of being in a *Star Trek* show consumed my thoughts. However, that wasn't long lived for I was then led to another room. There I was given a book that contained small multi-coloured dots which filled each page. I was asked if I could identify any shapes, letters or numbers within the pages of the book. I was amazed; I could not see anything they were describing. I went so far as to argue there was nothing there.

The technician in her wisdom outlined a letter on one page. I saw it for a moment, but when I blinked it disappeared. Then I was given a small rectangle box approximately one inch high, one inch wide and I estimated twelve inches long. The contents within this box were small, cylindrical, coloured disks. The technician asked me to study the arrangement of the disks in the box carefully. I was given ample time to do so and then I was asked if I could remember their positions. It looked easy and I did have a good look at the discs as well as having a good memory, so I said yes to her question. She then emptied the box and asked me to arrange the disks back into the box in the same order as they were in before. It looked easy and so I did as she asked but was unsure if I got it right. It looked right to me; blues went to green, green went to gold, etc. Then without giving me the results of my efforts, she told me I was finished with the test. I was also told I was finished for the day. Before leaving she also informed me a future appointment would be arranged within the year for more testing and also to see Dr. Johnson again.

An hour and a half had passed and the effects of the drops had almost completely worn off allowing me to see more clearly. However, I decided to stay in the city longer and allow my vision to completely clear before heading home; safety took priority for my family and myself. The Avalon mall was a short distance away and with the aid of Valerie's eyes and my almost clear vision I headed there with my family. After we had supper and did some shopping, it was time to drive home before darkness took over. With my eyes completely clear, the ride home was uneventful except for the upbeat conversation Valerie and I had about the day's events.

It was late evening when we arrived home. My parents were waiting our arrival and the outcome of my visit. I filled them in with what I knew which wasn't much. I also told them I felt good about the appointment and how transparent Dr. Johnson was. Still, there were questions I should have asked, such as what was RP? These questions would have to wait until another year. I would get a better picture along with a diagnosis in another year and so my craving for more information would have to wait. Sleep came a little easier that night as tiredness took over my body.

# Chapter 9

# Fortitude and Strength

I returned to work the following day not fully satisfied with the previous days events but not devastated either. I would not allow myself to be so vulnerable again as I was when I saw Dr. McNicholas. My thoughts remained on him and I wondered why didn't he recommend an ophthalmologist when I saw him so many years ago. Again I felt a foul taste in my mouth; the bitterness had not left me. It was with great effort I finally surprised my feelings for him. With that notion, I promised myself, I would carefully move forward with my guard always up and at work my mind returned to doing my job. This was good in that I was accepting my past without major questions, but yet remembering its life-lasting effects on me.

The summer sunshine no longer uplifted the green leaves on the trees or the petals of the sweet perfume flowers. They struggled to maintain life during the change from summer to fall. It was obvious Mother Nature soon would lay her winter blanket of fluffy white snow over the ground. In time autumn to would soon fall victim to winter's beauty. The winter months passed slowly and I felt a strange awareness. It seems I had feelings of being watched by certain work colleagues, and this of course left a sour taste with me. There was nothing I could prove they were just feelings. I truly felt certain colleagues were talking about me. I trusted my sharpened senses on this matter but dismissed it as just blind intuition. Still, dismissing it was quite difficult; I truly felt I was the target of an unknown conversation. The answer to my feelings came in a surprise to me. I was called to the office for what I thought was just general business concerns. I was wrong for I was issued a layoff notice which totally blindsided me. I questioned their reasons and was provided a bunch of falsehoods. I tried to defend my position but the young manager had made his decision and stuck with it. I was to leave my position immediately and I would be given a week's severance for time accumulated. It seemed one or more of my colleagues decided to tell management I couldn't do my job. They also trumped up their own evaluations on several times because I was off work. I was a scapegoat for someone's opportunity to move up the ladder of security and favouritism with management.

The acting manager, whose ambition was much larger than his cranial ability to adapt, saw an opportunity to impress the upper management as well. He had decided my faith without even asking me what was wrong. I wasn't even given the opportunity to defend myself. He was a cold, rigid, unforgiving person and it didn't matter what I said. Again, my ignorance of my basic workers' rights left me without any direction in which way I could turn. Fuming with internal anger, I bit my lip and proceeded to leave with the thought someone had discovered my functional disability and used it against me.

It was a frosty cold March morning. I once read a passage in high school from a Latin course which came to me almost immediately, "Beware the Ides of March." I thought wasn't this true. I had acquired a ride all winter with another person who worked in the mall as well. He was a trusted friend and knew of my functional disability. He would hear and understand my side of the events without judgment. Talking to him would be a release of some emotions which I needed right then. I went to him and told him of my plight and said I was going home. He nodded in agreement and wished me well after a small chat of support. I felt somewhat better after venting my frustrations, but was fully aware there was nothing he could do but hear me out. It then entered my thoughts that maybe in some way he had unknowingly in a conversation with others mentioned I had a sighted disability; this hit me hard for I hoped it wasn't so. However, the possibility was there and I couldn't and wouldn't dismiss it.

The reality was real; I was stuck there with no way home but to walk. I felt the pain of heavy loss and my family was about to suffer because of my functional disability.

Still full of mixed emotions including self-pity, I left to walk home. Out of a job, with a family still to support, I was devastated. Self-pity took control and for the first time I truly felt the feeling of hate. It was an ugly feeling and unfortunately the only one that brought me comfort at that moment.

It was a long walk home, some twelve miles plus in the bitter cold, but I didn't find the biting of the frost on my skin for I was too hot under the collar, full of anger. The breath I saw bellowing out of my mouth was no doubt the venting of steam from being so angry. I was also sinking further into my own stew of self-pity. I don't know when it began to snow or when the wind freshened but soon the road was white and the wind whipped up a drifting winter's storm. Mother Nature was replenishing her white blanket to cover her precious plants.

The walk home soon became one of perseverance and determination. I was going through a terrible ordeal, unable to breathe comfortably as the snow and wind threatened to smother me. I became snow blind, unable to see anything only a blinding white glare. Yet I struggled on freezing and all alone. My focus switched to surviving; slowly self-pity and anger subsided as I forged ahead. My boots became heavy with wet snow stuck to them as I laboured through the snow drifts. The snow piled higher and walking became extremely difficult, very taxing on my stamina and strength. Everything became white; I lost visual focus and became disoriented. Snow blindness was near completeness.

It was then I wondered if all the people who were out in such weather would be snow blind as well. My question was soon answered for passing vehicles debunked that thought because drivers needed to see if they were driving. There was nothing for me to follow; I struggled to maintain a straight path ahead only my internal compass and adaption kept me going.

Often, I got turned around and lost my way almost completely but thank goodness, I knew the compass and how to utilize my surroundings as a guide. I would use my adaptive skills to continue. There was no sight left; snow blindness had taken it all. The remaining senses I had left filled the void and it was through these other senses I put my dependence of survival upon. I needed to walk in a northeast direction if I wanted to get home.

Earlier that morning the forecast called for brisk northeast winds; if I kept my face directly into the wind, I would be going in the right direction. My sense of smell identified the existence of a salty sea breeze which told me where I was in relative position to the location to the salt waters of Conception Bay. My taste buds also confirmed the findings of my smelling sense for the salt rich air left a salty taste in my mouth. I could also hear the lapping of the waves as they rolled over and over finally crashing onto the beach with a roar. By keeping the waters of Conception Bay on my right I would be fine, if I didn't freeze or smother.

My mind returned to why I was out in the storm; silently I cursed the decision of the young manager to send me out in a storm and mostly I cursed my functional disability for being the cause of my plight both at work and being mobility restricted. Even though I was blessed with extra sharp senses, my every step was a complete struggle. I had to turn away frequently from the northeast wind to avoid smothering and regain my focus. Getting my bearings back would help keep me on my desired path. To keep myself from going astray, I pictured all of my surroundings in my mind, so if I did go astray, I could identify where I was in location to that mental picture. The problem was I really couldn't see my surroundings. There were many markers to keep me on the straight and narrow; this was when my adaptive skills took control. I really didn't have to see at all; it was like walking in the dark. It was good I was dressed warm and being young my stamina was top shelf, otherwise I wouldn't have endured so much for so long.

I hadn't heard any significant amount of traffic since I had left the mall. I knew most people were at work or at home, in any case they wouldn't venture out in such a storm.

Time didn't seem to be relevant; I didn't know how long I was walking. My pace was slow but steady and yet it seemed I was getting nowhere fast. I estimated I had walked about half the distance towards home when a loud voice pierced the blinding winter storm. "Come here, come here." Thinking I was gone astray, I followed the sound of the voice and found myself at the door of a building. It was a plumbing and electrical shop, L & F Sales and Service. Somehow, I had managed to stumble onto their parking lot. The man with the loud beckoning voice saw me struggling to find my way. He recognized it wasn't fit for anyone to be out in such a storm and immediately called me to come inside. The owner of the store directed me to a chair by a baseboard heater. "It's too stormy to be out there," he said, as he closed the door leaving the storm outside to fight its own battles. Although I was inside, my eyes were filled with a dark shade over them; I really could only see shadows at that time. In time I hoped my vision would clear but I didn't know how long it would take.

I was wet, cold, my face was burning from the frost, biting snow and drifting northeast winds. I was tired from the strenuous walk, my feet were freezing, my hands were completely numb with no feelings at all. They had gotten cold many times before and always the same reaction followed when warming up. The process included excruciating pain with pure burning sensation for about twenty minutes before any relief at all. With my gloves off, I knew I would soon experience those feelings as my hands and fingers began to regain life and sensitivity in the warm.

"Louis Sheppard is my name," he said extending a hand in a friendly greeting. I offered my hand in return, which he took, although I couldn't feel it but with a quick shake we started a conversation. I introduced myself through chattering teeth, not yet completely thawed out. From time to time I apologized for outbursts of colourful vulgar language as the life began to return to my hands. He noted I must have had them frost burned at some point in time. It then hit me, all those years ago when I was a little boy in school on Bell Island. The horrifying memory of a teacher (Ms. Reese) exerting her power and will over me with a yardstick. She used that yardstick as a strap and then forced me to place my hands in the icy cold waters of a small brook. Her excuse was to wash them but her real reason was the delight she felt from the punishment she inflicted upon me.

I would always remember that day and the mental scares it left with me. The pain, burning and suffering I was feeling in my hands were the physical effects and scars she left me with. We had been chatting for about fifteen minutes, I was happy he saw me and called me in, and by that time my eyes were clearing as my vision returned. With the clarity of vision, I could plainly see Louis standing by me looking out the large shop window. He was not as tall as myself, maybe five feet, seven inches or a little more. He was heavy set, much heavier than me; in my mind I framed my first impression of Louis as a compassionate man with a great personality. I told him my name and where I was from. As I was thanking him for his hospitality in providing shelter for me in the storm, my mind filed away a mental note stating that I would not forget this act of kindness.

Half an hour had passed and I was still suffering from the burning pain in my hands; my face had thawed leaving a burning hot feeling there as well. In time the burning and pain subsided and I felt more comfortable. I estimated the time for my hands to come completely back to life was a little more than half an hour, almost twice the normal time it generally took. Slowly, but surely, I dried off and warmed up, meanwhile we chatted idly over everything from the ever-changing weather conditions in Newfoundland and Labrador to politics, etc.

Louis was a few years older than myself and from a different town therefore a complete stranger to me. Still, we found equilibrium of topics to chat on. Although he had asked me earlier why I was out in such a storm, especially alone and walking. My answer at that time was short and unexplained, just that I was headed home to Bishops Cove from Bay Roberts.

It seemed Louis wasn't fully satisfied with my first answer and once again questioned me as to why I was out walking in such a storm. Although I didn't have to provide Louis with any information as to why I was out in the storm, I felt it would be prudent to tell him—after all, he provided me with shelter and warmth as well as offering me a ride home when the storm subsided. To this extent I answered him truthfully without hesitation.

At the end of my explanation, instead of questioning me further on the subject, he surprised me when he suggested I come to work for him. He explained to me because he was the sole employee, he had to close his shop when out on service calls. He continued saying it wasn't a good business practice to close his shop at anytime during business hours. He said, "I really need someone to take care of the shop during those times." I couldn't believe my ears. Here was a total stranger, providing shelter to me in a storm and then offering me a job. My answer of course was a firm yes. I was hired immediately and my duties would start right away. Louis produced a key from his pocket and advised me to open up in the morning. Life is sometimes horrible and sometimes wonderful; that day I had gone through both versions of life. I would work forty hours a week and be paid a minimum wage to start and if business picked up I would get a raise. Once the storm abated and the roads ploughed, Louis was true to his word and gave me a ride home.

I took home with me both the terrible and positive news of that day. There was only one thing to base the loss of my job on and it was my functional disability—of that, I was sure. Still, I felt the manager could have handled the situation much better. In reflection I tried every way to adjust and cope in my work environment and felt I was being successful but minor discrepancies were visible. I hadn't failed to measure up but I was sure other work colleagues noted my work performance and took advantage of my flawed inabilities to do a good job. Although I wasn't sure any of my colleagues knew of my functional disability, there were several people who worked in the mall knew of my condition and any one of them may have inadvertently let it slip. Still, I couldn't rule out the possibility I was reported in an effort to advance their own station in employment. Over the years I become very resilient. I knew I would bounce back more knowledgeable and much stronger than before. I hoped my new position would pan out much better then the previous one.

The small plumbing, heating and electrical business taught me a lot about its products and customer service. I was learning to become a sales clerk, which was quite a honourable trade. I also gained knowledge of installation and service repair solutions. What I didn't know was that I was acquiring talents and skills which would help in the future. I had only been with the company several months when things started to turn sour; the business soon fell victim to a depressed economy. Within a few months most of the small business in the area closed and so did L & F Sales and Service. Once again, I found myself looking for work suitable for my personal situation.

It was the summer of 1978, much longer days and a more suitable time to secure work. I was also looking forward to seeing Dr. Johnson again; I had received my appointment by mail earlier that spring.

Luck seemed to be on my side; a position with a major building supply dealer became available. I submitted my application and resume hoping for an interview. My resume included work experience as a carpenter apprentice, retail sales in a supermarket and of course sales and service in a plumbing, heating and electrical business. I also included on my resume I lived close by and could work in a team environment, which was complemented with a good education, a positive attitude as well as strong people skills especially in dealing with the public. I was selected, screened in and interviewed for the position. I must have made an impression for I was offered a long-term position as a sales clerk with Mark Gosse and Sons Ltd.

This company was a major building supply dealer in the area. This was a good position for me; I had the knowledge and experience to be a successful employee. My functional disability wouldn't have any significant impact on my work-related duties as far as I could see. I was wearing glasses and reading wasn't a major problem unless I was subject to bright lights, darkness or reading for extended period of time. The work hours were from 8 a.m. to 5 p.m. daily. During the late spring, summer and early fall months, I would be able to drive to work myself which boosted my moral and gave me a sense of independent and freedom. During the late fall, winter and early spring months, I would need to catch a ride with a co-worker who worked the same schedule and lived in the same community as myself. I never had to work in a dark or dimly light area; my work was always in a well-lit area.

Still there were minor adjustments. I tried not to go out into the bright sunshine as it reduced my vision when I returned inside again, but the effects were only short term, lasting for about five minutes after being out. This was my first work position where I truly felt totally incorporated as a mainstream person. No one knew of my functional disability and no one needed to know. I could manage quite well providing work of quality and quantity, which was acceptable to my employer. It seemed I had found my niche in the type of work I could do without having to expose myself to the ever-continuing adapting and adjusting in order to accommodate my functional disability; I was definitely in a comfort zone. One of the sales persons was near retirement. If I remained steadfast in my work ethic, I was sure to fill his position thus solidifying an indeterminate position for myself. I was extremely comfortable with this employer and if I was to become an indeterminate employee, I would consider telling my employer about my functional disability. I was confident they would be receptive to the knowledge that I was functionally disabled.

The day finally came when I was to go see Dr. Johnson again. This time only Valerie and myself went. It meant a full day at the eye clinic of the Health Sciences Centre for not only myself but Valerie as well. It would indeed be long day one of which would be extremely stressful for me. However, I prepared myself for the challenge and was willing to subject myself to whatever strenuous testing was ahead.

It was an early drive to St. John's; my first appointment was at 9 a.m. sharp. Because it was early morning, parking spaces were plentiful and I was able to secure a one close to the main entrance. After parking we headed inside. I registered at the eye clinic around 8:45 a.m. and waited to be called. In no time I was called to the eye chart testing room. Eye drops were administered to dilate my eyes before my vision was tested. I read the eye chart down four lines with confidence. However, I stumbled over the fifth line quite unsure of the lettering. Each eye was tested individually as usual with several lenses that were exchanged for my glasses but no improvement was found at least not in my judgment. My next test was in the colour testing room. As in the previous year, I was shown the book with the pages full of multi coloured dots. This test was the same as the previous year with the same results. Then I was given the box full of coloured disks. This too was a repeat test of the previous year with again the same results as before. Over an hour passed and my eyes were feeling the effects of the dilating drops. Another hour would pass before the next test appointment.

Both Valerie and myself took this time to go grab a mid-morning coffee at the cafeteria. I was sure she was somewhat bored, having to spend the whole time just sitting and waiting for me. It was just as stressful for her to wait in silence, not knowing what I was going through, as it was for me to get the testing done. It was during those breaks between tests and cafeteria visits I would tell her everything that happened during my tests. In this way she knew what was happening, how I reacted and how I felt myself. Within the hour we returned to the eye clinic and awaited the next test.

A technician called me to another room and informed Valerie I would be 45 minutes to an hour before I returned. Valerie nodded in acknowledgement. What she did to pass that time was up to her and I wasn't sure what she would do, but I was sure she would be present when I returned. I was led to the fields testing room where the big concave dish lived. This test would be the same as the previous year, so I knew what to expect. However, this time I was tested with glasses on and glasses off.

It took about an hour to complete the test for both eyes. Then, I was asked to wait outside for the next appointment. As I carefully found my way through the door across the waiting area, I heard the familiar voice of Valerie call me directly to her.

I was glad to get a break if even for a short while. The dilating drops had done its work; everything within my field of vision was disorienting. The fields test was long and stressful on my eyes as well. Trying to keep my eyes focused on a central point while identifying flickers of light not only stressed my eyes, but created a sense of nausea inside me. I also felt the twinge of a tension headache coming on.

By the time I was called to my next appointment my eyes were completely dilated and seeing completely disorienting. Trying to cope with fuzzy blurred vision magnified my nausea and tension headache that much more.

As I chatted with Valerie while awaiting the next test, a technician approached me with a box of tissues and a small bottle of eye drips. She checked my eyes and added some antiseptic drops as well as some freezing drops. "You are free to go to lunch," she said. "Come back in an hour and check in." Of course, I couldn't go anywhere; driving was out of the question and there wasn't anyone in hospital we could visit. Our only option was to go to the cafeteria. We were hungry and the smell of cafeteria food was quite alluring. We headed for the cafeteria and ordered up some lunch. The hour passed quickly and soon we were back at the eye clinic.

It didn't take long for a technician to find me after checking in. She led me to another room where a weird contraption sat idly awaiting me. There was a chair to set in and a chin rest. Also, there was a headband to rest my forehead against.

On the opposite end was also a chair and a rectangular frame containing a tiny purple light in the center. I was asked by the technician to place my chin in the chin rest and allow my forehead to rest in the proper place provided. The technician sat directly across from me on the opposite side of the frame.

I was asked to keep my eyes open as the purple light was inched closer to my eyes. Soon the light was touching my eyelids and eye itself. This was done with each eye individually. The extra drops and the stress from focusing on the purple light increased the nausea feelings and my tension headache. How much more could I handle, I didn't know, but I remained steadfast to see it through. Once again, I was told to wait outside for my next appointment. Valerie questioned me, "How much longer will you be?" I gave her the only answer I had, I didn't know, but I hoped it would be soon. I told her I was yet to see Dr. Johnson but was sure once I saw him I would be finished.

It didn't take long for Dr. Johnson's secretary to call me into his office. In front of him he had a chart folder full of papers. I am sure they were the results of the testing I went through the previous year and maybe the results of the testing I had just went through as well. After we exchanged pleasantries, he opened the folder and scanned through the papers. Then he turned to me and asked me to sit back as he looked into my eyes with the small handheld light. Again, this light was very bright which only irritated my nausea and headache that much more.

He turned back to the folder and began to fill in some forms. It was then a woman with a folder full of papers in her arms entered his office. "Oh, hello, Jane," he exclaimed. "Mr. Mercer this is Jane Green; she is a geneticist. I asked her to drop by to have a look into your eyes if you don't mind." I knew this meant more irritation and stress for me but I wanted answers and so I agreed.

Jane was a woman several years older then myself. She was of average height with a slim body. Jane stepped forward and carefully looked into my eyes with Dr. Johnson's bright light. After she withdrew back a few steps, she and Dr. Johnson chatted about what they saw in my eyes. "Salt and pepper," Dr. Johnson said, "like or similar to RP. However," he continued, "it's different in some other ways. I believe we are seeing something new and different. It still may be RP but I am not totally convinced it is. Officially until otherwise clearly identified, my diagnosis will remain as an unconfirmed type of unknown RP."

Jane agreed and suggested she follow up on it from a genetic perspective. "I hoped you would get involved," said Dr. Johnson. Not wanting to be left out of the conversation, I interjected with some information I thought they should be aware off. I told them about my younger sister and brother both having the same night blindness as myself. I also told them of one other person who had a similar condition but I couldn't confirm it was the same disease. Jane Green listened intensely as did Dr. Johnson. Jane turned to me and said she would check it out. "I will be in touch soon," she concluded. They then continued to chat openly using very technical terms which were well beyond my comprehension.

After a short period of time, Dr. Johnson turned to me again and said, "I am finished. However, you must have some photos done of your eyes. I will arrange to get them done before you leave. My staff will also arrange next years appointments as well,." Before removing myself from the examination chair, I directly asked Dr. Johnson what RP meant.

Dr. Johnson apologized for not explaining to me what RP was. "RP is an acronym for Retinitis Pigmentosa, a genetic eye disease. There isn't any cure at present for RP. It affects the rods and cones of the eyes causing possible loss of central or the fields of vision or even a combination of both. Also included along with night blindness, color blindness and finally deteriorates to total blindness. However, you are a long way from going blind yet. I have chosen RP as my temporary diagnosis because at this time it best suits your condition. Still, I am not totally convinced if it is RP and that is why I have asked Jane Green to get involved. I am hopeful she will in time identify the genetic flaw which is causing your condition." He continued, "Only then will you have a true diagnosis of your eye condition. So, until then I want you to continue to get testing and see me regularly. One more thing you, should contact the Canadian National Institute for the Blind (CNIB) to see if you are eligible for any of their services and possibly registration. I believe you are."

I was flabbergasted, so much I found it difficult to digest and deal with all at once. Still disoriented from the drops, I couldn't think clearly and the revelation I should go and connect the CNIB weighed heavy on my thoughts as well as my heart.

This was a revelation for me. I was barely aware of the existence of the CNIB. What could they offer me? They were for blind people only? I questioned myself, was I ignorant of my knowledge about the CNIB and the service they provide? I wasn't blind yet. Dr. Johnson seemed to think they could help me.

I made note of his advice and would consider it later when I could think clearly. "Thank you," said Dr. Johnson, "I will see you next year."

I removed myself from the examination chair and noted both Dr. Johnson and Jane Green remained chatting as I left his office. I went out to the waiting area and chatted with Valerie; she was full of questions. I answered her as best as I could, but clarity of thought still eluded me and so I stumbled through my explanations for her questions. I told her when my thoughts became clear I would explain all in complete detail.

Valerie was understanding and knew I would tell her all in due time. After waiting a little more than five minutes, a male technician called me to another room where photos were to be taken. I was directed to a chair in front of a frame that contained a camera. The lights were switched off with only a small night light on to provide enough light for the technician to see; it was only a blur to me.

Like most of the other tests, this frame also had a chin and forehead rest. After I settled myself into place, the technician said there would be a bright light shining directly into my eyes as he took individual pictures of each eye. He wasn't kidding; I had experienced nausea and a headache with several of the tests earlier, but this was the extreme. One eye was patched while photos were taken of the other eye and then the patch was switched while photos were taken of the previous patched eye. The camera's flash came to life fast and furious. My eyes were stressed to the limit; water flowed from them freely. The nausea and headache I felt were at a breaking point and I told the technician so. He asked me to try to hang on a little while longer. I gritted my teeth and forced down the urge to throw up as he flashed more photos.

I noted to myself the right eye wasn't as sensitive to extreme bright light as my left eye was. I noticed this earlier when Dr. Johnson was examining my eyes with his handheld light, but paid no attention to it. However, this time, I made a mental note to tell Dr. Johnson the next time I saw him.

There must have been twenty or more photos taken of each eye before the technician was finished. He immediately turned on the lights and what a shock I felt as the bright lights flooded into my eyes. I was overwhelmed and became completely disoriented. I was unable to move without aid; I was completely blind or so I thought. There was a huge round black spot blocking my vision; however, some light filtered through around its outside perimeter. It was as if I was seeing a solar eclipse with the dark moon blocking out the sun. The technician called Valerie in who helped me from my seat and out of the room. I remarked to her I couldn't see anything at all. I suggested she take me to a seat until the blinding effects wore off which the technician assured me they would. Valerie suggested we go to the cafeteria and grab a small snack and wait there. She would guide me there and we could chat as we waited. It sounded like a good suggestion; I agreed and so off we went.

This was the first time outside of being snow blind that I experienced blindness in the daylight; it wasn't a good feeling at all. We sat and chatted as we ate our snacks. The knowledge I was finished with the eye clinic for the day relaxed me somewhat. My mind cleared quickly as I emptied my mind answering Valerie's questions. Time passed quickly as I totally explained each test in complete detail to her. I finished up with Dr. Johnson's evaluation, diagnosis and advise.

I explained about seeing Jane Green and her role as a geneticist. I also told Valerie about Dr. Johnson's advice on connecting with the CNIB. My final explanation dealt with Dr. Johnson's unconfirmed diagnosis.

It was a lot of information for both of us to digest all at once. I needed time to think clearly and sort things out. Valerie also needed time for her to deal with the massive information I gave her.

One thing was for sure; I was satisfied with Dr. Johnson and his transparency. Although I had mixed feelings about his temporary diagnosis and possible outcomes, I felt confident his diagnosis would change. Still, the thought of connecting with the CNIB wasn't something I wanted to hear or deal with. However, it was a reality and I would deal with it as I dealt with everything else.

Our stay in the cafeteria I estimated was well over an hour. I took some aspirin earlier for my headache when we first arrived at the cafeteria. Its effects soon became apparent as my headache wasn't as severe. My eyes began to clear from the dilating drops and the blackened-out vision disappeared. It was a full day for us and so we left for home. Unknown to Valerie, I thanked my lucky stars for her understanding, compassion and company. I took my time driving very carefully with the aid of my co-pilot Valerie who kept an astute eye out as to where I was and what I was doing. Of course, we continued our discussion on the results of our visit at the eye clinic with Dr. Johnson as we drove along. The clarity of thought replaced my headache and soon we were discussing the possibility of connecting with the CNIB. For me this thought was a huge step backward. I had come so far only to be faced with degrading myself by reaching out to the CNIB. What would my friends think? What would my parents say and how would it affect my relationship with them? For a young man with so much to look forward to, yet the words Canadian National Institute for the Blind left me feeling insecure and incomplete. I wasn't that person; I was strong and confident for I could carry so much stress and worry without any assistance. Still, it seemed to me everything was upside down and inside out. However, through a lengthy conversation with Valerie, I agreed to at least hear what the CNIB had to say.

Chapter 10

# Breaking the News

It was late Friday evening when we arrived back home from the eye clinic. I had a headache but it was easing off. Mom was waiting for Dad to get home from work. Although Dad was a member of the Royal Canadian Legion, he very rarely frequented his branch; however there were times when he did and that evening was one of those times. Dad was a WWII veteran and Friday evenings after work most all of his comrades generally met at the Legion. It would be a time to catch up on the latest events within the Legion as well as to socialize with other veterans. Supper would be late for everyone including us, I thought. Mom had graciously taken care of our son Scott while we were gone; she also managed to cook supper for everyone.

Mom was outside in her flower garden where she and Scott were admiring the beauty of Mother Nature. She was anxious to know how things went at the eye clinic. It would take a long time to fill Mom in, so I suggested we chat about it over supper. The smell of a cooked meal lured us into the house. With Scott running around, both Valerie and I played with him until Mom prepared the table for that evenings settings. "God knows when you father will be here," she said. "I assume he may have stopped at the Legion. If that's the case he may be a while, so when supper is ready, we should eat before it gets cold. Still," she concluded, "he generally doesn't be too late, so let's hope he is here soon."

We had only been in the house five minutes or so when we heard Dad's car in the driveway. It was a beautiful evening so we took Scott outside to greet him. Mom followed us out but was still in the dark regarding the results from today's visit at the eye clinic.

Our house was next door to my parents, not fifteen feet away, on the land my parents gave me. There was a set of steps leading up to our back entrance; Dad went to sit on those steps as Scott ran to him. Taking Scott into his arms, he looked up at us and asked how things went at the eye clinic. One could tell he had been drinking for there was a huge smile on his face with a glow of warmth in his eyes as he played with Scott. He was in a great mood; I guess his spirits were uplifted after socializing with his comrades at the Legion, for the veterans' comradeship was an accepted form of relief. One couldn't blame them for having a drink or two on occasion for it was their way of dealing with post-war memories; sanity for them was in their comradeship and a social drink to depress the unwanted memories. Mom stood at the back door entrance of their house with smiles of happiness to see him home safe. After a few minutes Valerie retrieved Scott from his arms at which time he once again asked how our day went at the eye clinic. Dad wasn't a man to be put off with his questions; he expected to be answered immediately so I started to explain. However, I should note, he was also a quiet man who much like myself was a very quiet and private person. Still, when he spoke most often it was of great importance and not a trivial conversation. He was well respected for that quality and as such well respected by all who knew him.

Dad remained sitting on the steps as I began to tell him all of what I knew. I told him of the many tests I had and described each one at length. I told him of Jane Green and how she was going to be involved from a genetic perspective. I told him my visual acuity was fairly stable and my glasses were still fine. I also told him I was temporary diagnosed with Retinistis Pigmentosa, "RP," for lack of definite diagnoses. RP is a genetic eye disease which affects the rods and cones of the eyes; it is a disease at present considered incurable and leads to complete blindness in time. If Dr. Johnson's temporary diagnosis was correct, my eyes would degenerate as I got older. How soon I would expect to lose my sight depended upon the rate of degenerating. He expected I could be blind at age forty. However, the diagnosis wasn't totally confirmed; it was only a temporary one. More testing would have to be done first, including genetic testing, before a final diagnosis would be confirmed. Finally I told him about Dr. Johnson's advice concerning the Canadian National institute for the Blind "CNIB."

I was watching my dad's facial features from the time he first arrived full of smiles and laughter then changed to one of disbelief and sadness. He rubbed his forehead profusely and finally huge pear-shaped droplets of tears emitted from his eyelids. They flowed down his cheeks freely as he went for a handkerchief to wipe his face.

There we were, the five of us. Mom was now holding Scott close. Her face had changed as well; she too shed unwanted tears of sadness. Her immediate reaction was to pull Scott close into the folds of her apron, holding him tightly as she sought the comfort of her grandson. Valerie moved and was now standing by Dad with her hand on his shoulder. "Jim will be alright, Mr. Mercer. I will take care of him. I love him and we are in this together," Valerie said. With that Dad took Valerie's hand in acknowledgement of her compassion and love for me. It was then I saw a hint of relief on his face as Valerie remained holding his hand as she helped him stand.

I glanced at Scott still buried in the folds of Mom's apron; there were low chuckles of delight coming from him as he buried himself deeper into the apron. I just stood alone with my pain choking back tears that wanted to relieve me of the internal pressure within my body. There was no comfort for me at that time; only my inner strength kept me standing.

It was then I realized how much hurt my functional disability affected others, especially Valerie and my parents. In time my children would bear the same effects as well for my functional disability would impact their lives too. This troubled me greatly. How would I cope and deal with it? Everybody had some form of release— Mom holding Scott, Valerie comforting dad—I realized then it was left up to me to remain strong for not only myself but for everyone else. Indeed, my burden was heavy to bear and so as I cried internally and later openly in private. However, no one would know for I continued to project a positive outlook outside in public. It was then I realized parents feel the hurt, pain, suffering, happiness, failures and successes of their children not only through childhood but through their child's adult life as well.

My eyes were also on my wife; she showed strength above and beyond her own individual needs. She too not only carried the hurt, pain, suffering, happiness failures and successes of our life together in marriage but also in her extended family unit. In certain times it would fall on Valerie to fill my role as a parent because of my inability to do so due to my eyesight or lack thereof. I could feel no prouder of Valerie for this display of true family values. What I took from this was a true understanding of what it meant to be a parent. I understood the true meaning of family values from a parent's and spouse's perspective. I would not forget that moment. I promised myself I would carry it through my life until the day I died.

That night, before sleep replenished my body with renewed strength, Valerie and I once again discussed the possibility of contacting the CNIB. I was hesitant to commit myself but fell victim to the positive urging of Valerie. "We could check it out," she said, "and if you decide it's not for you then there is no loss if you decide against it." She was so persuasive I agreed with her and with that sleep came much easier.

The next day I returned to work still not fully satisfied with the knowledge I had acquired from seeing Dr. Johnson. I made a call to the CNIB a few days later; they informed me a District Administrator would visit me within a few weeks. I would be contacted when he was available. Less than a week had passed when I received a call from Mr. John William Drover a CNIB District Administrator for the Avalon district, the district in which I lived. I accepted an appointment for the upcoming weekend on a Saturday evening. It would be an informal interview conducted at my home. He explained he was out travelling through his district visiting current clients and could fit me in at the end of his scheduled visits. I thanked him for his promptness and waited for the appointed time for him to visit me.

He arrived shortly after 2 p.m. in the afternoon; a woman his driver and guide accompanied him. Valerie answered the door at which time they introduced themselves by first names only. Valerie replied in kind introducing herself as she shook their hand. Then she escorted them directly to the living room where a comfortable sofa awaited them. I noted his female guide was linked to his arm directing him to his seat. I couldn't help thinking this was the first totally blind person I had ever saw. It seemed to me my functional disability paled in comparison to his disability.

Memories flooded my thoughts from my past when I felt down over my functional disability and my parents would always remind me no matter how bad I had it there was always someone worse; although it was true, it was also cold comfort. I then made a mental note not to mention his blindness unless he brought it up first. I thought to myself this was the most respectful way I could acknowledge the presence of this man without offending him.

Once seated Valerie introduced me as her spouse. Mr. Drover extended his hand; I took it with a firm grip and a quick handshake. "Good to meet you, Jim, I am sure the commonality of our sight impediment will no doubt be our topic of first discussion." The procedure was then repeated with his female guide who introduced herself as Mr. Drover's spouse. The seating arrangement was such that we sat directly across from each other allowing the conversation to flow easily. The conversation began with opening pleasantries of the day and personalized identification of themselves. This was meant to be an ice breaker between strangers but also to establish respect and confidence in the formal interview to follow.

Mr. Drover spoke first identifying he was born in Upper Island Cove, where he received his early education only to finish up with a degree from Memorial University of Newfoundland. He introduced his guide and driver as his wife of many years. My response was to acknowledge I too was born in Upper Island Cove and my family moved to the community of Bishop's Cove when I was very young. I indicated to him I knew his family because his dad was the custodian at the local school in Upper Island Cove where I enrolled in grade seven and eight before moving on to the high school in Bay Roberts. From there I tried a college course and finally a formal education at Memorial University of Newfoundland, both of which never worked out.

The conversation then reverted back to him as he acknowledged he too knew my family and so the conversation began to flow without restrictions. This of course opened up a familiar atmosphere of comfort and trust, which eased tensions. To further identify us, the conversation led to marriage and family in general. Valerie acknowledged we were married for five years and we had a three-year-old son who was spending the afternoon with his grandmother next door. Valerie then told them she was from Little Hearts Ease, Trinity Bay, a small fishing community. However, at a young age she befriended a young girl who had a developmental disability, and they became inseparable. Her friend's family decided to move to St. John's where there were more benefits available for their daughter. Because their daughter enjoyed playing with Valerie, she was asked to move to St. John's with them as part of their family. Her parents agreed and so she moved to St. John's to be a playmate for the young girl as well as to care for her. Both Mr. and Mrs. Drover acknowledged it was a great thing she did and it took a special person to commit their young live on such an important role.

The conversation shifted back to Mr. Drover who urged his wife to confirm how many years they were married, after which she told us where she too was born and the size of their family. The conversation switched back and forth covering all aspects of life including sighted disabilities leading to blindness.

I told him for a long as I could remember, I was night blind. I also told him of how I was a shut-in at night until well into my teens. I continued with explaining to him reading was always a problem during schooling; even though my glasses were prescribed at a young age I didn't find them of any value until I was in my twenties. My explanation continued as I told him the glare of sunlight from being outside and even through windows to be stressful on my eyes. Then after being blinded by the outside glare, there were extended periods of time adapting to the changing light conditions, both inside and out. Given my adaptability, I could reduce the effect's glare had on my sight but the transition from daylight to darkness was totally different and unadaptable.

Mr. Drover remained silent as I talked about my functional disability. I felt it necessary to tell him about the reason why I left university. I began my explanation by telling him I was preparing for exams and because everything I had tried failed, I went to see Dr. McNicholas in hopes he would provide glasses which would help with my studies. I told Mr. Drover about that appointment and what Dr. McNicholas advised me to do. Mr. Drover was astounded at my explanation. As a matter of fact, he knew Dr. McNicholas and thought it was highly irregular for him to offer advice without including the CNIB. Although I could have elongated the conversation with him much more on Dr. McNicholas, I elected not to, so I finished up with explaining some of the problems I was experiencing at work, at home and in my social life. With that explanation I followed up with the adaptive steps I took to address them. I also included in my summary my visits with Dr. Johnson, and the testing I had done in relation to my appointments with him. I also included the diagnosis he tentatively settled on as well as his advice to contact the CNIB.

Silence was heavy for a brief moment and then Mr. Drover went into a brief description of the CNIB and the services it provided. He noted, if I had been referred to the CNIB by Dr. McNicholas years ago, I could have utilized the CNIB low vision services to aid me through my university studies. I was dumbfounded to learn I could have been helped with readers as well as tutoring and writing assistance. "These services are still an option for you should you decide to go back to your studies," he remarked. My thoughts returned to Dr. McNicholas and his advice—go find work, your eyes are as good as they are going to be. It was a bitter pill for me to swallow back then and even more bitter with the information Mr. Drover just gave me.

He then explained that registration with the CNIB was considered at two levels. The first level would be a person who was totally disabled by complete blindness and the second level being a person which has a disability leading to limited sight. The person who was totally blind would be registered as blind. The person with limited sight would be registered as legally blind.

He also outlined the level of sight loss which CNIB considers to be eligible for registration. Of course, medical documentation would have to confirm the level of sight loss before registration was approved. I listened carefully to all the information he provided about the CNIB but wasn't totally convinced the CNIB was for me. He then indicated I could avail of some of CNIB services outside the realm of CNIB registration. These services were, of course, limited and subject to availability of staff. These services dealt with minor adaptive information and were of no value to me because my adaptive skills were further advanced than what they offered. I felt secure in my adaptive abilities and couldn't see any area where improvements could be made. Therefore, the non-registered services weren't relevant to my decision-making process in seeking registration with the CNIB. However, the many services offered through registration were indeed enticing.

I was posed with a major decision to make; my most private secret would become public it would be out in the open. I wasn't too comfortable with that thought. After hearing my concerns regarding registration with the CNIB, he then assured me my privacy would be respected; the CNIB was mandated to be totally committed to confidentiality by law. Mr. Drover interjected and noted I may not even be eligible for registration and even if I were registered it would be up to me to identify my registration with the CNIB to anyone. However, he continued, I should apply anyway and see how things work out.

I still had some hesitation on moving forward with an application for registration. I was strong and could adapt, maybe I would apply later in the future.

Mr. Drover must have sensed my reservations and then proceeded to tell me of how he became registered.

"As you are aware," he said, "I am totally blind myself. I was working as a teacher when I started losing my sight," he declared. "I was so angry with the world; I couldn't understand why it affected my job and forced me out of teaching. Then my anger crept into our marriage," as he glanced towards where his wife was setting. "I told her to leave me, for I was no longer able to be the husband she wanted me to be." He paused for a moment to regain composure.

In that moment his wife took up the conversation. "It was a difficult period in our life together," she said. "However, he is my husband; we had a good marriage with children. Of course, there were hurdles to overcome," she continued. "I was just as angry as he was but for different reasons. I could cope and accept his oncoming blindness but couldn't accept our marriage coming to and end. It was only through the CNIB with their counselling and life adaptive services that we understood it wasn't the end of the world for us both, but a new beginning."

I glanced at Valerie and wondered if we would go through the same thing. I acknowledged Valerie's thoughts were similar to mine and what I wanted would be what she wanted for us. It was this personal testimony by Mr. and Mrs. Drover that helped me over my decision-making process to apply for CNIB registration.

It wasn't an easy decision at that time. I wasn't sure if I met the eligibility criteria to be registered. However, if accepted, I would be registered with the CNIB and eligible to avail of their services whenever I needed them. Also, if things turned sour for me with my eyes, I would be able to access immediate help from the CNIB regarding counselling. It was then I finally realized registration was a win-win situation. After some minor paper work, our interview with the CNIB District Administrator concluded. Before leaving Mr. Drover told us he would submit my application when he returned to his office on Monday morning. He noted I should know within a two-week time frame if my application was accepted. If so, I would receive a registration card in the mail later. Both Mr. Drover and his wife bid us good day and left to return to St. John's.

Both Valerie and I discussed the implications of CNIB registration including the interview as well. We both agreed it was a very productive afternoon for both of us. Two weeks passed before Mr. Drover phoned me and confirmed my registration with the CNIB was approved; he congratulated me and advised me he would be available to me for any help or services I needed.

Within a month I received a CNIB registration card in the mail; I was now officially registered with the CNIB as a legally blind person with all the rights and privileges afforded to its members.

Unfortunately, things soon turned sour for me again. I found myself within the unemployment ranks yet again. The economic downturn gobbled up smaller business and was now affecting the larger businesses as well. The least little thing will throw even the best of companies into disarray, closure, insolvency, and even bankruptcy. Which is what it was for Mark Gosse and Sons Ltd. One by one employees were cut from their payroll. Of course, last in was first out. I fell into that category as I had little seniority.

Being unemployed didn't affect me as much as it did in the past. I was a strong-willed person with a personal drive to move forward to find work and if there was anything available, I would do my best to get it. I considered going back to university and take advantage of the CNIB services at that time but ruled it out. The reality was simple; I was married with family commitments that needed to be addressed. It would be a tremendous financial strain on my family plus we would have to relocate to St. John's. Then there was my functional disability. It would play havoc with my studies even with the assistance of the CNIB. After leaving Dr. McNicholas's office, I vowed to myself I would make my own way leaving behind my hopes and dreams of an educated career.

Life for me did not stop; in spite of the layoff, within a week I had a new job similar to what I did at Mark Gosse and Sons Ltd. It was with John Bishop Ltd.; the job was in their hardware store at Bay Roberts. Again, this was a job I could do and my work colleagues were great to work with. Everyone was at the same level working for the same pay. There was no competition for higher positions. The logistics of getting to and from work also worked itself out. Thank goodness, with all my adaptive skills and my growing work experience, I found it easier to find employment.

My job at John Bishop Ltd. was fantastic to say the least! I could work exceptionally well with my inclusive adaptability. No one was the wiser my functional disability existed. My functional disability finally had a label; it was defined as being legally blind. I could confirm this if need be, by producing a CNIB registration identification card. My most valued secret was still intact despite my fears of it becoming public knowledge.

I again saw Dr. Johnson in the early spring of 1979. Of course, I would go through a battery of testing. When I registered at the eye clinic, I was informed Dr. Johnson had ordered a new test called an ERG test. It was to be done at the end of my day's appointments. I reminded myself to ask Dr. Johnson what the test was and what it was for.

I knew what awaited me with all the testing. I knew my eyes would be subjected to an extreme amount of stress. I knew I would develop a pounding tension headache, a feeling of nausea and I would be disoriented for most of the day including a period of almost total blindness. Still, I was prepared for it all. However, I didn't know what was involved with the ERG testing and how it would affect me. I would drive to St. John's as well as drive home once my eyes and headache cleared. The one thing that bothered me was not knowing what the ERG testing was like. I worried about what the effects of the testing would have on me and how long the effects of test would last. If I couldn't drive home, we would have to utilize our alternate plan and stay in St. John's all night. It was an option we were prepared for but not a preferred one. Still, we would make that decision when it became necessary.

The day went as expected; the technicians got their testing done and I suffered through it all, never once complaining. There was no change in my appointment with Dr. Johnson; I would see him before I got the ERG test done. When I got to see Dr. Johnson, he had all the test results except the ERG test. He would have the results from the ERG test the next time I saw him. As usual he instructed his staff to arrange for the following years appointments. It was then I asked him to explain what the ERG test was.

Through his soft-spoken voice he briefly outlined what an ERG test was. "An electroretinography," he answered, "or ERG for short is also known as an electroretinogram. It's to measure the electrical response of the light-sensitive cells in a person's eyes. These cells are called the rods and cones. They form part of the back of the eye which is called the retina." He continued with his response by noting the preparation for the test would be longer than the test itself. He assured me it wouldn't be longer then twenty minutes with no lasting effects if everything went as expected.

I was still in a state of being completely disoriented with a pounding headache and nauseous enough to throw up when a technician from the eye clinic staff led me to the elevator. He explained, "This test will be done upstairs." Valerie accompanied us and helped guide me along. The test would be conducted on the fifth floor where the equipment was set up and ready to go. I was led into a dark room and seated by a machine with a viewing screen. It sat on a table in front of me. In preparation for the test, more drops had to be added to my eyes. I thought, oh my goodness how much more could I stand! The eye clinic staff person who helped me to get there preceded to administer the drops while the testing technician prepared his equipment. Valerie sat quietly beside me as they got me ready for the test. "This first vial of drops is to help numb the eyes and the second vial is to help prevent any infections in the eyes," explained the eye clinic staffer. "Let me see your eyes before starting," the ERG technician said. "It looks like your eyes are fine and there's no need for any more dilating drops," he concluded.

Once all the drops were administered, I would have to wait another fifteen minutes before the testing began. My eyes began itching and burning almost immediately upon impact of the drops. Thank goodness, it subsided in a few seconds. For me, I sat in complete silence trying my best to maintain a stiff upper lip, so to speak. Valerie also sat in silence; I felt her eyes on me and knew she was concerned. The technician chatted with the eye clinic staff person while he prepared the equipment.

The room remained darkened, with only enough dim light for the technician to do his work. After the appropriate time had elapsed, the technician confirmed I was ready for the test.

The technician asked me to open my eyes as wide as I could. I followed his instructions and as soon as my eyes were open wide; he pinned back my eyelids with small pinch clamps. The idea was to keep my eyelids open which would prevent me from blinking. Then another type of solution was added to my eyes. He explained he was going to place contact lenses over my eyes. He explained the contact lenses had wired electrodes attached to them. The solution seemed to me to be an adhesive which was to help keep the contacts in place. The wires led to the testing equipment. It must have been a frightening scene for Valerie; for me I couldn't see it and only relied on the technician's explanations. In front of me was a viewing screen in which I was supposed to look into. Thank goodness, all of what was happening was explained to me in vivid detail. I was told I would see a coloured light on the screen and to focus on the coloured light during the test.

I wanted to blink so much; my eyelids were continually twitching. This test was just as uncomfortable as the photograph test, I told myself. If the preparation was this uncomfortably intrusive on my eyes, how difficult was the testing going to be? Suddenly, one of the pinch clamps lost its grip on my eyelid; the result was an immediate blink. The eyelid closed covering the oversized contact lenses with the metal electrodes wires and all. Within a millisecond

the second pinch clamp lost its grip as well ending with the same result. The pain from this was immediate and excruciating. With the wired electrode contact underneath my eyelids I felt faint. I gritted my teeth and grunted with acknowledgement of pain. I persevered still unwilling to succumb to the pain.

No doubt, my eyeballs and eyelids were scratched. How much damage was done, I didn't know. My eyelids remained tightly shut and I couldn't open them.

Try as I might they wouldn't open. Each time I tried to open them the pain would increase. I knew my eyelids had to be opened to allow the wired electrode contacts to be removed. The technician tried to help me but each time he touched my eyelids, I pulled away instinctively. This was the most terrifying ordeal of my life thus far. All sorts of things passed through my mind. I could be blinded; my eyes would be so damaged I would possibly need surgery to repair any damage. Then there was my sanity. It was taking a beating; emotionally I was at the lowest level I had ever experienced. I wondered if all this testing was worth it or if I should discontinue seeing Dr. Johnson, which would in effect end the testing.

I felt the warmth of Valerie's hand in mine and a renewed strength filled my body. Several minutes had passed before I allowed the technician to assist me and try again to open my eyelids. He explained to me if I didn't open my eyes soon there could be excessive damage done to my eyes. It was that realization that brought me to my complete senses. I needed to have my eyes open and soon. I told the technician to do what he could to help me open my eyes. The technician gently with both hands pulled my eyelids away from my eyes. He then instructed me to open them. It was most difficult and painful but I managed to get them open. Immediately he clipped them wide open once again with the pinch clamps. My eyeballs and eyelids still hurt, remained sore, but the excruciating pain was gone.

I thought the technician would remove the electrode wired contacts then but instead he instructed me to look into the viewing screen again. "It will only take a moment," he insisted I did as he asked and saw a red line travel across the screen. I remained focused and fixed on watching that red line. Within a minute the test was complete. I was glad for I so much wanted to rub my eyes which I thought would help relieve the burning, the pain and the soreness. I sat back into my chair trying to relax and not blink. I was also aware of the ongoing twitching of my eyelids and the realization if those small pinch clamps lost their grip again, I would once again suffer great pain and discomfort. The technician gently removed the electrode wired contacts and then the pinch clamps. Instantly my eyelids closed over my eyes. Again I felt pain and hurt almost as if something was in my eyes underneath my eyelids. I was told I would have this feeling for the next 24 hours or so and if it continued, I should go see my family doctor.

What amazed me was he never checked my eyes to see if any lasting damaged existed. He was more interested in the readings produced by the testing machine. I was told the test was successful and I was finished.

Valerie led me to the elevator and as usual we headed for the cafeteria to wait until I could see well enough to drive. She had been quiet through the testing but the cafeteria provided privacy and that gave her the opportunity to expresses her concern over the possibility of damage to my eyes caused by the ERG testing. I reassured her I would be fine in time, although I kept secret my thoughts regarding damage to my eyes. She also confided there were several times she wanted to tell them to stop the test, but thought better of it because she knew I would have stopped it if necessary. The drive home was no different than any other time with one exception. Although my eyes were clear, I still felt as if something was stabbing into my eyes. Every time I closed my eyelids or blinked, it felt like something was underneath the lids.

As usual when we got home, I relayed the day's events to my parents. I felt it was important for them to be kept informed of any updates or changes in my eye condition. The one important bit of information which was new was the resulting damage to my eyes caused by the testing equipment during the ERG test. Although it wasn't known how significant the damage was or if it was just a minor irritation, but I hoped it would clear up in a few days. Their concern showed on their faces but remained silent for they knew I wouldn't want them to worry. All night long I kept cold wet cloths on my burning, itchy eyes in search of some relief. Sleep was difficult to find that night but tiredness from a most stressful day forced my body to shut down and relax into the mode of sleep. The following morning it hurt when I opened my eyes but the sensation of something being in them was almost gone. I only felt it when I blinked or closed my eyes. I also noticed the day's light seemed to be brighter with more glare than usual. The following morning, I felt no ill effects from the test, and to my relief, my eyes seemed to return to their state of normalcy.

# Chapter 11

# New Life with a New Beginning

Life from then on became mundane. I felt totally integrated into the main stream of society with my own acceptance of normalcy. In my job I was able to adapt to most any work situation which faced me. Of course, there were drawbacks and there always would be, for I could be blind by age forty; I was still night blind; I was still colour blind and I had a slightly marked restrictions on my daylight sight. If things remained the same throughout my life, then I would be satisfied given my ability to adapt. However, if things went sour, it would be difficult to maintain a positive attitude.

The year 1979 was also a memorable year; I felt good and I didn't notice any major change in my eye condition. I was still adapting and coping well. Yes, even my spirits were extremely high and I was happy with work. It goes without saying I had a wonderful wife and a fantastic son. Yet these were not the things which made that year most memorable. What made it most memorable was the pending new addition to our family. Valerie would soon give birth to a beautiful baby girl. After she was born, everyone told us we had a gentleman's family; both Valerie and I were so proud and overjoyed with the new addition to our family. We named our adorable baby girl Valerie Deanne. From that moment on, I personally promised myself I would work harder than ever to provide a good living for our family; they would always have the best I could give them. I also knew my functional disability would always be there and would always present problems for my family; I would have to find ways to adapt and strive on. It would be difficult for me because I wasn't like other dads. I was restricted during the darkness; I couldn't give as much after nightfall like other dads. My heart ached; I would have to deal with it every day of my life. I challenge any father to place themselves in the role of an incomplete dad. It made me feel so inadequate and incomplete. However, to dwell on such a lack of completeness would no doubt be devastating for everyone in my family so I hid my feelings and moved on with life as it was.

The following year, I once again prepared to subject myself to the rigorous testing at the eye clinic and the presentation of the previous results from Dr. Johnson. I also hoped he would have a definite diagnosis of my eye condition or any news regarding breakthroughs in science to treat RP.

The day we arrived at the eye clinic, I was informed I would see another doctor as Dr. Johnson was no longer at the clinic and another doctor had taken on his patients. Of course, this came as a surprise to me. I had formulated a good rapport and a liking for Dr. Johnson. I trusted him with complete confidence in his ability. I was a person who hated change especially when change comes right out of the blue. I was not impressed but stressed and I wondered if the change would cause any dramatic effects on my functional disability. I had my own reservations on whether or not the new eye doctor was as capable as Dr. Johnson. I hoped I could put my trust and confidence in him as much as I trusted Dr. Johnson. My mind reflected back to many years before when I put my trust in an eye doctor. That trust was ill founded because in time I came to believe that doctor in conjunction with my functional disability was the reason for my current station in life. The belief was one I accepted reluctantly but one I never was completely happy with.

When I was ushered into the inner office to see the new doctor, I noted a tall man with a smile almost as broad as his shoulders; his voice was soft and quiet putting me at ease almost immediately. He introduced himself as Dr. Bense, the replacement for Dr. Johnson. He told me I would be his patient from that point on. After careful examination of the previous year's testing results along with the results from earlier that day, he looked directly at me and said. "There aren't any results from the ERG testing in yet." He then noted there wasn't any significant deterioration or change in my eye condition since my last visit according to the testing results. "It's too bad," he said, "there isn't any cure, new developments or breakthroughs with respect to RP at this time." He ended by asking me to come see him the following year at which time he would check my eyes again.

I couldn't help but wonder had I hit an end to any real help in solving my eye condition, for it seemed to me Dr. Bense had accepted the temporary diagnosis of RP as being the correct one. For me there wasn't any indication he believed otherwise. I formulated that opinion after hearing him say there wasn't any cure or treatment for RP at that time. What solidified my opinion was his suggestion I make an appointment before I leave the eye clinic with no mention of any future testing at all. I was not totally impressed with him but gave him the benefit of the doubt; after all he was the only champion I had besides my wife and family. I needed a break from the yearly testing barrage which I welcomed, but I hoped he would change his mind. I left his office still in the dark about my eye condition and its future ramifications on my sight—most especially my life itself. It seemed the diagnosis Dr. Johnson gave me remained stuck in my memories, "It looks like RP but different," "I can only give a temporary diagnosis it could be RP." Any diagnosis Dr. Bense gave me would be irrelevant if not confirmed by factual conclusive testing, which he didn't seem to follow up on.

Soon the visit with Dr. Bense became faded into a blurred memory; it seemed he didn't leave much of an impact on me. Life for me would go on as usual and as normal as possible.

A work opportunity presented itself that summer following my visit with Dr. Bense. A call from the CNIB employment services stimulated my collective thoughts with an intriguing offer. When I registered with the CNIB, I indicated if an employment opportunity presented itself and I was qualified to fill they should notify me. Of course, to reinforce that request I supplied them with a complete resume to keep on file. From time to time, I would update that resume periodically when necessary. This action was my way of networking every opportunity to advance myself wherever possible. The CNIB provided many employments service-related opportunities, through sponsored training, employment networking with private enterprises, as well as with all levels of government. With the CNIB's ongoing efforts to provide employment opportunities for their clients, the CNIB in conjunction with government funding engaged into starting up a business. The business was called Viking Tools, a small hand tools manufacturing company. A market study was done for the CNIB and it identified a market potential for such a business. Separate components of small hand tools would be imported by Viking Tools and assembled by visually impaired employees' current clients of the CNIB. I was one of several people selected to be interviewed for the position of Staff Supervisor. My education, experience in customer sales and service, along with product knowledge of hardware flagged my resume to the attention of the hiring committee. My interview identified the full potential of my suitability for the position. I was knowledgeable in the hardware product line including hand tools, warehousing, inventory control, shipping, receiving and working in a team-oriented environment. My personal suitability identified I had great communication skills with a positive attitude and a willingness to succeed. Within a few days after the interview, I was offered the job and given enough time to make my decision.

My job at John Bishop Ltd. was secure; however, I felt the need to elevate myself to a higher level of achievement. Of course, the increase in pay and opportunity to supervise a small staff helped me with my decision-making process. My job would be less hands-on and more supervisory. I would be utilizing my educational training and people skills far more than before. I would need far less adaptation from the physical nature of work but an increase in intellectual adaption would be required. I weighed the pros and cons carefully selecting the decision I thought was best for my family and myself.

I decided to accept the offer and move forward with a new challenge. I submitted my resignation to John Bishop Ltd. and reported for work at Viking Tools once my tenure was finished with John Bishop Ltd.

Daily transportation to and from my work at Viking Tools wasn't a problem. Construction work was on the upswing in St. John's and a passage with a construction crew was easily obtained.

I settled into my job quite easily. The logistics of conducting the business end of my job didn't present any problems. Most of those elements would be conducted by phone or in person transactions at the office itself. I really didn't need any adaptation for this part of my job. I had the necessary skills to make it successful. However, the supervision of staff would present barriers I needed to address. I had often taken on the role of supervision at several of my previous jobs before but never with the inclusion of disabled people. Of course, I would have to adapt and create new skills to address the barriers which faced me. All the staff would be legally and totally blind people including myself with the exception of two other people, the manager Mr. Leonard Taylor and the Secretary Miss. Carol Ann Coombs. The manager to my knowledge wasn't disabled in any way. His job was to manage the company and take direction from the Board of Directors for Viking Tools. Miss. Carol Ann Coombs was hired as the secretary; she was born with a crippling disability known as spina bifida. spina bifida is caused from a birth defect caused during pregnancy leaving complications of poor walking mobility among other problems.

To my knowledge, baring the exception of the manager, most likely this would be their first job; I considered the possibility they only had life and social adaption skills to utilize in their work environment. They would be lacking in work-oriented adaption skills; it would fall to me to teach them those skills. Familiarity with their surroundings in the plant would be necessary. I would have to identify all possible barriers which would impede their mobility at work. Once they were confident where everything was located, they would be able to navigate easily around the plant. Everything had its place and would remain so for their convenience as well as mine. They would utilize all of their senses and adapt them to create new skills in the work place like I did through necessity and work experiences. I would take great pride in teaching them my acquired work adaption skills. I felt as if I had a calling to do this type of work. Of course, I too learned a lot from them sometimes it was a steep learning surve and other times a gradual one. Besides having to learn how to work with legally and totally blind people, I also had to respect and understand their personal barriers including the emotional ones.

For me this wasn't a major challenge; I too was a legally blind person who knew what it meant to be functionally disabled with a sight impediment and the emotional drawbacks attached. However, the secretary being the only one outside the manager without a sighted disability would be an exception. Understanding what a visible physical disability meant when it came to barriers was quite different than those of us who had a sighted disability. In that case, I urged her to identify any barriers of concern to me and I would address them as need be. The manager, not having any sort of disability, wasn't different than other non-disabled person who I worked with in the past; thus, I knew how to address his concerns.

In the time I worked with the manager, there was nothing said to me concerning my disability. However, I had a feeling of bewilderment under his watchful eyes. Maybe it was because of the minor degrading chores he assigned to me when I first started there or maybe he felt I couldn't handle a supervisor position. I couldn't help but feel somewhat subordinate not only from the status of work but on the scale of humanity as well. In the past while working with non-disabled people, no one knew of my functional disability and thus no one looked down on me. This was different in that everyone knew of my disability including the manager, which caused me to wonder if he had any prejudices against disabled people or was he totally ignorant of what it was like to be disabled. Now matter how much I tried to keep my thoughts in check, it would be a feeling which would linger in my memory unsolved. I may have been wrong but I couldn't help feeling of being somewhere below his status as a human being. However, my concerns were not what the manager thought of me for I could deal with that; my main focus was with the employees who I was to supervise and who needed my help.

I soon learned of their frustrations and challenges in learning new adaptive skills; like me they were into a new learning curve. However, they made it easy for me to teach them as I was accepted as one of their own without question. It showed in their tolerance and patience with me as I encouraged them to open their mind and be more creative to find new ways of getting things done through alternate means.

I gained a better understanding of myself through their efforts. They saw me as being normal within their understanding and definition of what it meant to be normal as it related to their own realm of reality. I felt extremely comfortable around these people; to them I didn't have to prove anything.

I found adapting to working with these people not as challenging as I had thought it would be. When speaking to them, I learned to address them by name always facing them directly as I spoke. This was a way to identify I was speaking to a certain person directly without interruption from anyone else. I always had to ensure any potential obstacle prevented their path of mobility to be removed, even though everything had a place. However sometimes they would themselves create obstacles for others. A complete list of verbal instructions was necessary to address the issue. I was not amazed at their memory skills and realized like me the removal of sight only heighted their other senses which of course including memory retention. All in all, I was adapting to a new way of communication. Being legally blind, I could bridge the gap of communication between the perceived normal and the sighted impaired.

Because of the very nature of their affliction, there were times they would get into an emotional state of frustration. If I was to be successful as a supervisor, I needed to find ways to reach them and offer guidance. The first thing I needed to address was how to deal with their emotional state and second, I had to find out the root cause of their frustration. I soon realized I was doing a job part of which would have been related to my dream of being a Social Worker. It felt amazing; even though I wasn't educated or trained in that area, I met the challenges head on and adapted on the go.

My time at Viking Tools broadened my knowledge of the blind and legally blind people and how they faced day-to-day challenges. For the first time in my life, I didn't feel my functional disability was an impediment. It was through bonding with these people I learned something very important. These were people with different personalities from different walks of life bonded by one element of reality a disability, whether it was physically seen or unseen like in my case. In all other aspects of life, like me they fell into a category of being normal. As normal in their way of thinking about themselves and how they defined it. I came to realize and understand in some ways everyone has a functional impediment, even the perceived normal person. I challenge anyone to find a perfect person with no impurities or impediments. The answer is quite simple; there isn't anyone. My upbringing as a Christian taught me there was only one perfect person. We in our wisdom considered him a threat and crucified him.

The staff I supervised at Viking were labeled, ridiculed, belittled, and abused by those outside the circle of their own normal reality. I saw this firsthand through the arrogant, non-visible, self-perceived normal stream of people who labelled themselves as being normal and everyone else as being abnormal. It would be untrue if I said everyone within the perceived stream of complete normalcy were abusers. However, what was true and alarming to me was the fact some of these abusers existed within the CNIB itself. I discovered early as a result of my close contact with the CNIB there were staff who considered themselves superior to the clients they served. This perceived superiority often resulted in client abuse. The resulting factor in my estimation was a failure of the CNIB to recognize those issues and address them. What was most distressing to me were the stories I was told of intellectual abuse. In most cases the CNIB registered clients were poorly educated and lacked the intellectual academic training to defend themselves. Even those CNIB registered clients who were of an equal intellectual academic capacity weren't immune. They too, whether or not they were aware, were subjected to the labelling, ridicule, belittlement and abuse.

The CNIB was coming apart at its seams and in the process losing the respect the clients they served. The outcome, as told by the employees I supervised at Viking Tools, led to distrust and lack of confidence in the services offered by the CNIB.

I spoke to a CNIB staffer about this and was informed it was just office politics, an acceptable part of their job. This was new to me; I knew what office and work politics was like; it was nothing like that. I guess the staffer thought I was intellectually subordinate as well and couldn't understand what was happening. What I saw and experienced was something different. In my opinion the CNIB needed a change and soon if the institute was to survive.

Besides a few close friends, the mainstream of society had no knowledge of my functional disability and therefore no reason to label or inflect any abuse my way. However, being registered with the CNIB extended the knowledge base of my functional disability to the staff of the CNIB. Despite Mr. Drover's assurance of privacy and confidentiality at the CNIB there were those staff who continually abused that policy. Due to my registration, I was completely open to ridicule, belittlement, taunting and abuse from a larger base of staffers. I was fair game for those who would try and abuse me but my strong will remained in place to defend myself at all times. I am sure, like me, there were others who could defend themselves and demand respect from would be abusers at the CNIB. However, I am unsure of their success or failures due to the CNIB privacy policy. I later came to realize office politics of such a nature did exist at the CNIB, for unknown to me, I am sure those who I had scorned fed me to the top management where future reprisals would come back to haunt me.

Viking Tools was funded through the CNIB with its own Board of Directors. Most of these directors were also members of the Board of Directors from the CNIB itself. All of our management meetings with the board of Viking tools were conducted at the CNIB boardroom.

As a Supervisor of Viking Tools, both the manager and myself attended these meetings. It was in one of these meetings I was first subjected to a belittling comment by a CNIB staffer who was also a board member of Viking Tools itself. It was an embarrassing experience for me as I had never been subjected to such a degrading comment before. I felt the need to retaliate immediately but thought better as I scanned the faces of the remaining board members. I ascertained they had ignored the comments or readily accepted comments like that as being normal. I decided to do the same and so I moved forward with my presentation. However, I planned to take up the issue with the staffer later in private.

It was the first time a staff member of the CNIB tried to belittle me. I filed it away as a reminder to be always on guard and ready to defend myself. Before I got the chance to discuss the issue with the staffer, it happened again. However, I was ready; the outcome was much different as I defended myself and my station as an equal to that person. I also told him I could have challenged him before in a board meeting when he exhaled derogatory comments towards me. I told him I could have belittled him then but chose not to because I felt I was a better person than that. From then on, I was never challenged again.

In daily conversations with the employees of Viking Tools, I found out they faced many challenges in dealing with the CNIB especially on a financial assistance basis. There wasn't much I could do for them except to lobby on their behalf directly to the Executive Director of the CNIB. Once case in particular, an employee approached me seeking some help in securing financial assistance to acquire new prescription glasses. I reviewed his budget and noted he couldn't afford them unless he got some financial aid. I decided to take up the challenge and so I wrote a letter to the Executive Director of the CNIB outlining his concerns. A week later the employee told me the CNIB would assist him with financial aid. However, the fall out over my interventions on their behalf would have significant future ramifications for myself.

In my first week of orientation with Viking Tools, I concluded I had made a mistake in accepting the position. I did have a long-term position with John Bishop Ltd. However, I was no longer in their employment and therefore, I would have to make the best of where I was at that time. My intuition after the first week told me my position with Viking Tools wouldn't last. I carefully examined their business plan searching for flaws and solutions. One aspect of the business plan which concerned me was the Board of Directors and the funding agent, "the CNIB." I deduced their over involvement in the day-to-day operation of the business would contribute to its downfall. Another major concern of the business plan was the lack of positioning, marketing, market strategies, sales, product pricing and distribution. All this was absent from the business plan and the manager of Viking Tools never had a chance to move forward in a positive direction. His mandate was to make Viking Tools a viable business success but without the existence of the basic business elements his failure was assured.

I knew in my heart I would be soon out of work again. This of course was based upon a poorly designed business plan and business-related insight. In my determination for a business to be successfully established with continued growth, it depended upon good planning, business sense and insight from its founders. Viking Tools, as I predicted, within two years of its conception, fell victim and ceased operations. Even though their intentions were of a good nature, their inability to foster a viable sustainable business fell directly upon their lack of planning, business sense and insight. I knew this too be true for I always worked in the private business sector where business savvy is a must to survive. The Viking Tools board of directors came from the CNIB staff, government public servants, publicly run utilities and non-business oriented wealthy philanthropists. There was no business savvy within this conglomerate of directors to ensure success even though their hearts were in the right place. With respect to Viking Tools, the incomplete business plan and their board of directors weighed heavy on its downfall. I was not asked why I thought the business failed and as such my conjectured opinion remained unknown. As I predicted, Viking Tools did fold within two years and I was left treading water while searching for a new job.

The one thing I gained from that experience was supervisory and management skills, which I could add to my ever-growing resume of education, people skills, work experience and talents. It would be a useful addition to my future work endeavours.

During the time I spent with Viking Tools, I continued to see Dr. Bense who monitored me annually for any changes. There wasn't any testing only the response, "There is no change in your eyes; see you next year." However, my spirits got a boost when I was contacted by Jane Green. Jane was the geneticist whom I first met two years earlier. She questioned me as to who I knew had a similar eye condition as myself. She also wanted information on my family tree along with a request for blood samples to be taken for genetic testing. I also provided her with a short list of people I personally knew who had a similar eye condition as myself. Although, I wasn't quite sure their eye condition was the same as mine. I also gave her an update on the status of my eye condition as last told to me by Dr. Johnson and later Dr. Bense. Although she probably knew more about my eye condition than myself. In some way I guess I was trying to cover all aspects of information she would need to conduct her study of my genetic eye condition. Jane Green informed me she would arrange a specific time to come to my home with a qualified person to retrieve more blood sample.

Within a week Jane Green and her companion appeared at my home on an arranged appointed time. Her companion was a registered nurse who took the blood samples from me. After the blood was taken and I got to relax, Jane asked about my family tree and recorded all the information. She also informed me she would be collecting blood samples from other members of the family as well as questioning them on our family tree to get a complete record. When Jane and her companion left that day, she informed me she would be in touch if any break-throughs in her research became known or if she wanted any more blood samples and further family information.

I was still unemployed at that time and was actively seeking work. Through all of my networking search it did not elude me for very long. Within a short period of time, I secured a temporary position with Scotia Bank in Bay Roberts through the assistance of Jim McDonald head of the Opening Doors program with the Provencal Government. My job at Scotia Bank was to assist their loan's staff with an ever-expanding workload. The job was quite different from what I was used too; it would be a steep learning curve for me. It was more of a clerical position with lots of paper work to be done. There wasn't much physical work attached to the position and I was always in a well-lit area. This, I thought was the type of work best suited for me at a non-supervisory level. I hardly ever had to adapt to any situation. I became quite familiar with bank accounting skills, filing and recording of official legal documents. I was also in a position of trust where I could provide personal service in a one-on-one basis. I found this part of the job most satisfying. Like in school, I stayed away from any area which amplified any glare of light from the outside and also from any dark dim lit area's where my sight would be restricted. All in all, I enjoyed working at this position.

The forced decision I made to leave a formal university education years be-fore and seek work had worked out well for me but not completely to my liking. I felt I was still lacking something special. Yes, I did have the skills, talents, abil-ities and experience to work at most jobs but I didn't have an official document certifying I was qualified or trained in any specific area required to fill any legit-imate positions of substance. Therefore, in most cases where I applied for work, I was screened out for lack of certifying documentation. I was only successful in securing interviews for positions which required either certified documentation or an equivalent combination of on-the-job training and work-related experience. It is said that a rolling stone gathers no moss, but to me this saying was the com-plete opposite. Indeed, I felt like a rolling stone going from job to job and only staying long enough to absorb important work experience and indeed, I was gath-ering moss. Prior to my work ending with Scotia Bank, another person was hired to work as a teller leading to a permanent position. Although I was already work-ing there as a temporary employee, I wasn't considered for the permanent teller's position. I questioned the Banks decision to hire someone else when I was already an employee and their answer fell into the category of excuses and more excuses. In fact, I felt, because I had a functional disability it was the one and only factor in decision not to hire and train me. This was the first time I felt the stigma of perception as being a ladled person.

After my temporary position with Scotia Bank ended, work became more difficult to find. So for an alternative and temporary measure I turned to the construction field of employment until I could secure more suitable employment. The job market was changing; employers were looking for better educated and more qualified applicants with specific skills to fill their employment openings. There were jobs I knew I could do but was continually screened out. In time, I stopped applying for those positions and looked for jobs seeking work experience only as a requirement. These jobs were mostly attached to organizations specifically designed to service the identified disability community.

Several positions came open with several different disability organizations but each time I was screened out mainly because my disability didn't fit into the category of disabilities they were representing. The only positions I was successful in securing interviews with was the CNIB through their Employment Services Program or the Provencal Government through their Opening Doors Program. Of course, this was logical in that I was a registered member with both organizations.

I had come so far and achieved so much only to be stonewalled by lack of formal educational training. It seemed I couldn't find any position within the main stream of society other then physical construction work which wasn't really suitable for me. In those cases, there was too much for me to adapt to and so my performance was somewhat lacking. Although I still maintained an eagle eye on seeking suitable work within the main stream of society, the only opportunities I found was with the service groups whose mandate was designed to assist the disabled community in seeking work. With every position I applied for at the CNIB, I either met or surpassed all the competition requirements for the position. Each time I had an interview at the CNIB, I felt confident the results would be positive for me. However, I was wrong and each time the position was offered to someone else. I later found out from Mr. Drover the true reason why I wasn't hired. It seems I was being punished for being proactive in my dealings with the CNIB and its staff some years earlier, so much for office politics. In the meantime, I struggled from temporary job to being unemployed for lengthy periods of time. It was during these breaks from work I got to spend some extra quality time with my family.

The joys of being a husband and father are so often taken for granted. Work commitments often consumed too much time and thus family time is neglected. In most cases family time for a father or a working mother is available only on weekends and nights after work. Too often the rigours of work are very taxing on a body, leaving either parent tired at the end of a days work. This of course leaves very little energy to provide quality time with a spouse and children. Even on weekends daily chores neglected all week long would take up quite a bit of adequate quality family time.

With my functional disability severely restricting my life, any quality time with my family was welcome. However, in the evenings after work during the fall, winter, and spring there wasn't enough daylight to spend outside with my family. After dark reading to my children, and board games were never an option due to sight restrictions. I couldn't drive them anywhere or walk anywhere with them at night. I could only play oral word games, as well as some card games, made-up fairy-tale stories or hide and seek to entertain them. However, the summer season was much better with the extra daylight I was able to be outside with my family doing most everything other families did but in a shortened version. Still, I was very thankful for the summer season and the joy it gave me. Other then driving, walking, or playing after dark with my children, I felt like a complete dad. No matter how much time I could commit to my family, my functional disability still had an enormous impact, one that disturbed me greatly. The emotional challenges were not only stressful but also depressing. I often cried in silence internal tears of a parent who couldn't provide that 100 percent of parenting or the duties required of a husband and father. Sadly, no one knew how I felt because of my strong will to keep things buried inside. My only reprieve was that inner strength which kept me moving forward.

# Chapter 12

# A Physical Disability

We humans live a life of one direction, forward only. Unlike the natural ability to walk backward or the engineering ability of a car to drive in reverse, we cannot relive our past. We can only retrieve memories from the mental capacity of our mind or documented material. Memories are forever etched in the doldrums of time. Retrieval of these memories is possible but there is no way to make corrections or change outcomes to our past. However, we can learn from our past, build upon it by carrying knowledge forward with us. The mistakes our parents and grandparents can be corrected as they are brought forward through each generation. Once brought forward, corrections and adaptions are made in real time as improvements.

The present is forever evolving and creating a future for us to live in. In my case, the functional disability I inherited was not known to my parents and grandparents. Therefore, there were no existing corrective measures for me to build upon. It was up to me to learn from my own past and make corrective actions suitable to accommodate my functional disability. As the present is forever evolving and creating, we are able to make corrective actions within a defined period of time. Once a decision is made, implemented and accepted then it becomes a path to our future. As the future becomes reality, our decisions and actions become our past. It is then through evaluation we are able to make corrective actions.

For me, I was continually analyzing my actions and decisions in hopes to incorporate my functional disability as part of a perceived normal life. Sometimes the corrective measures were suitable for long term use while other times only suitable for short-term use. Still, this was my life and only I could determine its direction and outcome. I had laid the building blocks of corrective actions which allowed me to move forward. I had met the challenges of my life thus far with limited success. However, there would be many more challenges for me to face in my future.

It was the late spring of 1983 and as usual I found myself working for another company. This position was again within the field of retail sales. However, this time I held a manager's position. I managed the day-to-day operation of a small general store which sold a variety of goods including, building supplies, hardware, paints, electrical, flooring, plumbing, garden supplies as well as farming supplies and animal feed. By now I held a wealth of knowledge in retail sales and thus it seemed to be my station in life as it related to employment which was definitely on the up swing. The business was known as K&R Variety located in Bay Roberts, well within my radius of mobility. I could drive to and from work when daylight allowed and, in those times, when daylight wasn't sufficient, I booked a passage with other people who were working in Bay Roberts as well. Things went well and it seemed I would be employed for a very long time. However, my luck didn't hold out for into my second year with the company, I sustained a physical work-related injury.

During the month of November 1984, the company received a huge shipment of animal feed, sacks of oats to be precise. It was at the end of a long day and I was helping off load the feed from the truck a tractor trailer. We were almost finishing off loading the truck when I placed a sack of oats on my shoulder only to experience the oats being loose in the sack shifted. It all went to the back of the sack immediately. In doing so, the shift of its weight twisted me around and I fell to my knees in pain. I had injured my back and I knew it immediately. I wasn't sure how bad it was but time would tell.

A friend of mine who also worked in Bay Roberts and provided me with transportation to work had just arrived to pick me up. Through enormous effort I managed to get into his car after which we headed home. I was in a tremendous amount of pain; no seating position was comforting. I had to grin and bare it. I told my companion about what had happened and that I would not be going to work the next day because I needed to see a doctor. Within ten minutes we were home. I opened the door of his car and with a tremendous amount of profanity and physical exertion I got out of his car in a crouched position. There was a wire fence not more then three feet away. In desperation I lunged for it to hold onto; I couldn't stand upright; I was in a precarious position unable to move. My companion asked if I needed help but I refused and sent him on his way. I was to prideful to accept any help. I was a man and it was my burden to bear. As his car drove out of sight, I remained hunched over holding on to a wire fence across the street from my house. The question to me was obvious how would I manage to get across the street and into my house!

It was a cold late November evening and total darkness was just beyond the next cloud. My eyes struggled to find enough light to navigate a straight line forward for the next 100 feet which led to the back door of my home. Thank goodness the light over the porch door was on, a beacon for me to head for. Frost began to bite into my exposed flesh and still I was unable to walk upright and forward. The pain was overpowering with no relief; every breath of air was beyond my endurance of acceptable pain levels. My eyes were filled with tears of pain which also depleted my ability to see.

I couldn't stay where I was and yet I couldn't move; my legs wouldn't work for me. If I let go of the wire fence, I would lose my balance and fall off that; I was sure it would happen. If I fell, I would no doubt cause more injury to my back or even cause another injury such as a broken bone or a head injury. At least ten minutes passed and I was yet to move one step. I looked at the frozen ground with the black pavement glistening from the ever-increasing frost forming as darkness swallowed up the eastern sky.

In my clouded mind of pain and confusion, I devised a plan to get down on my hands and knees; I would try to crawl the 100 feet necessary to get me where I need to be. I needed to by laying down taking the stress off my back and relieving the pain I was in. No human should be in so much pain. Furthermore, I thought no one should have to resort too or be subjected to a crawling motion in order to move forward. Slowly I lowered my self down to the ground ever mindful of not allowing the movement to be to fast but rather deliberate and purposeful.

It was no easy chore but I managed to accomplish the task but not overcoming the sickening pain my body was engulfed in. Thank goodness I had gloves on otherwise my hands would be not only frozen but also bruised and cut from the heavy weight they held above them. I was a man of 230 pounds plus; it would be no easy task to crawl carrying such a weight while enduring so much pain. Slowly, I began my crawl towards that light over the porch door. I was in the middle of the road when I realized where I was. Thank goodness there was no traffic.

It was dusk that time of the evening when the transition of daylight to darkness poses a visual problem for even the best drivers to see what was on the road ahead of them. I needed to be off this road and into my driveway very quickly. I was a helpless target and surely an accident waiting to happen. My fear for my own life quickened my pace and soon I was off the road into my driveway. I maintained my quickened pace and slowly etched closer to my goal. I stopped at the bottom of the fourteen steps leading up to the back door of my home. I glanced back into the black abyss behind me thanking my strong will and determination to get this far. Surely if I shouted for my wife to come to my aid, she would for she was within hearing distance. I dismissed the thought as not necessary, after all I had gotten this far myself and would go the remaining distance myself as well.

It may well be said I was a stubborn person, prideful and independent, unwilling to ask for or accept help. This of course would be true; I would agree 100 percent with that analogy. Due to my functional disability, I had moulded my life based on independence, not asking for help but rather being stubborn and steadfast in my ability to find my own solution. I adapted and overcome most of my sighted problems to a level of personal acceptance. This was no difference to me; I would draw from my ability to overcome and once again feel the completeness of a perceived normal person. My thoughts returned to the task at hand crawling up those fourteen steps. This proved to be more difficult than the crawl from the road to where I was. The crawl from the road was mostly level on pavement. However, the crawl was more difficult than what I had expected. The road was tattooed with remnants of crushed stone and a sand salt mixture which was spread sometime earlier to affect ice control on the road. With every movement the sand, salt and crushed stone bit into my hands and knees adding to my pain. However, I would not be denied and after overcoming that challenge, I was facing another challenge: the steps.

It was an uphill climb one hand then another stretching out my body over at least two steps at a time. This of course forced my body into a more erect like position increasing the level of pain even more. This caused me to wonder how much more pain I could tolerate. With only my arm strength I took my body weight on each hand one side at a time. Then I moved my knees up one step at a time, first the left knee then the right one levelling out on the first step and so the process continued until I was levelling out on the deck above just in front of the back door to my home. I can recall that climb as being the most difficult thing I ever had to endure. The pain and nausea threatened to take away my consciousness and leave me in an unconscious state. However, I persevered and achieved my goal once again. The sense of a fulfilled accomplishment eased my pain somewhat as I stared at the closed door in front of me. Before me lay another obstacle how could I stand to reach and open the door. It would be impossible; I had exerted all my energy to get to this point and to push myself any further would mean I would black out right there.

With my last ounce of strength, I knocked on the door from a kneeling position. I had not yet cried out loud but knew it would soon come. The sense of failure as I presented myself to my wife on my knees when she opened the door would be too much for me to endure. The sound of the doorknob turning and creaking of the door hinges informed me I would be soon inside.

Tears began to fall freely not from pain, which would have been no shame, but from the emotional state which was upon me. I saw the look of bewilderment on Valerie's face and I heard the questioning words, "What are you doing, Jim?" I didn't respond as I tried to get inside where it was warm. With a forward motion my trembling hands and numb knees I managed to crawl over the doorstep into the porch. I still heard the questioning words from Valerie. Words I could not understand for my mind was clouded with physical pain, emotional distress and numbness from the cold. Instinct took over, and a determination to get inside became instinctive. My forward crawl continued as I headed for the couch.

Almost immediately my hands began to burn with unbearable pain as the warming sensation penetrating the exposed skin of my hands; my gloves were torn and ragged. Instantly my thoughts recalled my early school years and the severe ordeal I endured under Miss Reese. Her strapping with a yardstick on my hands and then forcing me to insert them into an ice-covered running brook would forever remain with me. The damage she left me with was not only mental but physical as well, for every time my hands got cold and started to warm up, I would suffer greatly with a burning pain in my hands.

I was indeed marked for life with a burden of pain as a constant reminder of how cruel some people were. My thoughts were interrupted with over whelming spasms of pain. A human should not have to endure so much pain and misery I thought.

I finally managed to respond to Valerie, telling her I injured my back and I needed to get on the couch as soon as possible. Valerie said, "You need to see a doctor immediately." I agreed with her but wanted to get warm and into a more comfortable position first. Once on the couch I lay flat on my back relieving a lot of pressure, which in turn relieved a lot of pain. Within fifteen minutes the level of burning pain in my hands also subsided, for that I thanked God. I was feeling much better and was able to talk coherently with Valerie. Being strong-minded and of course stubborn I got Valerie to agree to allow me to rest for the night and see the doctor the next morning. Once everything was agreed to, I was left to rest. Although my pain was still great, I had to think things through. If my back injury were serious, how would I earn a living? I had always depended upon my physical ability to work because my functional impairment was a barrier to most jobs. With this physical injury a reality check loomed large. I put the thought out of my mind and focused upon the primes my injury was only temporary. I remained positive, focused only upon a return to work in a few days.

I saw my family doctor early the next morning. He recorded all the details, examined me and ordered blood work and x-rays. Because it was a work-related injury, he sent an initial report to Workers Compensation. He then furnished me with a report for my employer. Finally, he gave me an absence from work note stating I would be absent from work for an indefinite period of time. It was a trying time for me; I was in limbo needing to work and yet unable to do so due to a physical injury not to mention a permanent functional disability. Because of my functional disability, I had to find and develop ways to adapt to all aspects of life including employment.

The questions I asked myself were logical. Would I heal and return to work? How long would it take to heal? When would I return to work? Would I have to overcome and adapt to this physical injury as well? Time is ever-evolving and changing. I had a serious physical injury to deal with. The days added up to weeks and then months. Finally, eight years of my life was consumed. Apart from the continued positive support from my wife and children, I struggled internally with physical and emotional pain no human should endure.

There were no positive outcomes for me during that time frame. I had two operations on my back with very little success. I was deemed physically disabled and unfit to work. Of course, this was the conclusions of the so-called health experts and not my conclusions. Deep inside I knew I would overcome somehow and return to work. Also, in that time frame my level of vision had deteriorated to the point I no longer was able to drive. Indeed, I had very little to look forward to.

The one positive constant element was my family "my wife and children." I thank them for their understanding, love, support I would not have been able to cope and maintain a focus forward. Deep inside I knew I would find a way out from under an unwanted burden, one of life's tragedies.

From the day I was physically injured and the following ensuing years my functional disability took second stage as I tried to deal with a physical back injury. At the end of eight depressing stressful years, I had slid to a point of almost no return. My life was in great turmoil; it was then I recognized there was still a way out. My future was in my own hands and so I made the first conscious decision for myself in some time. I would not be a burden on my family any longer; I would not be a burden to society any longer; I had my pride.

I was in a deep dark place with only a thread of light keeping me from falling into the abyss of no return. It was this thread of light I held onto tightly and hand over hand I pulled myself towards the light of life above, like the day I pulled myself up the steps to our back door. I promised myself I would become a more productive member of society and most especially return to the parenting joys of a father and husband. I didn't know what the way forward would be but I was sure if there was one, I would find it.

At 41 years of age I would have to start over; I knew it would be difficult but I was ready, of that I was sure. I made a mental list of all the things I could do and the things I couldn't do. I would have to take into account my visual impairment along with an unwanted physical back injury which became part of my functional disability. I decided there wasn't anyone out there who would hire an untrained person with multiple disabilities no matter how much work experience they had. It soon became apparent the time had come for me to clearly identify all of my functional disabilities to potential employers. Once I accepted that premise, I knew any potential employer could be receptive and open minded to hiring me; this was my hope.

My journey to a new beginning had begun in earnest. The thread of light, which held me in check from falling into the abyss of no return, was as thin as a single thread of spider woven silk. Like the silky spider woven thread it was strong and dependable. I had my life line and each progressive motion forward would bring me closer to my ultimate goal. I wasn't naive for I knew there would be many challenges ahead. One of those challenges included the possibility of total blindness from the degeneration of my sight. Even though it was a projected medical possibility, I elected to place it into proper perspective and only deal with it if God forbid it happens.

Taking stock of my personal assets would be critical in any future plan as well. I no longer had the strong physical ability to do heavy physical work. However, I could do light physical work. I was still ambulatory able to walk and stand for at least short periods of time, this was an asset. I still had all the adaptive skills necessary to utilize all my senses in aid of my loss of sight. However, I recognized I needed to upgrade and refine those skills to meet my current level of vision loss, once the upgrades were complete this would also be an asset.

The one positive unblemished asset I still retained was a strong will with a logical mind. However, I needed to upgrade my level of educational training that would further enhance my intellectual asset. I always had a personal drive to succeed and enough patience to see any plan through. Finally, I had a wealth of work experience, which could be applied, to most work positions.

During the time from 1984 to 1990, I depended upon the medical establishment to heal me and provide me with a strong healthy physical body again. A body that would allow me to return to work. After two major back surgeries and six years of recovery, the medical establishment determined they had taken my recovery as far as they could. This, of course, was less then eighty percent of where I was prior to my injury. During that six-year period I maintained a positive attitude on a recovery while the level of my sight still maintained a slow deterioration. Because I wasn't working my need to utilize my sight beyond acceptable social living wasn't necessary, I hadn't noticed any major change in my sight. Still, I accepted what change occurred. I chalked it up as a natural progression of age.

Prior to my back injury I noticed a slight change in my sight while driving. From the time I noticed the change, I took precautions and only drove when necessary.

It was February of 1993 when Moms took sick and passed away much too early in her life. It was a major blow on the family; each family member dealt with it in their own way. I have often had the feelings of deja vu as well as seeing things beyond explanation. One such happening occurred when I was about ten years old; it seemed that I saw a close friend of mine carrying a bucket of drinking water from their well. I spoke to him but he just ignored me and went directly towards his home. What I didn't know he had been found three hours earlier drowned in the salt water of Conception Bay near his home. Later in my life I pondered on my ability to see and experience the unexplained. The only answer I could come up with was simple: I had an extra sense, one which also gave me the feelings of my surroundings in the dark.

My way of coping with the loss of my mother caused me just as much grief as the remainder of my siblings; however, there was some comfort in my grieving for from time to time I would see Mom full of smiles and happiness. I spoke to an Anglican Minister about it and his answer was simple; it was normal and part of a grieving process. I had no reason to disbelieve him and so accepted the premise.

Even though I moved on after Mom's passing, the grieving process stressed me a lot and left me with a major drop in my sight. I knew the day would come when I would stop driving and it seemed that day had already arrived. I took it in stride as an accepted change in my life and made a mental note stress did affect my eyesight.

Valerie would have to be the designated family driver from then on. Although I still had the confidence to drive, I recognized the importance and moral obligation to take the initiative not to drive for the safety of all concerned. It was a decision not easily made, but one I never regretted. It was time for me to move forward and I knew it.

I soon felt the emotional sensations of being active once again. Methodically, I researched all the private and public educational institutions within an acceptable distance for me to go to. I would upgrade my gained work experience by enrolling into a relevant course which would complement my level of skills and work experiences. Because I no longer had the sight necessary to drive a car, getting to an educational institute would be a challenge. Either Valerie had to drive me or I had to secure a passage with someone going in that direction. Of course, getting back home at the end of a day would also present the same problem. Ultimately, I chose a private college for a number of reasons.

The main reasons why I selected a private college came from a well thought out plan. I could enroll into the program which best suited my interest and complemented any skills training and adaptions I already had. I submitted my application early thus ensuring there wasn't a waiting list for the program I was applying for. This of course ensured acceptance was guaranteed. The college campus I selected was in St. John's, some sixty miles away; transportation would be an issue. I needed to secure a passage to and from the campus on a daily basis. This didn't present a major problem because there was always someone needing to fill their car pool as seasonal construction workers are laid off and jobs become redundant. Once my ride was secured, I would be picked up at my home in the morning and dropped off at the end of the day. I would only experience darkness early morning and at the end of the day. Because, I was comfortable around my home after dark my confidence navigating the darkness didn't present a problem. However, I would have to make note off all my surroundings at the college campus before I could feel comfortable there. Fortunately, I have a great memory and exceptional observational skills which would help me adapt quickly. Within a couple of days, I was just as comfortable at the college campus as I was at home.

The program I selected was to study was Business Management. The program consisted of courses in Business Math, written English skills, Consumer Behaviour, Organizational Behaviour, Accounting, Marketing, Target Marketing, Market Research, Communication skills, typing and computer program applications. Although the course was very in-depth and challenging, I committed myself to its completion. The Business Management program was delivered over a period of six semesters by highly trained educators. I settled into the program amongst a much younger class of students. Some of these students were barely out of high school while others were converting from a university education to a more suitable college education.

Although, I could avail of CNIB services to aid me in my educational challenges, I rejected the notion and stuck to my own devices. Still, I didn't completely disregard the notion of using them if necessary. In no time my existing sight adaptive skills were finely tuned, I even developed some new adaptive skills. From that point on, I realized the need for assistance from the CNIB services would not be necessary at all. My new skills helped me learn more efficiently as I digested the required course load. At the end of the program, I was one of three who graduated with honours from the total enrollment of business management students at that time. I was also honoured by being selected and awarded two scholarships. My level of pride and confidence on my achievements was huge, through the roof so to speak. I was never prouder of my accomplishments and myself. It was then I reflected back on the time I spent at MUN and the reason why I dropped out. If only circumstances were different back then; if only I wasn't ignorant of what was available to me; if only computers were available; if only professional advisers would have provided me with proper guidance. I would have proven myself and achieved my original career goals. Of this realization, I was certain. Still, Dr. McNicholas had sealed my fate; it was something I wouldn't forget or forgive.

At age 43 I was ready to start living again. It would be a new normal for my family and myself. This was the second time I had to start over; time and destiny had defined my life's path which I would follow wherever it went. However, it was my own determination which brought me success in the Business Management program. I didn't utilize any of the existing established crutches to help me through the program. I attributed this as being self-aware of my own capabilities and having my own solutions to see me through. I wasn't the man I was when I left university so many years ago.

Also, with age comes wisdom and I believe that wisdom played a major role in self-guidance.

With a wealth of talents, personal suitability, skills, work experience and formal training in business management, I would soon find out what potential employers would offer me in the form of employment if any at all.

What I discovered about most employers disturbed me greatly. Prior to my back injury I intentionally hid my functional disability, because I didn't want to be labeled as a person with a disability. I also thought my chances of securing a job was far greater if my disability was hidden. When applying for work employers considered me on an equal basis with other applicants.

In this way I had an equal chance of finding work. However, my decision to disclose my disabilities put me behind many barriers. What I would experience in my new normal was discrimination in its ugliest form. With most jobs I applied on I was screened out, in most cases with no explanation as to why. I know in my heart I was discriminated against and not given a chance to prove myself. I knew most of the successful applicants and I also knew my own credentials, which were equal in all aspects with one exception. I had a disability and as a matter of fact not one but two.

One disability was hereditary while the other was due to an injury.

When I did get a return response, I was informed only the top applicants were selected for interviews. What I generally received was a standard rejection letter. It was their way out from the shame of acknowledging their discriminating practices.

Then there were the times I did receive interviews only to be screened out. In those cases, I felt those potential employers only fulfilled their obligation to be pro-active in screening applicants for people with disabilities as a cop out; equal opportunity employers they called themselves. There were also many groups of employers willing to hire a disabled person if the government subsidized their salary. Unfortunately, the end of the subsidization period meant their employment was terminated. I saw the disabled community treated differently than other employees in those roles. They were given demeaning work; duties not relevant to my skills, work experience and training. In other words, they were taken advantage of by those employers.

Their only reason for hiring a disabled person was to further their business agenda. In the eyes of government, the business establishment and disability support organizations projected an image of progressive equality. But, beyond that stellar image, hidden deeply, were the true motives of those employers.

Their abuse of those programs and the misuse of the tools which were available to incorporate disabled people into their work force ran rampant in order to further their own business concerns. Profit by any means was their only interest. I know this for a fact because I witnessed these abuses firsthand. I felt the cold callus decision-making process from private employers as they took advantage of their disabled workers. Knowingly or unknowingly this decision-making process was flawed and discriminatory.

I had never felt discrimination before, yet it was alive and doing well. This reality caused me to question my decision for declaring myself a disabled person.

I reluctantly accepted the discriminatory practices of private employers as a reality because I needed the work. I had a family to support; however, in public employment I didn't anticipate that discriminatory practices would exist considering equality legislation for its work force. Because of the existence of discrimination in private employment, I continually sought employment in the public sector considering their insertion of an equal opportunity employer. Still, getting a public sector job wasn't easy to secure. To that end I forged on through the private sector employment opportunities hoping to secure some meaningful work until I was successful in securing a position with the public sector work force.

The taste of discrimination was extremely hard to digest. For the rest of my life, I would not forget its unsavoury flavor.

Chapter 13

# A Flawed Program

In time, I hoped perseverance towards obtaining a public sector job would become a reality. It didn't matter how often I applied for Provincial Government jobs; I was never successful. The Open Doors Program of the Newfoundland and Labrador Provincial Government seemed to be my best opportunity. It was set up to champion applications from the disabled community. Their goal was geared towards aiding disabled persons gain employment positions within the Provincial public service. This program worked fairly well for most people but not for me. I submitted an up-to-date resume with all my credentials to the Open Doors Program for inclusion into their database. If a position matching my resume became open then my resume would be sent to the Provincials public service commission for consideration as a preferred applicant. Of course, there would be other applicants whom I would have to compete against for employment. The intent was for an application from an inventory of disabled people to bypass the preliminary screening stage into a Provincial Public Service testing stage. If successful, a total of up to three successful applicants would be sent for a final review by the hiring department head for a final selection depending upon ranking of first, second, and third by the Provincial public service commission. I never got past the testing stage for during this screening process I was always screened out.

This screening process was designed to test certain skills, including education, knowledge and intelligence of the applicants. It soon became apparent a visually impaired person whose reading ability was very much restricted compared to a normal sighted person never had a chance. The testing was not adapted for a person with a major sighted problem who was legally blind. These tests had a time limit with regular normal size font of printed material. Also, the stress of lighting in the examining room varied from dimly lit to bright blinding light. For me the stress of adapting to this type of environment no doubt played a part in the overall outcome of my performance in the application, testing and interview process.

There was never a test with large printed fonts or extended time limitations to give a visually impaired person an equal chance. The lack of controlled lighting in the testing rooms to mimic normal daylight was never addressed, also there was never any adaptive equipment available for a visual impaired person to use while being tested. In other words, Open Doors hadn't gone far enough to create an equal opportunity for all. It had ensured inclusion up to the interview process; however, it didn't address the adaption problems further through the interview process itself. This program may have been a step in the right direction but it had its flaws.

I am sure the opening doors program was designed by a non-disabled person(s) with no input from the broad spectrum of disabled people, otherwise there would have been total inclusion throughout the process.

I recognized these flaws but my focus was on securing employment for myself and not to be a critic on the process. It seemed to me there were better-educated people in positions of power to identify and address these problems. Besides, I didn't need the stress of getting politically involved myself. After several failed attempts to secure a Provincial Government job I decided, the Provincial Public Service Commission wasn't completely compliant with the equal opportunity employment program it so proudly exhibited.

The existence of indiscriminate discrimination within the entry level application screening, testing and interview process of the Provincial Public Service Commission existed, either knowingly or unknowingly; it seemed to me ignorance towards a disabled person's needs may have been the rooted cause of such discrimination. I postulated the possible cause was a lack of proper training and education for their staff, as it related to the inclusion process of persons with disabilities. My thoughts often centered on the successful applicants who did secure employment; I wondered how much discrimination existed within the jobs they filled. However, I would not find out if such discrimination existed for I was never successful in securing a Provincial Government job. Still, I wasn't deterred from continuing to apply for all levels of public sector jobs.

Over the years, since the time I found out I was legally blind, I was told by doctors my eye disease was incurable. However, it didn't deter me from asking the question at each annual visit to the eye clinic. My appetite to seek out and digest new information on breakthroughs in medical treatment or advances in new adaptive technology remained a priority in my life.

My contact with the CNIB was almost non-existent, especially after the way I felt the CNIB treated me. I didn't have any confidence in their ability to assist me in any way whatsoever. However, I still received a monthly newsletter from them with articles outlining existing medical success stories. The articles included breakthroughs in medical science and technology, a topic I was most interested in. It was in one of these newsletters that a story caught my attention. The story was a reprint from a reputable daily newspaper in Ontario. The story centered on a medical procedure for persons with RP. The story noted a new procedure was being conducted in Cuba. There were testimonies from people worldwide claiming success in sight improvement. What was missing from that story disturbed me. There was nothing official from the medical scientific establishment to support their claims.

Eventually, one such Canadian testimonial story appeared in the CNIB monthly newsletter which piqued my interest. It outlined the story of a man from Ontario with ties to Newfoundland and Labrador. He had recently travelled to Cuba for this experimental procedure and related his story to the press. What the article didn't include was if the procedure was successful or not. This was confusing to me for a national organization such as the CNIB had printed an article or story in their newsletter without any factual evidence to support the story. I found it very misleading for an experimental procedure existed but it didn't offer any statistics of it being a successful breakthrough for people with Retinitis Pigmentosa. I don't know why the CNIB newsletter didn't provide an article in its circulation debunking the factual implications of the Cuba RP medical procedure. I concluded that he CNIB newsletter was nothing more than a social gossip publication with no basis in fact at all.

Although I didn't have any faith in the CNIB newsletter, the article still haunted me. Finally, the urge to know more about the RP medical procedure in Cuba burned deep within me. The seeds of curiosity and hope were planted by the CNIB newsletter. Here was something at least I could investigate myself. An opportunity to travel to London, Ontario that spring presented itself. Both my sister and myself decided to go see the person who had been to Cuba for the experimental treatment. It he would agree to see us it would provide first hand knowledge gained directly from a person who had received the treatment.

I could hardly contain the excitement growing within me as we headed to the town just outside London, Ontario. It was there we would meet the man who had been to Cuba and submitted his story to the CNIB newsletter for publication.

The meeting with this man left me somewhat disappointed. He never discussed the medical procedure, other then it was of a surgical nature and that a second visit would be necessary to complete the treatment. He never offered any endorsement of the procedure or encouraged us to get the treatment ourselves. He had the initial treatment himself but wouldn't confirm if he would have the follow up treatment. He didn't even provide us with any information on whether he had regained any sight, instead he provided us with documentation of testimonials from other people who also had the treatment. Also, there was an overview document of the cost of the procedure, the length of stay and the doctor who would perform the procedure.

We left the meeting with mixed emotions. For me, I had more questions then answers. I think it may have been because of my own deductive skills and reasoning facilities. Upon returning home, I made a firm decision I wouldn't go to Cuba for the treatment. I couldn't bring myself to believe that the treatment offered any hope at all; there was too much unknown for me to commit. However, I did follow the Cuba story and its ongoing treatment into the future.

I gained that information in real time from my sister, "Greta." She decided to take the risk and get the Cuba treatment. In time, the mainstream medical professionals collectively came out against the Cuba treatment claiming it lacked factual medical information on its success and failures. The Cuba cure for RP soon faded into the abyss of nothingness. Dealing with the disappointment of the Cuba treatment took its place in my memories of the many disappointments I had endured in the past. It seemed I was programmed to accept rejection and disappointment in an almost emotionless way. To dwell on setbacks was of no value to me, so I forged ahead. My main focus returned to seeking employment and supporting my family.

Finally, an opportunity opened up with the Federal Government and I was screened in and selected to write an entry level test. Again, there was no extra time limit or enlarged print on the material I had to read. Also, the testing rooms were not ideal for a person with a sighted problem. However, through share determination I focused on getting as much as possible done on the test. A week later I received a letter informing me of a pass in the test but my mark wasn't high enough to forward my application for any further examination on the competition. The letter also highlighted a numbered list of names that were to be retained for future placement into employment positions if any openings became available. It was a list of twenty names and the list was to be in place for five years inclusive.

I knew the low-test score was directly related to the inability of the Federal Public Service to have in place accommodation elements to allow equality in testing. Still, the test score would be in place for any future job opportunities. I was elated at this aspect and I hoped my dreams of a public sector job would soon become a reality. I had attained a foothold towards a Federal Government job. Within a year, a job opened up for an entry level clerical position with the Income Security Program department of the Federal Government. My application was accepted and I was hired after further screening by the Federal Public Service Commission.

My experience of discrimination in the private sector of employment remained fresh in my mind. Either knowingly or unknowingly, I compared the employment environment between the private and public sectors of employment as it related to discrimination, inclusion, adaption, and accommodation. My findings were quite eye-opening so to speak. Although legally blind, one should note sight is more than visually acuity. Sight also includes perception, understanding, identification and recognition.

I have always collected, stored and analyzed information for self-accommodation, so it was a natural response to continue that process going forward. The entry level testing was not totally accommodation friendly for people with sight disabilities. This, of course, was my first taste of incomplete compliance in policy and best practices for inclusion of equal opportunity employment for all. Of course, for example, if I was confined to a wheelchair and people could see I had a disability then an accessibility ramp along with an accommodating work station would be provided. By the same reasoning, if I was totally blind and my disability was visible, I would be accommodated. But for the person who was semi-mobile, there was no accommodation, not even ergonomics to make that person comfortable while working. So, it was with me, my low vision was not visible, unless I told people I was legally blind otherwise they would not have known and so no accommodation for me. I considered this a lesson in awareness. I would not forget this lesson, but would ensure to address it if future accommodations were needed in all aspects of my job.

My life would always be a life of adapting and coping. I was getting older and the slow deterioration of my eyesight was almost unnoticeable in my daily life outside of work. However, at work the need to update my adaptive tools became more frequent. This alerted me that my loss of sight was more serious than I thought. Still, I maintained a stubborn attitude I could be a productive member of society.

If I were to remain a productive employee, something had to change. To do this, I looked inside myself to find the solutions. My plan was to let my co-employee know of my disability. Next, I ensured every time a competition opened up suitable for me to apply on, I would apply, and I would self-identify myself as being a legally blind CNIB-registered member. This of course forced the Federal Public Service to ensure I was accommodated in all ways to make sure all testing and interviews were suitable for all members of the disabled community. I was often contacted to find out what type of accommodation I required. In time the Federal Public Service developed accommodation tools for all.

At work it was always myself who had to identify my accommodation needs and myself who had to find the solutions. Even though all my adaptive and accommodation needs were forwarded to my superiors, they never ever took action; it was always returned back to me to act upon it alone. I was always the one who had to find the solutions and then seek permission to implement them.

Although my eye disease was deemed incurable, technology with its adaptive devices was becoming more promising than ever. I hungered continually for information regarding whatever new technology was available and where it could be obtained. If I were to go completely blind, then new adaptive technology would be my companion for life. In time medical postulation and theory coupled with science and technology offered a glimmer of hope for a cure or a similar outcome.

However, the ongoing research offered nothing substantial to base one's hope on. All of the research was still in its infancy stages, from conception to early-stage laboratory trials. Most promising advances were years away from major scientific breakthroughs or human trials, which may have been focused on ongoing research into blindness, its causes and possible treatments prior to the 1980s. For me my earliest recollection of any treatment began in the 1980s.

The existence of being educated in the language of braille provided the totally blind an avenue of communication through writing and reading in the braille format. However, the blind and low vision community longed for more mainly because braille wasn't for everyone. Also, it meant all products contain braille

172

labelling which for manufactures would be a logistical nightmare. Therefore, it was time to think outside the box and so science and technology edged its way to center stage. Healthy diets and natural health products became readily available. One such product I tried myself was a daily regiment of a product known as Vitamin A palmitate. After a measured period of time, I didn't find any positive improvement in my sight. My sight was still deteriorating and so after two years on that product I discontinued the self-administered treatment for lack of results.

Special coloured eyeglass lenses, with a reddish orange tint base color, ranging from a light shade to a darker shade of the reddish orange, were developed by Corning. My sources informed me initially they were developed for the United States Military during wartime; however, it soon became apparent they could be used for people with sighted disabilities such as RP. These special eyeglass lenses became the next promising product for visually impaired people to hit the market. They offered so much possibilities for sight enhancement the CNIB promoted them as a possible benefit for people who had a low visually impairment. Although these lenses could be obtained in one's own prescription, the sample lenses were non prescription and fitted over one's own glasses like sun glasses.

The CNIB provided a sample of these glasses to me for a trial use. I became one of the ones who took full advantage of the new Corning-tinted lenses on a trial basis, my findings were very encouraging, the crispness of my vision was greatly improved, likewise the enhancement of what little coloured vision I had. Also included in my sight improvement was the sharpness of my vision along with drastic improvement in the reduction of glare with a greater detailed definition of everything I saw.

After returning the trial glasses, I had one drawback with them; the extra lenses were too heavy over my own prescription glasses. So, I ordered a pair in my prescription just to eliminate the heavy weight on my face.

Corning offered the coloured lenses in several shades. Starting with a very light red orange tint, ending with a dark red orange tint, these shades were identified in the following way: Corning 511 was the lightest shade, Corning 527 was the medium shade, while Corning 555 was the darkest. Although Corning may have had a larger list of tinted lenses, these were the only ones which were known to me. I ordered a pair of Corning 555. I placed my order through the CNIB who contacted Corning directly to fill my prescription.

Within a month I received my Corning glasses. I found one drawback with my new Corning glasses, when inside the lenses were too dark for me and my sight inside was greatly impaired. Initially in the trial basis I had worn the sample lenses over my own prescription outside only removing them once I came inside. However, when outside I wore my Corning glasses constantly. The following year when I had my eyes checked for a new prescription, I ordered the two lighter Corning lenses in my prescription. I now had three pairs of corning lenses of which I found most useful inside and out. As time passed and my vision changed, a new prescription was needed. However, I couldn't find any one including the CNIB to order the Corning glasses from. I had to return to regular glasses. The one improvement in regular glass lenses was the introduction of the photocratimic lenses. These lenses would turn a dark shade of gray outside and after a brief time inside they would return to an almost clear glass lens. I found these lenses great for blocking out bright blinding light and glare. However, they didn't offer the sight enhancements which Corning glasses provided.

The Corning glasses had provided a major block against loss of sight due to eye stress and strain. The end result was significant in that once my eyes were no longer protected by the Corning Glasses the slow and stressful deterioration of my sight continued unabated.

Disappointed over not being able to obtain any more Corning glasses, I returned my attention to emerging technology in the adaptive assistant aids for the visually impaired. Some of which include items such as, CCTV or closed caption viewing screens, Beecher's or high-powered optical lenses, similar to opera glasses in style. Then there was the use of computers, which was versatile to modify text in colour and enlargement. Programs such as Zoom text which could offer greater flex ability when using computers. Computers became more useful as speech-oriented programs became available. The speech-oriented programs read whatever was on the screen back to the user. All in all, thinking and working outside the box these new technologies offered the opportunity of greater inclusion into the work force and society itself for people with sighted disabilities.

Personally, I only used the CCTV and the Zoom Text program for work. The cost of such adaptive technologies for home use was well beyond the financial reserves of my budget and I was sure the budget of other people as well. There were many other adaptive aids available but wasn't suitable for my use, still adaptive equipment was useful to some but not all. However, these adaptive technological aids provided a pathway for inclusion towards a normal personal and work life in society.

Of course, there were other ways to address the effects in the loss of sight. Health Canada's healthy diet to help preserve and maintain one's sight was one such way. I took up the challenge and began eating more fruit and vegetables which were supposed to provide more nutrients to the body and most especially the eyes in helping maintain a good eyesight. While on the diet I monitored my eyesight and found no change in any way of preserving my eyesight or the loss there off. However, because it was supposed to be a healthy diet, I stuck fairly close to it if only for pure health reasons.

As always, I reached back into my memories if only to see what worked and what didn't. There wasn't any cure for RP, only aids and hope. I had tried most of the adaptive aids and found some useful but not all of them. I had also tried the diets and vitamin supplement such as vitamin A palmitate for a prolonged period of time and found them not to be of any benefit at all. However, having disregarded most of the adaptive devices and health supplements, I remained positive. Through necessity, I used what adaptive devices worked for me but hungered for something more, most of all a cure.

My main interest for a cure peaked with the introduction of some new scientific technology and medical theory being fabricated into reality. It seems every so often something new just comes out of the blue and this was one of these times. Through the monthly circulation of the CNIB newsletter there were two topics dealing with scientific technology and medical research which piqued my interest. Although I had lost total confidence in the credibility of the CNIB newsletter to publish creditable factual news, I still resourced it as media gathering information within the social circle of registered CNIB clients. What heightened my attention was the fact an article was reprinted from a reputable scientific journal by the CNIB newsletter.

One such topic dealt with two different medical procedures. The implantation of stem cells and gene replacement therapy was postulated as a possible solution to restore sight.

For gene replacement therapy, in theory once a defective gene is identified it could possibly be replaced by a healthy gene. However, at that time, the process and logistics of moving forward to a clinical trial would consume decades of research and time. Still, for me this seemed to be an option I would consider if my sight remained in a status quo position.

The theorization that stem cells could be used to treat many forms of medical

175

problems including eye disease leading to blindness. This medical procedure presented a possibility it too could be a possible solution for my eye condition. However, like gene therapy, its reality existed in the doldrums of time. For me it too was hope but on the distant horizon.

The second article dealt with artificial sight. There were two new devices being put forward in that article as well. This first new technology was a device known as Argus 11 or the bionic eye. This product was comprised of a computer chip and miniature cameras. The computer chip was inserted into the retina while a camera attached to glasses captured the surrounding visual fields. If successful, it would provide artificial sight much as the eye would do. For those who were totally blind, this device offered hope in seeing again even if it was restricted artificial sight.

Clinical trials soon began showing up all over Europe but none in North America. It did provide some artificial sight to its user, mostly a dim light. However, the sight improvements would be directly related to the upgrading power of the computer chip. It would take time and many upgrades to the computer chip for this device to be an effective replacement of sight. The early upgrades increased the sight to the user from dim light to shadows of shape in black and white but no color.

Not soon after the introduction of the Argus 11, another product known as E Sight also showed up in science journals and subsequently in the CNIB newsletter as well. Digital computerized cameras attached to special designed glasses with a small power source were being tested to enhance existing sight no matter how low the vision was or where it was located in the eye. The camera would capture the visual field surrounding the user and direct it to the area of the eyes where the best sight existed. The end result was expected to enhance the complete visual fields for the user creating an impression of normal sight. However, like the Argus 11 or Bionic Eye as it was called, it too depended upon the existing power source and digital upgrades to be an effective device for the user in creating usable sight. Although there was more research in other areas, these ones were the only ones which magnified my interest because of their possible outcomes.

Through the Internet and social connections along with inquiring questions on my annual visits to the eye clinic, I kept myself informed on all the resent advancements in both medical research and technological advances. In time medical theory and technical devices became a reality as clinical trials started popping up in different countries. The future was shrinking what seemed to be decades to an end-state for a cure or treatment was fast becoming only years away. Personally, I became happier with my station in life for I was working at a job I liked and God willing, I would have the opportunity to at least keep the sight I had or maybe even regain it. In the meantime, I kept a keen eye on all possibilities. Then just before the end of the 20th century came new hope as research moved ahead in leaps and bounds.

Several years passed and the Argus 11 saw major improvements but far from being where it needed to be as a suitable solution for sight creation. Ongoing testing saw the implementation of animal trials in both Europe and North America, which was necessary for the foreseeable future if it was ever to go to market. The same was also true for E Sight. It seemed that technical adaptive devices would be the saviour for my sight as nothing new was forthcoming regarding gene therapy and stem cells implementation treatments.

The millennium was barley minted when medical journals published papers on clinical trials in animal for stem cell implantation and gene replacement therapy. This was what I was waiting for; the possibility of staying the deterioration of my sight or even restoring it loomed large in eyes. There would be no invasive artificial devices with intrusive surgical implications and its side effects for me to deal with. Over the years, I saw many ophthalmologists and optimists, including Dr. Johnson, Dr. Bense, Dr. McNicholas, Dr. Richardson, Dr. Moore, Dr. McNamara, ending with Dr. Whalen. Each one, in their own way provided advice regarding my sight. Some also provided updates on advances for sight enhancement tools as well as what was being developed. It was Dr. Whalen who advised me gene therapy would be my best option for a possible treatment. I also considered Stem cell procedures as a possible second option. As time progressed Human gene therapy clinical trials for different forms of eye disease began in earnest.

Originally, it was thought I had Retinitis Pigmentosa but the defective gene which my form of RP wasn't known. The clinical trials which were being conduct dealt only with known defective Genes. Because the defective gene which cause my eye condition wasn't known, I wasn't eligible for the gene therapy process yet.

In 1978 blood was drawn from my family and myself for testing. It was then sent to laboratories in Canada and the United States. The intent was to identify the defective gene which caused my eye disease. I should note since 1978 a small group of people having the same disease as myself was also identified. I should also note, that blood samples may have been taken from those people as well, if only for comparison reasons. The years passed with no response from any of the laboratories. In 2003, some 25 years after I first saw Dr. Johnson, a laboratory in Huston, Texas, USA discovered the defective Gene, "RLBP1" which caused my eye disease. It was identified as being a rare type of Retinitis Pigmentosa. It was so rare it didn't even have a name, so it was named after the place it was found. In the future it would be known as Newfoundland and Labrador Rod Cone Dystrophy Syndrome. I felt honoured to have played a major part in its identification. The bragging rights were mine as I was the initial guinea pig in its identification. If in 1978 I had not gone to see Dr. Johnson with the inclusion of Jane Green it may not have been discovered. It was them who started the process of trying to find out what caused my eye disease. It would be Jane Green's steadfast commitments to genetic research which helped in finding the elusive RLBP1 gene. From the bottom of my heart, I silently thanked Dr. Johnson, Dr. Jane Green and all those who worked so diligently to uncover the root cause of my eye disease.

I looked forward to the time a clinical trial for the RLBP1 gene to become a reality. My patience was being tested to its limits as clinical trials were being conducted in several areas in Europe and the USA but not in Canada. Soon the emotional high I was riding came to an end as reality set in. The reason there wasn't any clinical trial at all for the Newfoundland and Labrador version of RP was because other forms of RP had a larger population base then the small pocket of people with the Newfoundland version of RP. In fact, the possibility for any gene therapy clinical trial which included the RLBP1 was almost non existent. At that time, I scolded myself for relying solely on gene therapy as the best option. As usual not letting disappointments deter me from moving on; I turned my attention to seeking clinical trials on stem cell implantations for persons with RP. This procedure would cover the implantation of a healthy stem cell in the eyes which would include not only the defective RLBP1 gene but many other genes as well. One such clinical trial was being conducted in Florida.

Both my sister and myself applied for inclusion into that clinical trial. We were so excited especially my sister who had made the list for the second phase of the trial. I was sure I too would make that same list. However, it was not to be; disappointment once again showed its ugly head. An unforeseen slow down in the North American economy especially the United States forced that government to curtail their financial support for clinical trials. Also, the research, testing and development component of the major drug companies followed suit and suspended their activities in clinical trials. As a result, the trial we applied on was cancelled pending the availability of future funding. Although disappointed, I knew once the economy improved, the possibility of clinical trials would begin again.

I remained full of hope that something would happen in my lifetime and I would become part of it. I still had to face the fact my work needed my complete attention if I was to remain employed. The remainder of my tenure with Service Canada became more stressful as my sight continued to fail. Dr. Johnson had told me I would probably be blind by the time I was forty years old. I had surpassed that prediction and forged on well beyond forty years of age. However, with the faster deterioration of my sight as I grew older, I knew my time was shortened before total blindness would invade my world of sight.

The adaptive equipment I was using needed updating as my sight continued to fail. I followed protocol and requested updated equipment but once again it was delegated back to me to research and find the equipment. This irritated me greatly. Even though I maintained both a list on adaptive equipment and contacts where I could acquire the most advanced equipment, I felt my employer wasn't doing its job to support me. My employer had greater resources and could obtain the necessary equipment much quicker and easier than me.

The one problem I had in finding my own equipment was clear. It interfered with my work directly because I was forced to ignore my work while searching for the proper equipment. The quantity and quality of my work was impacted and my supervisors were always on my case because of this. Their lack of understanding and ignorance to the needs of a functionally disabled person were no doubt discriminatory.

There was no doubt in my mind the future was shrinking fast. What were decades to an end-state for a viable treatment in vision loss was fast becoming just a few years away. Despite the ongoing setbacks, I remained steadfast on a brighter outlook. I continued to look on the positive side for I had the ongoing support of my family and I was working at a job I enjoyed despite the discriminatory atmosphere. God willing, I hoped, I would also have the opportunity to at least keep the sight I had or maybe even gain some improvement in it. It seemed a genuine treatment was no doubt on the horizon.

# Chapter 14

# A Forced Medical Retirement

For me, it seemed, no matter if at work or at home, there was always something new for me to overcome. My life was that way for as long as I can remember. I learned at an early age to adapt and change. Even though I could utilize the tools of adaption to my advantage, I could never foresee the future and what it beheld.

The future can be defined as a manufactured creation of the present which is never ending, only creating. We all live in the present and so we can watch the creation of the future in real time. However, my creation for the future would be quite different than that of someone else. For this reason, the future is unpredictable even with the best laid plans. The past is but a product of the future. One such product is our memories. From the memories of my past and the ongoing creation of the present, I could postulate a future outcome for myself if I knew what everybody was creating for their futures. Although there is no factual evidence to support my postulation, I acknowledge the hard work all the scientists were striving for to achieve the same outcome regarding sight. So, I remained adamant a treatment for vision loss was near. I was also adamant there would be many barriers to overcome for the researchers as well. However, sight was but one element in my life; another element was dealing with the ups and downs of adaptation, inclusion and unwanted discrimination. It was the unwanted discrimination which I hadn't postulated as being a future obstacle in my life. I thought I had the ability to overcome any adaptive problems including discriminatory ones. I was wrong, for I was tested in July 2006. It came from my employer unknowingly regarding accommodation and inclusion for people with disabilities, shortly after the end of my annual holidays and my annual visit to the eye clinic in St. John's, Newfoundland.

Dr. Whelan's examination of my eyes indicated there were some major changes in them. He suggested, if I had medical leave benefits from work, I should consider retiring, explaining it would help reduce the stress on my eyes. This he suggested would allow me to retain what sight I had for a longer period of time. It made sense to me, so I considered his advice, but remained undecided in my decision for I still wanted to remain working until I was at least 65 years old. I needed to work until then in order to acquire enough pensionable time to retire comfortably. However, the retention of my vision took president. To help with my decision, I decided to advise the office manager of my revised eye condition and seek his advice first. I returned to work early August 2006 and before my first day was done I approached the office manager to discuss my future with Service Canada.

The office manager's administrative assistant was requested by the manager to attend the meeting as well. She was called to provide all relevant information regarding the human resource policy pay and benefits regarding medical leave. Also she was to provide and any other options which were available to me. The only program they discussed was one called medical leave. I was encouraged to take advantage of this program as it was my only option. With their strong encouragement and my eagerness to address the stressful manipulation on my eyes, I felt it was a good decision for me as they explained it. I also felt the information I was given was solid and I would be looked after until I officially retired from Service Canada at age 65. They made arrangements for me to go to Human Resources pay and benefits division for fast tracking of my medical leave application. Everything went through both quickly and smoothly. It was then I was reaffirmed I would be on the long-term medical leave program until I was 65 years of age with no change in my pay and benefits status. I would remain on the books as a Service Canada employee and therefore my service time would continue until I officially retired at 65 years of age. At that time, I would be transferred to a regular retirement program with a severance pay out and a retirement pension based on all my time with Service Canada including the time I was on medical leave.

Although the package they gave me included everything I wanted for myself and my family, I still felt the urge to reject it and remain working. I couldn't help thinking it was too good to be true, but not wanting to continue stressing my eyes, I reluctantly made the decision to leave work and go on the medical leave program.

I left the office a week later, this time for good, completely satisfied with myself and the decision I made.

Although the information I was given by human resources pay and benefits was of an oral nature, I was confident in what they told me was true. It was their job to know the policy, rules and regulations regarding long-term medical leave. I didn't have to worry about supporting my family financially, thank God for the Federal Governments pay and benefits program for their employees. Also the other major plus for going on long-term medical leave was the drastic reduction of stress on my eyes. All in all, it was a great decision for me and my family, given the information I was led to be true at that time (I would be transferred to a regular retirement program at age 65 and receive a retirement pension based on all my service time up age 65), which was exactly what I wanted. It would be the same as if I had worked until age 65 and retired with an ample pension to support my spouse and myself in our senior years.

With the reduction of stress on my eyes, I felt I was in a better position for any possible treatment for my eyes. For more then two years I kept myself apprised of ongoing advances in all forms of eye treatments. Being kept informed was much easier than ever; through the many supportive organizations throughout the world as well as the internet I gained a wealth of knowledge.

The Foundation for Fighting Blindness both in Canada and the United States was always on top of every new development, where and when it was taking place. Not to be denied any information at all, I registered with both organizations and through regular emails I was kept up to date on everything. Still, nothing was happening to address my eye condition. This was my life struggle to remain hopeful and patient, pending positive outcomes for my eye disease.

It had been a while since I last asked Dr. Whalen about my best options for a treatment so I decided to question him once again. At my next visit, I put the question to him concerning the best treatment for my eyes. His response was very strong in that gene therapy still remained my best option. With further questioning he completely ruled out the Argus 11 devise as well as stem cell implantation procedure. I felt somewhat disappointed over his answer; it seemed there was some form of treatment being developed for everyone except me and the people who had the same affliction as myself. However, I had strong confidence in his advice and felt maybe just maybe he was in the know of something on the horizon which would be beneficial for me. With that thought, I decided to swallow the urge to seek out any more alternate form of treatment for my eyes and await a gene therapy solution no matter how long it took. However, I did have a back up plan; baring any kind of treatment suitable for my eye condition, therefore, I kept an eye on the development of wearable sight enhancing aids as a fall back. The main drawbacks for these aids were its cost, suitability and wearability. The cost was well beyond the financial capacity of most people; also, most of the aids were heavy, clunky and clumsy to wear for prolonged periods of time; then there was the aesthetic suitability of adaption to one's appearance. All in all, it wasn't a plan I would choose lightly.

Shortly after I saw Dr. Whalen, I received a call with a follow up letter from Service Canada regarding my medical leave status. The letter contained three options with a demand to reply within two weeks. The first option was to return to work which of course wouldn't be advantageous to the health of my eyes. The second option was to voluntary take what they called a long-term medical retirement package. It would be based on the continuous service time I had accumulated form the date I was hired to the date I started a long-term medical leave of absence program. The continuous time of service meant I would also lose an extra four years of service time because my service was broken for a month eight years earlier. This package was different than what I was currently on with a lot less income support. The third option was a forced medical retirement program; with this option Service Canada would forcefully retire me on a long-term medical retirement and reduce my income even more then the voluntary medical retirement choice they offered in the second option. I was dumbfounded and lost for thought at what was happening. My employer, Service Canada, had taken on a draconian style of negotiations in dealing with people on a medical leave of absence. In any event, what was most devastating for me besides the reduction of income would be the loss of fourteen years of pensionable service time. If I took a voluntary medical retirement or was forced to go on one, I would loose four years of pensionable service time from the day I was hired by Service Canada up to a break of one month. After which my pensionable service time would continue again for the next right years until I went on a medical leave of absence program. At that time, I had turned 55 years of age and the remaining ten years of pensionable time up to age 65 would also be excluded in the calculation of my retirement pension. At age 65 the voluntary or forced medical retirement would transition into a regular retirement pension with only eight years of service to draw a pension from. To add insult to injury, I would also loose the severance pay out attached to the lost fourteen years. I was devastated. I would loose fourteen years of service time; if I chose to remain on a medical leave of absence and if I chose to return to work I would surely go totally blind due to the work related stress. All my dreams of financial security at the retirement age of 65 were gone. If I couldn't re-negotiate the package I was offered when I first went on medical leave then it became obvious, I would struggle financially after age 65.

I turned to my union and also to the pay and benefits division of Service Canada itself for answers. Once again the stresses associated with work came into play. In my heart I knew my sight would suffer and deteriorate more than it would because of the stress involved having to fight for one's rights. Being the type of person I am, I would no doubt challenge their right to do this to me. After all, I was told something completely different before I made the decision to take a medical leave of absence.

Luck was not with me for the person from human resources pay and benefits who helped fast track me onto a medical leave of absence was no longer with Service Canada. Therefore, I could not argue or prove my claim on what I was told regarding the medical leave program which I was put on. The Public Service union suggested I voluntary take the long-term medical retirement package but under duress. This would give the union the flexibility to submit a grievance claim on my behalf. The reason being, I was not offered any alternate work solutions adaptable to my disability at the time I first went to the office manager for advice; the union felt I was discriminated against. Due to this realization, I was also instructed by the union to submit a human rights claim. They felt as a disabled person my human rights were impacted negatively.

It would take four years before all the grievance process was exhausted and the human rights claim dealt with. Unfortunately, I was unsuccessful at every level of hearings.

My sight fell drastically during that period of time because of all the stresses and pressures associated with fighting Service Canada. I firmly believe I had not gained anything at all for the vision loss I experienced would have been the same if I had remained to work. However, I was not sure how Service Canada would have dealt with my continued vision loss and inability to deliver quality work.

I lost my battle with Service Canada, which greatly impacted not only my sight but also my family's financial position. I recognized it wasn't good to dwell on my losses; I needed to move on into the future and what it would bring. In some ways I was thankful for the fact I was done with Service Canada and the stress associated with it. It has always been that way with me, to accept my faith and move on in and effort to learn from the past and try to adapt.

My life soon returned to a mundane style of living. I did the things I enjoyed doing; my demeanour became relaxed and I felt good about myself once again. I concentrated on family life once again as well as on the vision care my eyes needed.

It was in a newsletter circulated by the Canadian division of the Foundation for Fighting Blindness when a specific article caught my attention. The article outlined a story of success with respect to gene replacement therapy. Gene replacement therapy finally, I thought, it's here, it's real, and I am ready.

A clinical trial was conducted in the United States on Leber eye disease. Leber eye disease is a Hereditary Optic Neuropathy, (LHON), eye disease is an inherited disease, caused by a defective gene. The disease progresses with time to a point where the vision in both eyes worsened with a severe degeneration in visual acuity (sharpness) and color vision. This condition mainly affected the central vision which is needed for activities such as facial recognition, reading, writing, driving, etc. Although, the symptoms were similar to the eye disease I had. There were some major differences in that I was night blind as well as having both my central vision and visual fields affected too.

The outcome was significant in that the persons who were treated had regained some sight.

This, to my knowledge, was a significant breakthrough in genetic research. My emotions were almost uncontrollable; I was beside myself. The doctor who conducted this trial was a lady named Doctor Bennett. I was so excited that I contacted Dr. Bennett by phone to see if she would consider conducting a study on the Newfoundland version of RP, "NLRCDS." Her answer came quickly as she explained all her research was in Leber's, "LHON" eye disease and that she would be continuing her work in that area for the foreseeable future. Dejected with her answer my confidence was badly shaken. My question to myself was simple, is anybody going to do some research on the Newfoundland version of RP, "NLR-CDS."

Time is no doubt a great healer and so after a few years with ongoing genetic research being conducted in many forms of eye disease, I felt confidence build within me again. Of course, with the optimistic attitude of Dr. Whalen and Dr. Jane Green gene therapy for "NLRCDS" would indeed become a reality, otherwise, I probably would have turned my attention to alternate treatments.

As I waded through the doldrums of time, I reflected on the many choices and decisions I had made. Some were beneficial, but most were not. I postulated, if I didn't have a functional disability most of my life's choices and decisions would indeed have positive outcomes. Still, with the choices I had, I measured my decisions against the choices and decisions my pears had. It was plain to see their achievements far exceeded mine and I didn't measure up; it wasn't even close. However, I guess it's human nature to be competitive and so I continued to strive for equality with my peers. I never strayed from the notion no matter what other people though about me, I could do most everything my peers could do despite my functional disability.

Life offers us choices which lead down many paths. Each path leads to only one outcome, a destiny. How we achieve or arrive at that destiny is based on direction or misdirection, good or poor choices, and the occurrence of any interruptions.

In my case, I started out with a functional disability which defined the path I would travel through life. People of a professional status also misdirected me. Through their ignorance and misguidance, I was given poor advice, which led to drastic changes in my life's journey. One major interruption was a back injury which caused me to lose ten years of work. I had to re-train which took away another three years from my life's journey and redirected me once again in another direction. It seems my station in life was to suffer even more for work related stress coupled with ignorance, knowledge, discrimination and a draconian style of negotiations sealed my faith going forward as a senior. Based on these elements I was forced to make difficult choices some good and some bad. Baring any change to these elements my destiny is still unknown and not yet predefined.

Just eighteen months after I left my job with Service Canada the passing of my father once again added unwanted stress in my life. He was my role model, my best friend, my counsellor when I needed counselling and advice. Most of all he was my hero, the best father anyone could have. Like my mother who continually showed up in my dreams and visions to comfort and console me so did my father. Even though they were gone, it felt like they were still with me. Through the grieving process over the passing of my father, I stressed and as a result like the effects from the passing of my mother my vision took a major hit. The reduction of daylight vision shrank drastically; it was quite noticeable. So much so I could identify the effects it had on me easily. Also my night vision or lack there of changed as well; the adaptation time it took my eyes to adjust to the darkness was much longer as well and artificial lighting inside wasn't as clear either. Blindness was overtaking my sight and if I continued to be stressed, I would lose it sooner than I wanted too, I thought. However, this self-recognition of what was happening with my eyes was something I knew would happen from the first time I saw Dr. Johnson and as such I could adapt and accept at the same time. The ability to adapt allowed me to accept the death of my father even though the grieving process continued. The stress also continued for it seemed my blood pressure climbed to a point where I was prescribed medication to control it. Only after the blood pressure was under control did my stress level drop off and the rapid deterioration of my sight slowed down.

Living next door to my father, I spent a lot of time with him after the passing of my mother. With him gone I missed those visits; it seemed during those visits, I felt independent and free. During those visits I was out of the house especially at night and therefore the feeling of being a shut-in was greatly reduced. Because I was no longer able to visit him, I needed to fill the void; I needed to find something to occupy my time.

To my amazement I took up writing, even though Language and English Literature were my worst subjects in school; I found the solitude of writing most comforting. Still, there were hurdles and obstacles to overcome, most especially the ability to read printed material. To adapt to this dilemma, I utilized my memory and listening skills to capture as well as store relevant information for future retrieval. I thanked my lucky stars for doing a business course years earlier. In that course, I was trained in typing and computer skills both of which I could use in my writings.

It was no doubt a great stress reliever for me. I also wrote poetry and songs for my own private entertainment. The next logical step in writing was to write a book. So after years of writing, I completed my first novel. Then I started research for the next one. I remember that time distinctly. It was mid-August 2013; I was networking some of my contacts to gather some information with respect to research for my book. During a phone conversation with my sister, "Greta," she told of some unconfirmed gossip circulating through the medical establishment. The information came from a mutual friend of ours; unconfirmed gossip was circulating about a large drug company whose name remained unknown at that time. It seemed the drug company was sniffing around to set up a clinical trial on genetic eye disease in Newfoundland and Labrador. The gossip indicated they were interested in gathering information on the rear RLBP1 gene, possibly for the clinical trial. Having been disappointed so many times in the past, I didn't allow my hopes to get too high. First, I would contact either Dr. Whelan or Dr. Jane Green to confirm or deny the gossip. Without hesitation, I immediately phoned Dr. Jane Green first; timing they say is everything and boy was my timing right. Dr. Jane Green confirmed a company named Novartis was indeed interested in the RLBP1 gene with intent on setting up a clinical trial. I then questioned her as to when it would start. In fact she was scanning her list of people with the RLBP1 gene for potential candidates even as we spoke. Immediately, I offered myself as a good candidate. What was even more astounding was the timing as to when the trial would start. She informed me it would start at the end of September that same year. It was mid-August and coincidentally I had an annual appointment with Dr. Whelan in the last week of September. Immediately Dr. Jane Green placed me into the trial. Instantly I felt a great weight lifted off my shoulders. It had become a reality. I was officially in a clinical trial, one specifically designed for the RLBP1 gene. My conversation with Dr. Jane Green continued concerning the drug company and their goals. I was also informed a similar clinical trial on the RLBP1 gene would be starting in Sweden at the same time.

This was the first time I became aware of people in Sweden with the same genetic defect in the RLBP1 gene. Immediately, I thought would any of those people be related to me because of them having the same defective RLBP1 gene. This was important for I only knew of a small pocket of people in Newfoundland and Labrador who were affected by the RLBP1 gene and with people in Sweden having the same defective gene the chances of having gene replacement therapy was greatly improved. Because it was given its own name, Newfoundland and Labrador Rod Cone Dystrophy Syndrome, I always thought it only existed in Newfoundland and Labrador, but it seems I was wrong.

Dr. Jane Green continued outlining how the trial would be set up and conducted. She told me the trial would be based on a two-part clinical trial; the first part would take approximately five years to complete, based on information gathering with respect to how the RLBP1 gene affects the sight over a period of time. This historical data collection would be necessary for the second part of the trial. The first part of the clinical trial would consist of a semi-annual visit to the eye clinic; the visit would be to see Dr. Whelan and get a series of different testing done. The testing would be conducted over a two-day period. The start of the second part of the clinical trial would begin shortly after part one of the clinical trials were finished. This part of the clinical trial would involve a medical intervention for gene therapy. The logistics of how that part of the study would be conducted wasn't known at that time; in theory the eye would be injected with a healthy gene carrying with it a virus which would kill off the defective gene and allow the healthy gene to take its place. Once the defective gene was gone and the healthy gene was in place it was theorized that sight would re-generate in that eye. With that explanation from Dr. Jane Green my conversation about the clinical trial ended but not before she rescheduled my appointment with Dr. Whelan from late September to the 5th of October. It would be my first day as a participant in the clinical trial for the RLBP1 gene.

After chatting with Dr. Jane Green, I immediately called my sister Greta. I told her the gossip was true and indeed a clinical trial was to start at the end of September. I also told her Dr. Jane Green had placed me into the study with my first appointment to start the 5th of October. I urged her to contact Dr. Jane Green to see if she too could be included into the study. I finished my conversation by relating to her all the information Dr. Jane Green told me. From then on, I was beside myself. The only exception was the day I married the love of my life, Valerie, and the birth of our two children. I don't believe I was any happier.

A few days before my appointment at the eye clinic, I was contacted by Kathy Whitten, a genetics nurse coordinator. Kathy would coordinate all my appointments for the clinical trial. She would even be conducting some of the testing herself. I was to meet her at 8:00 a.m. on Monday and Tuesday October 5th and 6th, 2013. This of course was the first of my appointments at the eye clinic. It would be the official start of ten regular scheduled appointments for the clinical trial spanning a defined period of five years.

My first day's appointment was a one-hour drive away; it was an early rise from a sleepless night. Excitement over took the tiredness as we drove to a new chapter in my life. Valerie would be my official attendant companion. She would not only drive me to my appointments but also to stay with me during the two-day event of testing. It would be two full days of testing from 8 a.m. to 4 p.m. each day. If not for Valerie, I would not have had the stability of knowing I could have attended each appointment. The logistics of finding someone to be my attendant for each visit would have been a nightmare. For her commitment to my plight, I was greatly appreciative of her undying support to me. As I said earlier, Valerie was my rock. I am honoured to have such a wonderful person in my life.

The drive to St. John's continued yet verbal conversation was at a minimum. My thoughts were flooded with wonderment of what the day would be like.

What seemed like a fleeting moment of time we arrived at the parking lot for the Health Science complex? Once parked we went directly to the general registration desk to register for my appointments at the eye clinic. To my surprise a nurse holding a clipboard with papers attached inquired if I was James Mercer. I responded by introducing Valerie and myself assuming she was the nurse I was to meet. She introduced herself as Kathy Whitten, Genetics Nurse Coordinator for the clinical trial to be conducted on the RLBP1 gene. After registration, we went to the eye clinic to await the appointments. When seated, Kathy told us what tests would be done that day. She was clear and concise in her explanation of the testing.

First, I would get an eye exam to measure how well I could see at a measured distance. This exam was the same as if I was being tested for glasses. This test is conducted on a Snellen eye chart and it tested a person's visual acuity.

Secondly, the second test was coloured photos taken on my eyes. This test is known as Fundus photography, which takes colour photos of the back of the eyes.

Thirdly, a test to examine all my fields of vision was conducted. This test is known as a Visual Fields Test and it measures how wide of an area a person's eyes can see when they focus on a central point. It also measures how much vision is in either eye and how much vision loss has occurred over time. It also could determine if there are blind spots in the eyes; as well as identifying where they were, as well as their size and shape. It would also identify if it was an eye disease or a brain disorder causing the sight problems.

Fourthly, an OCT test or Optical Coherence Tomography takes a cross section picture of one's retina using light waves to measure retinal thickness.

Fifthly, an ERG test, Ophthalmic Electrophysiology, Electro-oculography testing includes a series of tests, which are used to identify information about the visual system beyond the standard clinical examination of the eye. The primary objective of the electrophysiologic examination is to assess the function of the visual pathway from the photoreceptors of the retina to the visual cortex of the brain. Information obtained from these diagnostic tests helps establish the correct diagnosis or may rule out related ophthalmic diseases.

Sixth, I would see Dr. Whelan where he would examine and conduct some tests himself. Some of the tests would include a headlamp and magnifying glass to look into the eyes, as tonometry is used to measure the pressure inside the eyes, which are called intraocular eye pressure.

Seventh, I would get some blood drawn, which would be sent for testing at a genetics lab outside the province.

Test eight was designed to examine my colour vision. This test is known as the Farnsworth D-15 dichotomous test and it assesses colour blindness. It is done with two different tests; one was the use of coloured discs to be arranged in proper order and the other was a book where the pages are comprised of coloured spots. Each page would contain either letters or numbers; the client would have to identify them.

Test number nine, "the test is called a Skills (Smith-Kettlewell Institute Low Luminance) Card." She continued, "It is a way to measure your vision function at reduced contrast and luminance. There are two small eye charts on the wall approximately twelve by sixteen inches in size each. You will need to read those charts."

"Test ten consisted of reading two much larger eye charts with larger characters. The proper name of this test is called Pelli-Robson Contrast Sensitivity Test! It tests your ability to identify letters which are gradually less visible on a white background," she said. "It measures your ability to distinguish between the finer increments of light versus dark (contrast). In areas of low lighting, such as for glare, dusk and dawn, its one measure of a visual function where the background is often reduced!" she said.

"Tests Eight, Nine and Ten will be conducted in the Janeway Hostel building adjacent and connected to the Health Sciences complex itself." Kathy informed us her office was located on the fifth floor of the Janeway Hostel; this floor was designated solely for all the genetics staff connected with ongoing clinical trials. There were interview and testing rooms set aside for genetics use only. It was in one of these rooms I would finish the testing process for that day. Kathy finished by informing me the logistics of doing these tests would be discussed at the time of the testing.

I told Kathy I had some of these tests before and had experienced very stressful effects with those tests. Kathy then assured me the equipment had changed and was updated with new technologies that offered the same results in testing; however she was unsure how stressful the test would be on me.

As soon as Kathy finished her explanations, I was called into a room by an eye clinic technician. Kathy followed me while Valerie remained in the waiting area. The room contained an eye testing chart at one end of the room and a chair at the other end. I was instructed to walk up close to within five feet and read the chart. Then I was to move back to ten feet and once again read the chart. Finally, I was told to set in the chair some twenty feet away and read the chart. The results of the eye test were then documented and inserted into a file containing my name a copy of which was also presented to Kathy. Next the eye examiner placed drops into my eyes explaining it was to dilate the pupils for further testing. I was then instructed to return to the waiting area for my next appointment. Of course, Valerie questioned me on what the test was about. I explained everything to her and promised her I would keep her informed after each test. It was a promise I would keep; it was important for me to be open with it as well as for Valerie to hear it.

Idle chat between Kathy, Valerie and myself didn't last long as I was called once again. This time Kathy remained with Valerie as I was led off to get some colour photos on my eyes. I dreaded having to get this test done. I had this test once in the past and from that experience I knew I would be subjected to a lot of eye stress. However, I was ready and willing to do what it took to achieve my goal of improving my sight.

Once inside the room, I noted a camera was attached to a mounting station on one side of a frame while on the opposite side was a place to rest my chin. I sat in position resting my chin and awaited the start of the test. The camera had an extremely bright light which shined directly into my eyes. Each eye would be done separately with many photos taken of them both. Each time a photo was taken the camera flash increased the stress and strain on my eyes and left me totally blind. The tear ducts in my eyes released a continuous flow of water which uncontrollably flowed down my cheeks. My central vision was blocked out completely with a huge black ball, my peripheral vision was filled with a dark gray light. I couldn't see anything at all. To make matters worse, I developed a headache as an uncontrollable pulse beat steadily in my eyes. It was a struggle to keep them open as I was led back to the waiting area. Once seated, I lost that battle as they closed tightly. Instantly, I felt some relief as the stressful pressure began to slacken off. It was a relief to have the test completed. I felt more at ease setting in the safety and comfort next to my wonderful wife. Valerie was indeed my rock she was always there for me. I would never take advantage of her selfless support or would I ever forget her willingness to give it without question.

After taking a seat by Valerie and Kathy, I interrupted a conversation between them just to let Valerie know how the test went. Valerie listened quietly and asked if I was ok. I embellished the truth a little telling her I was fine; I didn't want to show any weakness in my resolve. I asked Kathy when my next test would begin. She checked her schedule sheet and advised me I had another twenty minutes to wait. In that time, my vision returned to my perception of normal. However, I still felt a heavy pulse beating in my eyes. This was amplified by an ever-growing feeling of pressure compressing my eyes. I felt as if my eyes were going to pop out of their sockets.

The next twenty minutes were consumed by setting quietly just listening to the sounds around me. Valerie and Kathy continued their conversation. People were arriving for their appointments, while still others were finished and leaving. The eye clinic staff were shuffling back and forth busy with their duties. My attention heightened with each name being called as I expected the next name would be mine. However, it didn't come, something was wrong, it was taking too long.

## Chapter 15

# Novartis Clinical Trials RLBP1

Kathy checked her watch and advised me I should have been called for my visual fields test. Another twenty minutes passed and still the three of us were setting. Kathy broke the silence saying it's taking too long and I should have been called long before then. She said she was going to check to see what the delay was. I was quite satisfied with the delay myself because it gave me more time to recover. I asked Valerie if she was tired just sitting; her response was what I expected. "Of course I am," she responded. I knew it was a long wait for her and suggested she go for a short walk to shake off the tiredness.

Valerie rejected that suggestion saying lunchtime was near and when I had a break from the testing, we would get a lunch somewhere. Our conversation ended when Kathy returned.

"There was a minor mix up with the next appointment," Kathy said. It seemed the technician who was to conduct the test was unavailable; however, another technician agreed to make time in her schedule to conduct the test. Kathy instructed me to follow her to the testing room. The room was dark except for some light emitting from a dish-like piece of equipment setting atop a table in the corner of the room. The dish was completely white in color and the light emitting from it was blinding to my eyes. I tried to avoid looking directly at the dish in hopes off shielding my eyes from the glare.

A chair stood alone awaiting my arrival and so I accommodated the awaiting chair and sat down in front of the dish. I remember this test a long time ago, I told Kathy. It was a much larger dish back then, I concluded. Kathy agreed saying, "Nothing has changed, except for the size of the dish and a computer generated program; however, the testing remains the same delivering the same results. This test will measure your fields of vision. It will identify area's in the eyes where there is sight impairment. It will show how much your central and peripheral vision is affected and where the affected area's are." It was only a few minutes when the technician arrived; immediately she checked my eyes and proceeded to administer more drops into them.

Then a small handheld device with a push button switch was placed in my hand and I was instructed to push that button when I saw lights of any size in the dish. My chin was placed on a chin rest and one eye was patched. In the center of the dish was a small amber coloured light. I was told to keep focused on that light all through the test. Once the test began, lights would appear and disappear all around the dish. I was to hit the button with every light I saw. Each eye would be done separately taking approximately fifteen minutes per eye to complete the test.

With one eye patched, I looked directly into the dish trying to focus on the small amber light in the center. The blinding white light from the dish itself immediately impacted my unpatched eye. Immediately, I felt the strain and stress increase multi fold as my brain tried to accommodate the glare. I could hardly maintain a focus on the amber light in the center of the dish. My unpatched eye wondered around the dish searching not for lights to appear and disappear but for a place to hide itself from the blinding glare. As my brain accepted the fact there was no place for my eye to hide from the glare, my focus returned to the centre of the dish again. This process of adjustment took only a few seconds as I realized lights were appearing and disappearing all around the dish. Instantly my thumb hit the button for each light I saw.

The test continued until each eye was done individually. My memory of having that test in the past didn't seem so stressful with as much glare. An answer to my thoughts came quickly as I realized my level of sight had declined as well as my ability to adapt to blinding glare. Kathy acquired a copy of the test for her folder and we headed back to the waiting area once again I had blind spots in my eyes but not as bad as the photo test. Valerie sat silently awaiting our return. Kathy went to check on my next appointed test just to see if everything was still on schedule. Before she returned, I told Valerie I was thankful that test wasn't as stressful on my eyes as the photos were. Her warm hand clasped mine and I felt her inner strength power my resolve. Kathy returned quickly advising us we had an hour and a half of a break. It was enough time to go for lunch as well as enjoy a welcome relief from the testing. Besides, I knew Valerie was as tired and hungry as myself.

We decided to leave the hospital and go out for lunch. It would indeed be a welcome relief for I really needed the fresh air to clear the fog from my eyes and brain. We selected a local restaurant for our lunch but mostly for the quiet and relaxing time. Here we could chat in private over how things were going. I knew it was hard on Valerie just waiting for me to finish each and every test. I could only imagine how she felt, as we chatted and conveyed her feelings to me. I was glad she openly expressed her feelings, for she too needed a release of stress. She reaffirmed her concerns about how I felt both physically and mentally stating it was of the utmost importance to her. I tried to shield her by embellishing the explanations on how each test affected me; I was wrong. It was then I decided to always be truthful in my explanation of how I felt after each test. Valerie listened carefully as I told her all; it was a welcome relief to share all the trauma that I was going through. We concluded our lunch, both feeling somewhat rejuvenated and ready for the remainder of the days testing.

Kathy was waiting for us at the eye clinic. Her smile welcomed us immediately. It was easy to tell Kathy was a warm, caring, compassionate pleasant person with a terrific personality. Both Valerie and I felt very comfortable in her presence. "Your next appointment is for an Optical Coherence Tomography (OCT) test. This test will take pictures of your eyes," she said. She continued, "It will take a cross section picture of your retina using light waves to measure retinal thickness. This test will only take a few minutes and should not be too stressful." Kathy must have sensed I was concerned about the level of stress I would have to endure getting through the remaining tests. It was then she initiated a trivial conversation I believe just to get my mind distracted and relaxed; it seemed to work. Just talking to Kathy seemed to relax me and her personality was no doubt the reason why.

After a short wait, a technician called my name asking me to follow her. I was led to another room where another piece of equipment was set up.

This testing device sat atop a small table stand. I was directed to sit on the chair by the table and place my chin on the chin rest attached to the OCT machine. I was then asked to look into the viewing screen first with my left eye and then the right eye. In the center of viewing screen, I saw a white X embossed upon a reddish background. I was asked to maintain focus on that X while pictures were taken. First the X was shifted to the right and then to the left. Each time I had to remain focused on the X until pictures were taken. The whole process took only five minutes or so and I was done. What was most significant to me was the lack of stress associated with this test. It didn't affect me in any way at all. There was no blinding white light or unexpected camera flashes at all. I felt good after the test and I told Valerie as much when I joined her. Kathy had been with me in the testing room and joined us a short time later. She informed me one of the pending tests was re-scheduled for later that evening and my next appointment would be with Dr. Whelan himself. It would be a short wait before I saw him and so there was time for a coffee break. I was glad for the break. I knew Valerie was tired and weary just setting around; the break would relieve the stress she was going through as well.

We picked up a coffee and decided to take a short walk around the hospital just to stretch our legs and shake off the tiredness. As we walked Valerie kept me on the straight and narrow because my sight was still fogged and disoriented.

After returning we once again met up with Kathy and awaited my call to see Dr. Whelan. My wait wasn't long Dr. Whelan's assistant called me to his office shortly after. Kathy followed both of us into his office.

The room was furnished with a small office desk and chair on one wall with shelving above it. The center of the room contained a large reclining type leather chair almost like a barber's chair, with testing equipment attached. I was instructed to set into the large recliner type chair while Kathy sat into an additional chair directly opposite me.

Dr. James Whelan appeared shortly and took a seat by his desk asking how I was. I embellished the truth a little saying I was fine, not wanting to show any signs of weakness form the effects of the testing and long wait. I saw Dr. Whelan fifteen years prior to the clinical trial and noted then he was a tall man, much younger than myself, possibly into his early forties . He turned to me and explained he would be seeing me every six months for the next five year. He told me this part of the clinical trial was designed to follow a subject for a period of time collecting historical data which would be compared against each visit and then recorded for future use. After the five-year clinical trial was concluded; a selected number of subjects would be chosen to receive an experimental medical treatment by way of gene therapy replacement. In that part of the clinical trial it would involve direct injections into the eye. The injection would contain a virus able to kill off the defective gene and replace it with a healthy gene. "For this clinical trial," he explained, "the targeted gene would be the RLBP1 gene."

He then turned to his desk and scanned through some papers in a folder. I assumed they were the results from the tests I had done earlier. He turned to Kathy and asked about the ERG test. Kathy informed him the appointment for that test was scheduled for later that evening. He suggested in the future he should have that test done before he saw me. However, because of the logistics of scheduling tests, he agreed to read the results from the ERG test the following day. Pending his analysis of that test, he would see me then, otherwise I would not need to see him until my next appointment in six months time. After concluding his explanation of the RLBP1 clinical trial, he turned to me and with and handheld bright light he looked into my eyes.

He then noted he would check the pressure of my eyes. He pulled a metal frame in front of me which contained a device that emitted a small purple light. He then placed himself in front of me only to be separated by the metal frame. It was then I noticed he was wearing a headlamp. Slowly he moved the purple light closer to each individual eye eventually touching them. He kept my eyes open with his hand as I tried to avoid the bright white light glare from the magnified blinding light of the headlamp. I was instructed to look up, then down, then left, then right and finally directly ahead. I found this test hard in that the glare from the bright white light from the headlamp shone directly into my eyes, which caused my eyes great stress. He then noted, "All looks good, no sign of cataracts. I will see you in six months." With that we left his office.

It would be another hour before I was to get my next test in the hospital. In that time Kathy went back to her office and agreed to meet us back at the eye clinic. Valerie and I went to the cafeteria for a coffee. When we returned to the eye clinic Kathy was waiting for us. "We need to go to the fifth floor of the hospital," she said. We followed Kathy to where I would have the ERG test. Along the way Kathy briefly explained the test. "An Ophthalmic Electrophysiology,

Electro-oculography test (ERG) includes a series of tests which are used to identify information about the visual system beyond the standard clinical examination of the eye!" she concluded.

Once at the fifth floor I was led into a darkened room where a small dome shaped piece of equipment sat atop a table. It too had a chin rest with a blinding powder blue light emitting from its ten-inch screen. A technical asked me to set on a chair by the ERG testing device, she then put drops into my eyes to further dilate them. Then she added anaesthetic drops which made my eyes feel numb. I was asked to place my chin on the chin rest and look directly into the viewing screen of the dome-shaped ERG testing device. It was explained to me this procedure would bleach my eyes in preparation for the ERG test. Once my eyes were fully dilated and bleached the test would be conducted. After fifteen minutes the technician then attached small electrodes on each eye with another electrode placed on the skin of my forehead to act as a ground for the faint electric signal emitting from the retina. The electrodes were attached by long wires to the machine so I was asked to be careful not to dislodge them from their attached positions. The technician then went to a computer terminal and prepared to do the test.

I had only removed my eyes from the ERG testing dome long enough for the electrodes to be attached then I returned to the position of looking directly into the ERG testing screen. The technician asked if I was ready and with my answer of yes the screen emitted bright wavy lights for a few seconds. This was done three times after which the technician said the test was finished. The technician then removed the electrodes. Kathy helped me leave the ERG testing room. I remembered having this test before but with different equipment and with much more devastating effects at that time. The only lasting effect were some blind spots in my eyes which was associated with the bleaching process for an extended period of time and the affects of the dilating drops which distorted my vision affecting my balance and mobility in walking.

Once outside the ERG testing room, Kathy stepped aside and allowed Valerie to assist me along. We then followed Kathy to the laboratory where some of my blood was taken before heading back to her office.

Once back at Kathy's office, we were directed to a small room where another piece of testing equipment for the clinical trial was set up. Kathy said, "This device is called a Color Dome LED simulator and is used for the Dark Adaption test; it tests how the eyes reacted to color flashing lights in the dark. The Dark Adaptation Test is a psychophysical test used to determine the ability of the rod photoreceptors to increase their sensitivity in the dark. According to the Willis Eye Hospital this test is a measurement of the rate at which the rod and cone system recover sensitivity in the dark following exposure to a bright light source," she concluded. "You will need to return tomorrow for that test," she said.

Kathy then informed me she needed to do some testing herself before I left for the day, as well as provide instructions on what was needed to know and prepare for the Dark Adaption test itself.

"It is time to test your colour vision," Kathy said. I was then given a small book filled with pages of multi-coloured dots. I had this test before many years earlier I told Kathy. She nodded saying, "We need to do it again because it is part of the clinical trial." I was then asked if I saw anything on any of the pages in the book. I couldn't pick out anything on either page of the book, even though I was assured there were numbers and letters there. Then I was given a long rectangle box containing coloured discs going from one base shade of color to another. I had done this test before as well, the box was approximately sixteen inches long and one inch wide. There were approximately fifteen coloured discs in total contained within the box. The coloured discs were arranged in order in the box. Kathy asked me to study them for a minute or so then she opened the box and spilled them out. Kathy then disarranged the coloured disc from their correct order. I was asked to put the discs in order of colour back into the box. I tried my best to arrange them but was unsure of the outcome.

Following that test Kathy explained, "The last two tests for the day will be short, I will instruct you on what is required of you for these tests."

"The first test is on the Skills Chart," she said. She then proceeded to ask me to stand and face two small charts on the wall. The eye charts were approximately five feet from the floor. They were no larger then twelve by sixteen inches in size. Kathy instructed me to stand one foot away and read them with one eye closed and then switch eyes. Next, I was given a handheld visor mask to cover my eyes. The visor mask was full of pinholes on one side allowing vision to one eye while blocking vision to the other eye. I was then asked to read the chart through the pinholes in the visor mask covering my eyes one at a time. The first chart I saw had a white background with small dark shaded letters. The second chart I saw had a dark background with small lighter shaded letters. I wasn't able to read any-thing on either chart with or without the pinhole visor mask.

Kathy then took me outside the dark adaption room to a place down the cor-ridor where a huge eye chart hung on the wall. I estimated it to be thirty by forty inches in size. It had two sections on a sliding mechanism with three-inch high lettering of different color contrast shading on a white background.

My first thought looking at the chart was this is another form of a colour test. However, my recollection of Kathy's explanation earlier in the day dispelled that notion.

"This test is Pelli-Robson Contrast Sensitivity Test!" Kathy said. "This test also includes reading this eye chart," Kathy asserted. Both sections of the chart had a white coloured background with the chart on the left having light shaded coloured contrast lettering while the chart on the right had darker shaded coloured contrast lettering.

For this test, I had to stand approximately six feet from the chart and read whatever letters I saw through each individual eye while the other eye was closed. This procedure was then done again with the pinhole visor mask. The letters were much larger than what was on the Snellen eye chart or what was on the previous skills testing chart. I noted to Kathy the charts had a bright white background which produced a lot off glare. I also noted to Kathy the glare from the fluorescent lighting above was quite blinding which affected my sight and reading ability. Kathy nodded, but I was unsure if she put any credence in what I was telling her. After finishing the test, we went back to the Dark Adaption testing room.

Kathy said, "It is time to prepare for the dark adaptation test which will be conducted tomorrow. For the dark adaptation test, you will have one eye patched blocking out all light for at least 24 hours. The eye to be patched would be the eye containing your best sight," she said. "It is very important to keep your eye patched and not to let any light in at all." Kathy then reaffirmed an earlier assertion, "The Dark Adaption test will be conducted here on the colour dome LED simulator machine." In a general conversation, Kathy explained, if I was selected to proceed to the second phase of the clinical trial I would probably receive medical intervention on the best eye. Of course, this wasn't official it was Kathy's opinion. The official reason why they would choose one eye over the other eye was still unknown and unexplained.

Unknown to anyone, I was worried. I questioned myself, what if I do get selected and the treatment doesn't work? The only answer I could postulate was not good; it would mean I might lose what sight I had in that eye. This would leave me with one eye which had very poor sight at best. It was too much for me to ponder at that time. I would think on it later when my mind was clear of stress and confusion. The day ended with Kathy finishing up patching my left eye and making an appointment for the following morning at 8 a.m. sharp. With all my senses severely impacted we left Kathy bidding her farewell for the day.

It was a very stressful day both physically and mentally, not only for myself but for Valerie as well. I thought it was going to be a stress-free restful night, but I was wrong. The effects of the testing still remained with me including the effects from all the eye drops. My eyes were still foggy and disoriented; my brain was in a state of utter confusion. My mind raced through each test over and over; it was a continuous loop. Then there was the headache which had developed from the onset of the testing earlier in the day. I scolded myself for not taking any medication with me that day. I knew I would develop a severe headache before days end. I made a mental note I would not forget medication in the future.

I could hardly see. Kathy had patched my good eye leaving the sight remaining far less then fifty percent of what I normally had. I thought to myself one can only imagine how much stress a person can be subjected to and still remain cognate of their senses and surroundings. Valerie managed to get me outside, God only knows how, for I was completely disoriented. I never felt so vulnerable in all my life. I stumbled over my own feet and everything else going forward. I couldn't maintain a straight line going from one side to the other side. It was as if I was under the heavy influence of alcohol or drugs. The only difference this time was my clarity of thought. It was obstructed by stress and tiredness creating a complete loss of confidence in my mobility thus rendering me helpless. Somehow, we struggled to the car avoiding objects of all kinds. There were stairs, sidewalks, pot holes, sign posts, vehicles of all kinds both moving and stationary as well as pedestrians. My heavy frame must have been quite a handful for Valerie. She kept me going straight and upright at the same time. The urge to throw up was over powering but I managed to suppress that urge. I still felt the enormous pressure and numbness in my eyes. This of course was caused by the eye drops, a freezing agent, antiseptic medication and dilation solutions that I was subjected too.

To me it was a complete nightmare, I didn't have any control of what sight I did have as well as the effects caused by a complete lack of control.

The drive home was a quiet one. I have always been a quiet person keeping my feelings and emotions hidden. This time it was no different. I told Valerie I felt uncomfortable and needed to close the only eye I had vision in to get some relief. Partly it was true; I needed to suppress depressive emotions and the overpowering urge to cry. Thank goodness when my eye was closed. I felt the relief I was longing for. The strain which was put on my one open eye was instantly gone. What remained was the internal tears and mixed emotions which I could deal with in a private secluded realm unknown and unseen. Darkness became my greatest comforter even though I considered it to be my greatest nemesis. It was over an hour before we reached home and the unwanted struggle to get from the car into our house was welcomed. Once inside, I found relaxation on the sofa where I could lie down and try to collect my thoughts. Valerie prepared a great meal and through trial an error along with her assistance I managed to find the food on my plate. However, finding my mouth was even more challenging. Still, through perseverance I managed to feed myself and curb the physical hunger feelings. However, the pain, confusion and stress remained unabated.

The night passed slowly; it seemed like an eternity, but in time the fogginess cleared and my mobility became much easier. I was able to see more clearly, thus reducing eye strain and stress which allowed my mind to function more clearly as well. My headache succumbed to the administration of medication, slowly but surely, I regained a sense of normalcy. Understandably the eye patch on my left eye was extremely irritating, so much so, I had to go into a dark room and remove it for a period of time. Immediately I felt relief. Once the irritation subsided, I had Valerie re-patch the eye. This time Valerie placed some softer material over the eye; she said it would help reduce the irritation.

In an effort to occupy my mind, the remainder of the night, I spent time pondering over the day's activities and wondering if it was all worth the effort. I also revisited the premise of possibly losing my sight in my best eye.

I found my answer in the memories of the past. All my life I had met every challenge with positive thoughts, never accepting failure but always finding ways to move forward. It was this positive attitude which moulded me into the person I had become and it would be this attitude which would see me through all future challenges including the clinical trial.

It would be an early start in the morning for both Valerie and myself as well as an early retirement for the night. Sleep didn't come easy but eventually tiredness forced my body into submission followed by sleep. Still, it wasn't a good sleep; the irritation from the eye patch along with being overtired as well as being hyper excited played havoc with what sleep I did get. Of course, being into a clinical trial that could possibly lead to regaining my sight didn't help much either. It seemed every time I awakened for whatever reason my mind immediately focused on the clinical trial and what it would be like to have the sight of normal vision. It was mind-boggling; I couldn't comprehend and settle my mind on any outcomes at all. The night seemed longer than usual and yet time never changes. When morning came, I was wide awake and ready for the day.

It was a bright morning with potential of lots of sunshine to come. My eye, which wasn't patched, opened to the natural light of day which filled the room, my sight seemed to be much better. I noted to myself, after waking from an extended period of sleep, the morning light seemed to be the best light of the day for me. With Valerie's help, I managed to get dressed and get a cup of coffee before heading to St. John's for another complete day of testing. Before leaving I took a day's supply of headache medication.

This time Kathy Whitten, Nurse Coordinator for Genetic Research would do the testing herself. It was a beautiful morning; the sun's light gradually introduced the landscape of another day. The temperature had fallen a few degrees overnight but remained just above the freezing mark. I couldn't see the wave action across the bay in real time because my sight was restricted with only one eye. My good eye was patched leaving my other eye stressed with reduced clarity, sharpness, crispness, depth and definition. Sight in that eye was almost non-existent. Still, clarity of thought retrieved solid memories of vivid crispness from every wave action I had seen in the past. I could still hear the roar of the sea's undertow, which was music to my ears. The taste and smell of the fresh salt air tantalized my taste buds while its aroma mystified my sense of smell. I combined both my memories with my other senses and postulated a depiction of how the bay looked that morning.

The trip to town was uneventful; my thoughts were centered on the day's testing. I wanted to remain focused on the testing and its outcomes. So to achieve this I remained silent blocking out everything including the small talk Valerie wanted me to engage in. Just before arriving at our destination, I told Valerie I felt good about the tests which lay ahead. I also told her I had apprehensions but I still remained positive the decision to enter the clinical trial was my best choice towards sight retention or improvement and as such the risk along with the stress was well worth it. I was healthy and I knew I could handle all the stress associated with the clinical trial that was a plus for me.

I had waited sixty plus years for this and I couldn't let it pass me by. It was the second time we had met Kathy in two days. Her office was located in the Janeway Hostel adjacent and attached to the Health Science Complex where the eye clinic was located. However, in this building we would find the room where the Dark Adaption test would be conducted. This time she would be the only technician and I would be there with her for the whole day.

The day before was the first time we met Kathy. We found her to be very friendly and personable. She made us feel very comfortable helping to put all our fears too rest.

As prearranged, we met Kathy at the registration area of the Health Sciences Complex. After a brief greeting, we went from there to the Janeway Hostel. We got the elevator and ascended to the fifth floor where Kathy's office and the testing room was located. Once inside the dark adaption testing room, the door was closed and the lights were turned off. Complete darkness surrounded us and the feeling of being claustrophobic heightened the tension and stress levels.

During the test, Kathy explained, the room would be completely dark and the patch would be switched to my right eye allowing testing on my left eye. Once testing was done on my left eye, the patch would once again be returned to my left eye. In no way was there to be any light penetrating the eye for extended periods of time. Suddenly a small glimmer of light appeared in the darkness. Kathy explained she would use a small light to aid her in her work; it would not affect the test in any way she reaffirmed us. It would only be on for a second or two each time it was used.

In her gentle voice Kathy spoke, "I am going to dilate your left eye before we start the testing. Please forgive me, I know how much the dilation drops stresses out your eyes but it is necessary for your left eye to be fully dilated for this test to begin," she continued. "Your right eye won't be dilated and when you are out of the dark room your left eye will be patched once again, therefore, the effects of the dilation drops will not affect your sight outside this room. The test won't start for another fifteen minutes or so, we must give the dilation drops time to work." With that Kathy removed the left eye patch and with the aid of her small light she proceeded to put dilation drops into my left eye. "There," she said, "that's not so bad, so while we wait let me explain how the test will work from here on.

"As you already know, I explained yesterday what the Dark Adaption test was and what it is used for, from this point I will explain the logistics of how the test is conducted. First I must re-patch your eye until we are ready to start the test."

Kathy then proceeded to re-patch my eye with a removable black leather type patch which was attached by an elastic band around my head. I could switch the patch easily from the left eye to the right eye very quickly. As Kathy had explained earlier, the dilated eye didn't pose any problem in the dark, but my right eye strained beyond its capacity searching from some source of light but was unsuccessful.

Kathy continued her explanation informing both Valerie and myself what to expect going forward. "Once your left eye is ready," she said, "I will ask you to switch the eye patch to your right eye. This should prevent interference from your right eye while the testing is ongoing. Then you will place your chin on the chin rest in front of the Colour Dome LED simulator screen and focus on the centre where a small orange light is there for you to focus on. This is similar to the Visual Fields Testing procedure in that you must remain focused on that centre point of light at all times. When the test begins, there will be coloured flashing lights in the Colour Dome. You will be given a handheld clicker to click each time you see the flashing lights. The test will take about seven minutes to complete but will be repeated a second time for a total of fifteen minutes duration. Then you will have a break for another fifteen minutes, at which time you will switch the eye patch back over your left eye before the next stage of testing begins. Each stage of testing will be the same as the first one; the only difference will be the breaks in between the testing and the bleaching process. The next break will also be fifteen minutes followed by and half an hour break. Then right before the next testing begins your left eye will be bleached. At the end of that test there will be a 45-minute break before more testing continues. The final break will be at least two and a half hours long at its end the last test for the day will be conducted. Yon can remove your patch and before you leave for the day I will give you your next appointment for six months time."

She concluded by asking if there were any questions or clarification which needed to address. Her explanation of what was about to happen seemed clear and concise, with one exception—what was the bleaching process?" Kathy responded, "The bleaching process is when the eye is subjected to an extreme bright light for an extended period of time. It would be like the light you experience when getting photos of your eyes. The testing from there on will be measured on how much the bleaching effects the eye sight during the test." With that explanation fully given, Kathy checked my dilated eye to see if it was ready. "Oh yes," she said, "your pupils are as big as saucers. You are indeed ready to start the testing."

After all was explained and Kathy had checked the dilated eye, she proceeded to move the eye patch from my left eye to my right eye. This allowed for the test to began in earnest.

With Kathy sitting at a computer terminal staring into its monitor, she initiated the start up process of the testing procedure. Like she explained, I did what I was asked to place my chin on a chin rest and stared into the center of the colour dome LED screen simulator. I was given a handheld clicker and asked to click the button with my thumb every time I saw a flashing light. The test lasted approximately fifteen minutes in total before a fifteen-minute break started. I thought this is a breeze for there were no adverse effects from the flashing lights. I then switched the eye patch back on the left eye as the break started. Kathy had allowed Valerie to stay in the room while I was being tested. I felt good about that because it was necessary for her to understand what was happening.

During the break, Kathy initiated a friendly conversation, which helped ease the tension. Both Valerie and I felt very comfortable chatting with Kathy. I was glad Kathy wasn't one of those stiff upper lip nurses who just goes through the motions of doing their job. From that point on, I knew, if Kathy remained with the study, any future testing would be much easier to cope with. After the break, the second stage of the testing began followed by another fifteen-minute break and some more idle chat. After the fifteen-minute break ended, the testing once again started. It too went without incident and then there was a half hour break, time enough for us to get a coffee, which we promptly did. Of course, the patch was once again switched to the left eye in order to protect any light from entering into it. Kathy added some extra eye covering underneath the eye patch to ensure there was maximum coverage on the eye.

After the scheduled half hour break, we returned to the Dark Adaption room where Kathy was waiting. "Are you ready to continue?" she asked. "Because if you are it's time for the bleaching process before we continue?" I nodded in agreement to the request but felt a little concerned about the effects of the bleaching process.

With the eye patch switched over to my right eye and my chin in the chin rest, I sat patiently awaiting the bleaching process. Then Kathy said, "Here we go." Suddenly, the screen lit up with the brightest white light I had ever seen. It was totally blinding, my eye stressed to an unacceptable limit creating tears to flow down my cheeks. It lasted for thirty seconds or more and with its sudden end came instant relief.

Kathy gave me a few minutes to regain my composure before she asked if I was ready to restart testing again. Ready or not, I was this far and to stop now wouldn't be conducive to my end goal. At the end of that test, I was given a two and an half hour break before final test would be completed. Once that test was finished, Kathy gave me an appointment schedule with a confirmed date for my next visit in six months' time. With my next appointment safely tucked away in my wallet, both Valerie and I left Kathy to resume her regular duties. It was late evening and the sun was still shining brightly. The dilation drops had almost completely worn off and with vision in both eyes, I marvelled at how well I could see. It seemed to me the patched eye which was in the dark for so long had exceptionally great vision. I told Valerie I could see well enough to drive but would still leave the driving to her. We chatted all the way home about the day's activities. I was so excited to be in the trial and even more excited to think at last I could possibly see with unrestricted vision.

The remaining visits to the eye clinic and the clinical trial testing on a semi-annual basis went without any problems; I knew what to expect with the testing and I knew I could handle it. However, during one visit, midway through the clinical trial, Kathy informed us she was moving on to another position. Before leaving she would train another nurse coordinator for the clinical trials (Krista Rideout) to take her place. Kathy continued by explaining that Krista was quite capable and would be at my next appointment. From that point on she would coordinate all the testing and appointments as well as provide the testing scheduled for the dark adaption test as well. It would be a change in personnel but not in the logistics of the clinical trial itself.

Just as Kathy had told us, Krista was indeed at the eye clinic when I arrived for the next semi-annual appointment. While registering at the eye clinic, a tall lady with dark hair approached me and introduced herself as Krista Rideout Nurse coordinator for genetic clinical trials. Up close, I noted, she was much younger then Kathy. Her youthful smile immediately filled the room as she asked if I was Mr. James Mercer. I acknowledged yes and followed up by introducing Valerie as my spouse and attendant.

"As you already know, Mr. Mercer, I am taking over from Kathy Whitten as your nurse coordinator for the remainder of this genetic clinical trial phase!" she explained. "I have all your appointments for today's testing scheduled as well as your appointment to see Dr. Whelan," she said. Continuing, she explained, "Tomorrow we will do you dark adaption test at the Janeway Hostel! Have you any questions before you go to your first appointment?" she asked. I couldn't think of anything I wanted clarification on so the answer was no. I noted to myself Krista seemed to be well organized and eager to start our day.

During the day we got to know Krista better and found her to be very respectable, understanding, informative and personable with a bubbly personality. There was no doubt Krista was a true professional well suited for her job as nurse coordinator for genetic clinical trials. It didn't take long for me to realize all future appointments would go smoothly.

Almost immediately, I gained total confidence in Krista's ability to organize and coordinate all aspects of the clinical trial. I also knew I could depend upon Krista to be totally honest with me if I had any questions regarding the clinical trial and any updates brought forward affecting the clinical trial. Like with Kathy, Valerie and I developed a friendly relationship with Krista, one I knew would continue throughout the clinical trial.

# Chapter 16

# I Sight the Power of Perception

It was December 5th 2017; I just finished my last semi-annual appointment for the RLBP1 clinical trial, phase one. My next scheduled appointment with Dr. Whelan would be forwarded to me once it was confirmed.

I felt very comfortable for the RLBP1 clinical trial phase one would end with that appointment and the second phase of the trial would begin once all the participants of the first phase were finished.

As usual the first week in the New Year 2018 brought us lots of joy and happiness after celebrating Christmas, New Years and Valerie's birthday. However, it soon turned sour for on the 10th of January 2018 I was scheduled for a colonoscopy scope. The test was done at Carbonear General hospital which is a community near my home town. The test was scheduled because I had surgery 6 years earlier for a medical condition known as diverticulitis. Regular scheduled scopes were needed to monitor the diverticulitis condition which would help keep it in check.

The results of that particular scope were immediate and gut wrenching. It wasn't the answer I was seeking for or wanting. The doctor who performed the scope didn't hold back; he told me outright I had bowel cancer and I would need surgery immediately; the sooner the better he concluded. He would make the arrangements with a surgeon which would contact me soon for the surgery. In the mean time he also scheduled a repeat bowel scope as well as a cat scan before seeing the surgeon. Within a month, I saw a Surgeon who scheduled me for surgery.

Six weeks from being diagnosed, I had my surgery on February 20th, 2018. After a week in hospital, I was sent home to recover. Two weeks later the surgeon called me in to check on my incision and review the test results from sample tissue he had taken during the surgery. The surgeon told me he had removed all of the tumour and the tissue samples didn't show any signs of cancer cells. In his medical opinion I was cancer free, however, I would have to go too the cancer clinic at the Health Sciences complex and be assessed by an oncologist doctor there. He would forward his report there and they would contact me.

The cancer clinic called with an appointment in late March with another one for the end of May. After the two visits and the results of several tests later, I was declared cancer free. I was informed I didn't need any further medical intervention or treatment because there wasn't any sign of cancer. Baring an incidental find of a blood clot near my liver, I was verbally given a clean bill of health and a discharge report would be issued pending a visit to the thrombosis clinic.

I was then given directions to the thrombosis clinic to see a specialist. In no time after leaving the cancer clinic we were at the thrombosis clinic chatting with the specialists. The doctor there reviewed my x-ray and concluded the blood clot was in a large blood vessel with plenty of blood going around it. The doctor told me it would dissolve on its own in about three months. She continued there is no need for treatment and I should not worry. She concluded by forwarding a report to the cancer clinic. However, before leaving, she noted if I felt any pain in the affected area, I should immediately seek medical help. I was then directed to return to the cancer clinic again. In no time I was led into her office where I was once again reminded I needed to maintain regular testing over the next five years, this would provide medical personal the opportunity of early detection of any return of cancer cells. At that point I was given a discharge report noting I was cancer free and I was wished good health for the future.

As we left the cancer clinic, I felt a huge weight being lifted off me. Although, my body still trembled with mixed emotions of uncertainty. With new vigour, I immediately contacted Krista to inform her I was completely healthy and totally free of cancer. The cancer clinic gave me a clean bill of health and I had the discharge report to prove it. This made me feel good about my chances with the clinical trial going forward.

I was finished with the semi-annual appointments but not the clinical trial completely for Krista had another appointment scheduled for me on January of 2019. It would be an annual appointment from then on where I would just see Dr. Whelan himself while waiting for further information on the second phase of the clinical trial. It was during that period of time shortly after my final semi-annual visit and post cancer surgery that I digressed back into my past in an effort to unravel all the things which had happened to me in my life.

I grew up in a Christian family; both my mom and dad were devoted Christians. Going to church on Sunday was a major part of their devotion to their faith. Working on Sunday was frowned upon; it was God's Day, a day of rest. It was also a family day for outings and visiting relatives. I enjoyed the family related activities more so than the spiritual ones. Nightly prayers at bedtime were expected but never enforced. However, going to church and Sunday school was a must.

My Christian education, so to speak, was in one ear and out the other. It wasn't very interesting and seemed so unimportant as a youth. Being functionally disabled with a sight impediment, the power of perception eluded me. I learned early in life to rely on my other senses. I could not grasp the significance of religion and faith. It was so intangible; it fell outside all my senses and as such it fell outside my realm of believability. I had major concerns in understanding and believing something which fell outside all my human senses. However, through reinforced teaching and the staying power of memory, the fabrication of my faith was instilled in me. Buried deep inside me for most of my life were those teachings of my youth as it related to Christianity.

It was always there, remaining silent and ready to emerge at a moments notice. But when called upon none of my prayers were answered. Or if they were, I didn't recognize the answers, therefore, my trust or faith in God was never reaffirmed. I had a life full of struggles, disappointments and unhappiness. I often coveted the successes and material things my friends and family had achieved. It wasn't easy for me in that respect.

I often blamed God for my affliction and all the effects it had on my life. However, in 2012 I had my first life threatening illness, "diverticulitis," which needed corrective surgery. It was then, just lying in the hospital, I turned once again to God and asked for forgiveness. In time my body healed but my faith in God faltered. I believed instead the skill of the surgeon was my saviour.

Time would pass and once again illness threatened my life and once again the surgeon performed his magic. This time however, like before I prayed for healing and in a dream of sedated drugs I felt warm inside; I felt at ease. My worries and fears were non-existent and I somehow knew I would be fine. Later in the clarity of thought, I realized the power of faith had touched me, opening my eyes and heart to believe. It was then I thanked God for the blessing which was bestowed upon me. If I hadn't had surgery for diverticulitis and follow up regular scheduled colonoscopy scopes, the doctors would not have known I had cancer. It wasn't luck; it was God's way of answering my prayers after that first bowel surgery.

With my eyes finally opened, eyesight became a reality and the power of perception became a part of my adaptability. I realized the many blessings which I had received in the past and hadn't recognized; things like the ability to cope, analyze and adapt. The luxury of having a fantastic memory as well as having the ability to remain confident in the face of adversity. The life long love and support of my parents as well as the continued love and support of my siblings. But, most important of all is having a tremendous loving supportive spouse and two very dear and precious children. With all my fears concerning my health set aside, I focused on the RLBP1 clinical trial once again.

I was worried about the clinical trial and how my health would affect any further participation in it. However, those fears were dispelled once I felt good about my health. My confidence in the future and the clinical trial remained positive. Dr. Whelan was always adamant I remain healthy if I wanted to stay in the clinical trial. The cancer illness had threatened to prevent my continued participation in the clinical trial. However, my cancer was professionally dealt with and to Dr. Whelan's joy, I remained healthy. Dr. Whelan's prerequisite of being healthy to remain in the Clinical trail was met which for me was a confidence-building factor. For that blessing I thanked God and prayed for his continued support in every aspect of my life.

After a five-month recovery from the life-threatening illness of cancer, we decided to spend some time with our daughter, son-in-law and grandchildren in Alberta. It was on the 26th of July, we boarded a plane and left our home province of Newfoundland and Labrador; our destination was Fort McMurry Alberta. I felt refreshed as my strength gradually returned. We saw nothing but sunshine and hot weather for the full month of August. It definitely added to the complete feeling of well being which I was experiencing. Life felt good again; I know I was given a second chance and I would make the most of it. I was so engrossed in enjoying life that I hadn't checked my emails for more then a month. When I did check my email, I noticed I received an email from Krista Rideout nurse coordinator for genetic clinical trials.

Her email was dated for the 23rd of July 2018; she had sent me an email informing me my appointment with Dr. Whelan was re-scheduled from January 2019 to October 15th 2018 and I would get all the clinical trials testing done as well; it would be a two-day appointment. She wanted to know if that appointment was fine with me. I responded back accepting the appointment and I immediately acquired a return flight to co-inside with the clinical trial appointment dates.

Things were happening and happening fast for on the 5th of September 2018, I returned a call from my younger sister, Greta. She had some updated information on the clinical trial in Sweden with respect to the RLBP1 gene. It seems her husband Winston was in hospital having a medical procedure. While waiting for him she encountered Krista in the cafeteria. Krista was excited to tell her about a new management position she had taken within Genetics Clinical trials division.

Krista was also excited to relate some new information on the RLBP1 clinical trial she had heard in one of her management meetings. In that meeting she was made aware of a person in Sweden who was formerly injected with a healthy RLBP1 gene. In other words, medical human clinical trials were started on gene therapy for the RLBP1 gene in humans in other words phase two of the RLBP1 clinical trial had become a reality. This meant it would only be a matter off months before the human clinical trial on the RLBP1 gene would start in Newfoundland and Labrador. Of course, this was pending the success or failure of the Sweden trial. It would be an ample period of time of study, testing and follow up on that person to ensure the success and or failure of that procedure. Of course, this was only preliminary news and not yet confirmed by any other ranking official associated with the RLBP1 clinical trial in Newfoundland and Labrador.

Still, it was astounding news for me. At last, there was a glimmer of light shining through the long and cumbersome RLBP1 clinical trial process.

My confidence level was so high I felt the urge to shout aloud thank you God at last, at last, eye sight was no longer a twinkle in my eye. It was within a grasp of time and God willing I would be included to receive the sight-producing gene I so much longed for.

The phone call with my sister ended on a more conservative note. I would see Dr. Whelan in a month's time and would ask him if there was any truth to the RLBP1 clinical trial news coming out of Sweden. Once I had a definitive response from Dr. Whelan, I would forward the information to her.

From the day we arrived in Alberta up to the day it was time to fly home for my eye appointments, the passage of time was quite enjoyable. First and foremost, precious time with our daughter's family, both our grandchildren, James 6 and

Quinton 3, was exactly what I needed in my recovery process. Quality time with our daughter Deanne and her husband Jason was most enjoyable as well; there is nothing like having family around to fill the hole of hurt. The many hours just playing with our grandchildren took centre stage as my mind became active and focused once again as all the ugliness of the world was locked outside.

I remember back in my own childhood when I had just as much fun as I was having then with the boys. I felt young again with the exercise, fresh air and stress free days. It all added to a complete feeling of well-being. The possibility of a start in genetic human trials coming out of Sweden on the RLBP1 gene was no doubt a major factor in the continued well being process of my body and mind. All in all, things were no doubt looking up again for me.

The day finally came to fly home for my eye appointments. I could hardly contain my emotions. As we drove to the airport in Ft. McMurry, my mind focused on the flight home. It would be a long flight, tiresome and no doubt boring for us both, especially me. There was nothing to see out the window at 38 thousand feet even with what little vision I had. Likewise, I didn't have enough sight to see the TV screen embedded into the back of the seat in front of me. Reading was also no longer an option either, for my sight no longer supported the capability to read printed material. Although there was music, it soon became boring and I was left to try and relax in silence. The only reprieve from total boredom for me at least would be to let my mind wonder and imagine all the possibilities of having the gift off sight.

I then wondered how much sight I lost because of the stress associated the cancer illness. Would I still be eligible for the second phase of the clinical trial? My mind remained on negative thoughts threatening to dispel all my hopes to be included into the second phase of the clinical trial. I guess God gave me strength and I gradually forced the negative thoughts to be replaced by positive ones. Ones that brought me back to the reality of the plane ride.

In no time we arrived at the airport and checked in; within a short period of time we boarded the plane. Both Valerie and I were tired, with the flight being the red eye overnight; we hoped we would get some much-needed sleep. For me, it was not to be for I was too excited at what the next few days would bring. Likewise, it was the same for Valerie, but for very difference reasons, insomnia most likely the cause in her case.

I had never flown at night; the quietness on the plane seemed so out of place.

Once boarding was complete, the plane was set for take off and began its ascent to 38 thousand feet. The flight had one stop in Toronto with an hour's break before continuing on to St. John's, NL. Aside from the low whimpers of a baby seeking nourishment and the sounds of people sleeping through the monotony of the flight there was no other activity to occupy my mind. As the plane perched the night sky at 38 thousand feet, the sound of the jet engines became mundane; there was nothing but total darkness outside. From time to time a glimmer of lights shone up from below indicating the many towns and cities which blessed the landscape of Canada. Valerie tossed and turned in her seat trying to find a comfort zone where she could relax and fall asleep. Her voice would break the silence from time to time in frustration. I would re-assure her sleep would come, if she could just relax, but I knew she would disagree with me. However, unlike me, she could watch TV, or do some reading if she wished but she was tired and wanted to sleep. In time, she would find some sleep but there would be no sleep for me.

I was too hyper as I thought I would be. The four plus hour flight from Ft. McMurry Alberta to Toronto, Ontario would seem like an eternity if I couldn't find something to occupy my time. So, in an effort to dispel the boredom, I receded into my subconscious, a place where I always found comfort and peace. It was as if I had fallen asleep, some might say I was in a state of daydreaming. Everything was blocked out; I couldn't hear or see anything except my own thoughts and the internal sounds of my body. Immediately, I felt very comfortable, free of stress, relaxed and active all at once. Boredom was no longer an impeding force on the progression of time. I was deep within a place I refer to as the service control center of my subconscious. Here, I could maneuver in an out from the many different functioning components of my brain. It would be like going from one store to another store gathering different things only available in those different stores. It is only in these places; I could access all the brain function I would possibly need. Functions such as stored memories, problem solving, analytical and creative skills, as well as imagination and fantasy functions.

With my eyes closed came the solitude of total darkness, my hearing would be on mute, everything external would be blocked out except self awareness, a state of mind where I would know when to return to reality. Apart from a few responses to Valerie's voice once in a while, I remained in a subconscious state until the pilot announced we would land in Toronto shortly.

I marvelled at how quickly time seemed to have passed, even though I knew time to be constant. During the time I was in a subconscious state, I retrieved memories from my past, imagined outcomes from my appointments as well as postulations on any future medical treatment.

The memories I had retrieved from my past were very vivid and clear. I recognized early I was different from my pears and how that difference affected me both mentally and physically. Although I remained positive and confident, there were times when I broke down and cried in the privacy of my own company. Like the time when I was a small boy of 10 years old glued to the window after dark listening to children including my siblings play outside while my tears stained that window pane. It was always a challenge for me to try and become part of my social peer group; no matter how hard I tried, I never achieved total inclusion. I was always on the outside looking in. In my mind I was a misfit, which caused me to wonder at an early age whether or not there would be a time when I would shed the restrictions of my functional disability and the insecure feelings associated with it.

For over six decades, I have lived with my functional disability, adapting and coping. In that time, I remained positive there would be something like a breakthrough of sorts before my life's end. With the announcement and my involvement in the RLBP1 clinical trial, it seemed a breakthrough was indeed possible, for the RLBP1 clinical trial offered that hope.

I could not predict what Dr. Whelan would tell me about the unconfirmed reports coming out of Sweden regarding gene replacement therapy for the RLBP1 gene. Personally, I could only wonder and hope it was true. If it was true then what would the next step be for the Newfoundland and Labrador RLBP1 clinical trial? I decided not to allow this thought occupy my mind until I had a definite answer and complete understanding on what was happening in Sweden. With my thoughts still focused on the possibility of the clinical trial ending with this my last visit, I remained positive I would indeed be selected for the second phase of the trial and be eligible to receive the sight restoring gene.

It was indeed within this realm of possibilities, possibilities I had fantasized years earlier. I allowed my imagination to run wild; the postulated outcomes were extremely uplifting. The possibilities were endless if my fantasies came true. I would no longer be night blind. I would be able to see colors and read again. I would be able to drive a vehicle once more with the added flexibility of night time driving. I would be able to socialize with others both day and night with no fear of being in the dark. I would no longer be dependent upon the assistance of others especially the burden my wife carried as my assistant. I would no longer be left behind by my friends when they went on fishing and hunting trips. The burden of my functional disability would be broken and both Valerie and I would have the opportunities to enjoy the best life could offer. It would be all I had wished for and then some.

The feeling of the plane descending along with the captain's voice on the intercom brought me back to reality. People were stirring; it was daylight outside and the city below was Toronto, which was our first stop. We were a little more than half way home. After a one-hour stop, we would be on or way again. The remainder of the flight would be the same as the first leg of our flight. Boredom would still be my nemesis. Once in the air, I closed my eyes and went again to my place of comfort. I would remain there until we landed in St. Johns Newfoundland and Labrador.

Scott our son picked us up at the airport; he was just as happy to see us as we were to see him. The drive home became immersed in conversation, which was a welcome relief from the silent flight home. My mind relaxed and the excitement of attending my appointments took second stage to our conversation. We chatted on many topics, most especially his family, Cheyanne 12 years old and Alexis 9 years old, our granddaughters.

After arriving home, we turned on the water and heat; it would only be a week before having to turn it off again. Once we were settled into the comfort of our own home we fell victim to tiredness and sleep became most welcomed. After a few hours of deep sleep, we awakened feeling refreshed. Once we collected our thoughts, the mundane activities of living home took priority; it was necessary for us to go grocery shopping but only to get enough food to last us a week.

It was Friday night October 12th. We had arrived earlier that day; my appointments were scheduled for both Monday October 15th and Tuesday October 16th of the following week. We had all the weekend to rest up from our jet leg. We also had enough time to get some visiting in and prepare for the appointments ahead. Our first chore was to go grocery shopping, after which we stopped at our son's home for a visit. Both Cheyanne and Alexis were excited to see us. Even though they were much older then James and Quinton it was still fun to be with them. However, our visit was short for the effects of jet leg still lingered; we were still tired and needed more rest.

The weekend went by all too quickly; we managed to get all our visiting in. It was an early rise Monday morning October 15th; we had to be at the eye clinic by 9 a.m. Sharp. It would be a long day, ending sometime in the afternoon, depending if all the testing appointments were on time with no delays. The most important appointment was with Dr. Whelan. It was scheduled for 1 p.m. that afternoon.

We met Krista and another lady who Krista introduced as Esther Mooney. Esther would take Krista's place while she was temporally filling a management position. I was aware someone had back filled Krista's position but hadn't met her or knew her name. Esther was a tall, slim lady with light hair. Her smile was as warm as the golden rays of summer sunshine. Her personality immediately took centre stage as she initiated a conversation with both Valerie and I.

Like Krista, her predecessor Esther was, in my opinion, well suited as a clinical trials nurse coordinator. Not that I officially knew what a clinical trial coordinator should be like; I drew that conclusion from my experience over the past five years as a participant in a clinical trial. Over the next two days we would get to know Esther even better. This would be important because if I were selected to continue into the second stage of the clinical trial, she would possibly be the nurse coordinator I would have most contact with.

To my surprise, all the testing fell into place without delays during the morning before it was time to see Dr. Whelan. After Dr. Whelan examined my eyes, he noted there wasn't much of a change in my eyes; as a matter of fact he noted there was possibly a slight improvement in my fields. I explained to him I had my eyes tested for glasses a few months earlier and the new glasses may have been the reason for the improvement. I also noted to him there was only one eye which needed an update in corrective lenses. That eye I told him was my left eye the one I had the best sight in and the one in which I patch for the dark adaption test. Dr. Whelan nodded as if understanding everything I told him. However, he never responded in any way except to listen and continue on with what he was doing.

As usual there is always ample time at the end of his examination to ask questions. It was then I took advantage of that opportunity and asked about the reports coming out of Sweden. His answer to my question was somewhat disappointing to me but still positive. "The unconfirmed reports from Sweden," he said, "aren't totally correct." He continued, saying, "It seems the reports were misinterpreted thus leading to a release of false information."

I have always found Dr. Whelan to be honest and transparent in his responses. To further explain and clarify what was happening in Sweden, he noted the Swedish clinical trial was on track. After some delays, they were ready to move into the second phase of the clinical trial but as of yet hadn't done so. "It would be soon," he said, "maybe within another month or maybe they have already started, I really don't have that information as of yet. In any case I have not been informed of any new developments. If they start it will be this fall. Most likely. Newfoundland and Labrador would follow within a year or less."

This wasn't totally bad news from Dr. Whelan. Nothing had changed, the clinical trial was still going ahead and the second phase would soon start in Sweden if it hadn't already started. The one unknown was my continued good health and how it would affect my eligibility in the selection process for the second phase of the trial. Dr. Whelan also told me it wouldn't be up to him for the selection process of the participants but the drug company itself who were doing the trial. It was out of his hands, although he would make every effort to have all the Newfoundland and Labrador participants continue into the next stage of the trial. With my questions answered, I left his office seeking the whereabouts of Krista and Esther for the final appointment of the day.

Esther met me at the eye clinic and provided me with some bandages to patch my eye for the Dark Adaption test scheduled for the following day. After receiving specific instructions for the following day's test, we headed home. Later that evening around 8 p.m., I got Valerie to patch my left eye; it would be patched all night and most of the following day in order to have the dark adaption test done. We would have to get up earlier then the previous day in order to get to my appointment in town. The appointment was set for 8:30 a.m. By 6 a.m. we were on the road. This gave us ample time to stop for breakfast leaving enough time to find suitable parking.

I went through this test twice a year for the past five years and I still wasn't comfortable being patched over one eye; still it was a necessity, one I welcomed. Yet, I couldn't help feeling very vulnerable, a feeling I had no control over and one I hadn't found a way of adapting to. With only one eye to see with, the fear of falling or bumping into something consumed my confidence. The loss of control affected more than my mobility; mentally I felt embarrassed at what other people might thing of me as I stumbled over my own two feet. It has always been important for me to project an image of normalcy. Thus deflecting unwanted stares that made me feel uncomfortable. I sight they say is 20/20 but I believe that I sight is in the power of perception. It was Tuesday Oct 16th, 2018, my last day as a participant in the historical component of phase one of the clinical trial. We arrived on time for my appointment. I was prepared both mentally and physically for a long day. We met Krista and Esther at the dark adaptation room where the colour dome awaited our arrival. After a conversation of small talk, Krista asked if she could draw my blood before we continued. This was done usually the day before, but due to my small veins, there was no success in drawing blood from me that day. Krista noted she would take my blood when I came in the next day. Once the blood was drawn and spun, it would be sent by mail to a designated laboratory for testing. After Krista had taken my blood, Esther closed the door and the lights were turned off. The dark adaption test would soon begin but first the patch was removed and dilating eye drops were put into my previously patched eye. I went through this procedure many times before; it would take about fifteen minutes for the pupil in my eye to dilate enough in order to continue forward with the dark adaption test. From here on the room would remain dark and my left eye would not see the light of day until the days testing was over.

Esther began the process of booting up the machine. As usual, I placed my chin in the chin rest of the machine with my right eye patched to block out any adverse effects on my sight from that eye. If the right eye wasn't patched it would contaminate the testing of the left eye and the test would have to be re-do ne over again. Patiently, I awaited the words 'we are ready to start, are you ready?'

Those words didn't come. There was trouble in getting the machine up and running. Several attempts were made but to no avail. I was told to re-patch my left eye again because the lights needed to be turned on to check out the machine more closely. After several more tries with the lights on it, soon became evident the machine wouldn't work.

Krista suggested they swap out the machine for another one that was recently repaired. The testing would be delayed approximately one hour but would still leave ample time to complete the test before days end. We were asked to leave the room until they were ready for us again. My focus remained on getting the test done until Valerie asked me what if you can't get the test done today; what are we going to do?

That thought hadn't entered my thoughts and suddenly it caused me to wonder what if? What if I couldn't get the test done then? What if they wanted me to come back another day? What if I don't get the test done at all? What if not getting the test done would mean I wouldn't be selected for the second stage of the clinical trial? All these what-if's troubled me a lot. I had come this far but at the last day of the historic component of the trial to see all my hopes destroyed because of mechanical problem with a testing machine.

Once the machines were changed, we were called back into the dark adaption room again. The lights were turned off before the patch on my left eye was removed and placed once again over my right eye. With my fingers crossed, I was ready to be tested but to everyone's surprise that machine failed to work as well. Finally, after several unsuccessful attempts to get the second dark adaption machine up and running, I was told testing was done for that day. I was then told I was finished.

Krista was aware of my situation regarding the time limits I had on returning to Alberta. "It looks like we are going to have to get a new testing machine, which will take more time than you have," she said. "There is no need for you to come back to do this test again; we can use the information we have taken over the past five years. No need to worry," came her response to my thoughts.

We were returning to Alberta early on the 18th of October and even if they could have gotten a new machine for the following day, I still would not have been able to do the test. Because, I needed to winterize our house on the 17th of October before flying back to Alberta early the following day. Therefore, it wouldn't have been enough time to do both the test and winterize our home on the same day. Krista had given me a way out for which I thanked my lucky stars and Krista's insight. Things were still on track and I was delightfully happy it was so.

The flight back to Alberta would be just as mundane and boring as the flight home was the previous week. However, this time, I got some positive answers from Dr. Whelan. He assured me nothing was true about the unconfirmed reports coming out of Sweden regarding someone being medically treated with a healthy RLBP1 gene. Still, he was adamant it was expected to happen and happen soon. He noted if it hasn't already happened without his present knowledge, then it should become a reality within the next three months. He continued by saying if there weren't any more delays and all else remains the same, he anticipated the following year Newfoundland and Labrador would do their first participant. The historical component of the RLBP1 clinical trial had come to a conclusion, at least for me.

223

There were still others who were pending their final appointments and until they were done, the Newfoundland and Labrador RLBP1 clinical trial would remain in the historical phase. Once that was done, depending upon the successes in Sweden with respect to the medical component of the RLBP1 clinical trial, Newfoundland and Labrador would follow suit. Of course, all the major health and government authorities would have to be on board. Strict protocols would have to be developed and followed. Finally all the selected participants would have to be healthy, willing and available to receive the sight-giving gene.

I have often wanted to know the future and how it would affect me. By revisiting my past, I have come to realize I had achieved that objective. However, having achieved that objective, I still felt something was missing. I had taken a virtual trip back in time to analyze the effects of a functionally sighted disability on my life, but not its underlying root cause. Yes, the identification of a defective RLBP1 gene is clearly significant. Still, it isn't the root cause; to identify that cause, I would need to travel back through recorded and unrecorded time to find an answer. Because I can only travel back through the virtual memories of my own lifetime as well as the verbal communicated memories from my parents and grandparents, my ability to confront that problem is totally restricted. Therefore, I can only postulate an answer given my limited knowledge on ancestry and genetics.

After the creation of human life and the dawn of scientific research the evolution of humanity was found to be based upon a strong desire to procreate and the uncontrolled mixing of the human genetic makeup. That strong desire to procreate resulted in a genetic pool of humanity which was doomed from the beginning to become tainted.

This process continues on through the centuries leaving its mark of genetic impurities on all humanity. However, scientists in all fields of study are continually working hard to identify and correct all forms of genetic impurities. It is through their efforts that we, who are most affected, await breakthroughs and treatment for our flawed genetic makeup.

As I have said earlier, the present is forever creating a future; the past is but a product of that future.

If we know what we want our future to be, then logic tells us we must put in place a plan to follow. Over the past five years with my participation in the RIBP1 clinical trial, I have been continually creating a specific future for myself. A future I know will happen according to the planned foundation I have created and will create in the evolving present. If all goes as planned, the future looks bright for me with a destiny of my own choosing, a destiny where the privilege of sight becomes a reality.

Going forward, my focus remains positive as I wait for the next phase of the RLBP1 clinical trial and its potential outcome.

# *Epilogue*

A sight impediment is none less disabling than any other disabling factor in a human life. However, the perception of other people towards a sight impediment may never known if that sight impairment is hidden from sight.

This book dealt with the perception of a visually impaired person as well as society itself on how both sides view and react to a disabling sight impediment.

Many true stories from our rich past often becomes a blurred memory and disappears forever; this story, however, will remain alive a published document in the recorded library of time.

James E. Mercer
2022